THE FUTURE OF HONG KONG

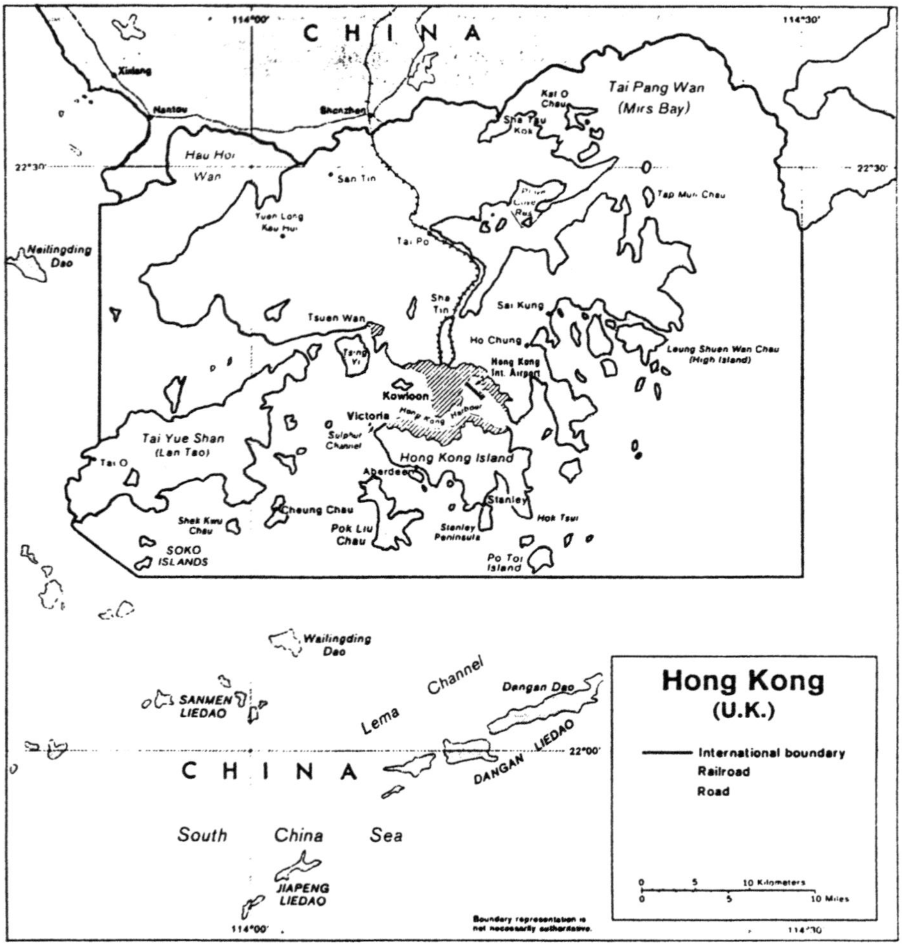

CHINA
Hong Kong
(U.K.)
International boundary
Railroad
Road
Tai Pang Wan
(Mirs Bay)
Hau Hoi
Wan
Tai Yue Shan
(Lan Tao)
Kowloon
Victoria
Hong Kong Island
Lema Channel
South China Sea
Boundary representation is not necessarily authoritative.

The Future of Hong Kong

TOWARD 1997 AND BEYOND

EDITED BY
Hungdah Chiu, Y. C. Jao, and Yuan-li Wu

Q
QUORUM BOOKS
NEW YORK • WESTPORT, CONNECTICUT • LONDON

Library of Congress Cataloging-in-Publication Data

The Future of Hong Kong.

Bibliography: p.
Includes index.
1. Hong Kong—Politics and government.
I. Chiu, Hungdah, 1936- . II. Jao, Y. C.
III. Wu, Yuan-li.
DS796.H757F88 1987 303.4'95125 86-25573
ISBN 0-89930-241-6 (lib. bdg. : alk. paper)

Library of Congress Catalog Card Number: 86-25573
ISBN: 0-89930-241-6

First published in 1987 by Quorum Books

Greenwood Press, Inc.
88 Post Road West, Westport, Connecticut 06881

Printed in the United States of America

The paper used in this book complies with the Permanent Paper Standard issued by the National Information Standards Organization (Z39.48-1984).

10 9 8 7 6 5 4 3 2 1

Contents

Tables

Preface

This book has its origin in a panel on the future of Hong Kong as a free-market economy. One of the coeditors, Yuan-li Wu, organized and chaired this panel for the Twenty-seventh Annual Conference of the Western Social Science Association in Fort Worth, Texas, on April 24–27, 1985. Two of the contributors to this volume, George Hicks and Y. C. Jao, presented papers at the panel, and another, Ta-ling Lee, served as a discussant. Because of the success of the panel, it was subsequently agreed by the participants that a book should be developed that would contain contributions from other interested scholars as well.

This volume, then, is, a collective work prepared over a period of nearly two years. It consists of essays on various aspects of the Hong Kong question from a multidisciplinary and multidimensional perspective. Although the situation in Hong Kong is changing rapidly, we hope that our general approach and analytical framework can stand the test of time, so that only specific details need to be revised as the occasion arises. In addition to presenting seven chapters, we also append, for the easy reference of the reader, certain important official documents in the recent history of Hong Kong, as well as a comprehensive bibliography.

It remains for us to express our sincere thanks to the Asia-Pacific Educational Fund, whose generous grant has facilitated the publication of this book. During the preparation of the manuscript, we were ably assisted by Shaiw-chei Chuang, Mitchell A. Silk, M. R. Rao, Lu Ann Young Marshall, Kathy Montroy, and Chih-yu Wu. To them we would like to express our sincere thanks.

1

Introduction

HUNGDAH CHIU

HISTORICAL BACKGROUND

British-administered Hong Kong is about 70.0 miles (100.0 kilometers) southeast of the southern Chinese city of Guangzhou (Canton). It consists of Hong Kong and the Lan Tau Islands, the Kowloon Peninsula, and more than 200 small islands. The total area is 400.5 square miles (1,037.2 square kilometers). Hong Kong has a population of 5.5 million, and with a population density of 13,149 persons per square mile (5,077 per square kilometer), it is one of the most densely populated areas in the world.[1] Before 1949 there was no border control to restrict the entry and exit of the people between Hong Kong and the Chinese mainland. The population then was about 800,000. After 1949 a large exodus of refugees compelled the British authorities in Hong Kong to institute a tight border control to diminish the large influx of people to Hong Kong. The control has become increasingly stiff in recent years, and all refugees who enter illegally are repatriated to China. Despite the tight border control, it is believed that refugees from the mainland comprise the majority of the population.

British administration of Hong Kong was established in three stages:

1. After defeating China in the 1839–42 Opium War, China agreed to cede the island of Hong Kong to Great Britain in the 1842 Treaty of Nanking.
2. After defeating China in the 1858–1860 Arrow War, China agreed to cede the southern part of the Kowloon Peninsula, about 3.5 square miles (9.0 square kilometers), to Great Britain by the 1860 Treaty of Peking.
3. In 1898 China was compelled to lease to Great Britain an additional 365 square miles (949 square kilometers) for 99 years. This part later was called the New Territories.[2]

GOVERNMENT AND ADMINISTRATION

Hong Kong's government and administration have developed from the basic pattern applied in all British-governed overseas territories.[3] The head of the Hong Kong government is the governor, appointed by the queen of the United Kingdom, who acts as her representative in Hong Kong and is also the titular commander-in-chief. Below the governor, there are the Executive and Legislative councils. The Executive Council consists of four ex-officio members—the chief secretary, the commander of British forces, the financial secretary, and the attorney general—together with other members who are appointed by the governor on the instructions of the British secretary of state. There are 12 appointed members, 10 unofficial and 2 official. Appointed members hold office for a fixed period.

The function of the council is to advise the governor, who is required to consult it on all important matters of policy, except those that are too urgent to allow the council to be consulted, in which case the governor must explain to the council as soon as possible what action he has taken. The council also considers all principal legislation before it is introduced into the Legislative Council, and it is responsible for making subsidiary legislation (regulations) under a number of ordinances. If the governor decides to act against the advice of the majority of members of the Executive Council, the governor is required to report his reasons to the British secretary of state.

The maximum number of the Legislative Council is 61, comprising 29 official members, including the governor, who is the president; 3 ex-officio members—the chief secretary, the financial secretary, and the attorney general; and 32 unofficial members appointed by the governor with the British secretary of state. Official members normally remain appointed for as long as they hold office, whereas unofficial members can be appointed for up to four years and may be reappointed for a period of not more than four years each. The main function of the council is to enact legislation, including appropriation of public funds. A bill passed by the council must receive the governor's assent before becoming law (ordinance), although the queen of the United Kingdom has reserved power to disallow an ordinance. However, the power of disallowance has not been used for many years.

Below the central administration is the Urban Council for the urban areas, the secretary for the New Territories, and seven district officers with political, executive, and liaison responsibilities. The Urban Council is composed of 30 members, 15 elected from district constituencies and 15 appointed by the governor. Its functions include the control of street cleaning, refuse collection, food by ginesse, foot shops, markets, abattoirs, liquor licensing, and park and recreation facilities. The director of the Department of Urban Services in the central administration is the council's chief executive, and the department is charged with carrying out the council's policies and implementing its decisions.

There had been no comparable council in the New Territories, which are run by the central administration directly. In 1985 a proposal to create a regional council similar to that of the Urban Council was introduced and was established in April 1986.

In 1982 district boards and district management committees were set up in each of the 18 administrative districts. The boards consist of government officials, appointed unofficial members, elected members from the constituencies, and urban councilors or rural committee chairman. The function of the boards is primarily advisory, although they are given substantial responsibility for the management of district affairs.

The district management committees, whose membership comprises government officials, provide a forum for interdepartmental consultation to produce a more effective government at the district level. They are in effect responsible for servicing their respective district boards.

Election to the Urban Council and district boards are on a constituency basis and through a very broad franchise. Every individual who is 21 years of age and who has been a resident in Hong Kong for seven years, or who was born in Hong Kong, is eligible to apply for registration as an elector in the constituency in which he or she lives. A candidate must have been a resident in Hong Kong for ten or more years, and his or her nomination must be supported by ten voters in that constituency. Voting is by simple plurality.

A special feature of the administration of Hong Kong is the existence of an extensive network of government boards and committees, which now number 368. Advisory bodies are found in nearly all government departments. The function of these organs is to obtain, through consultation with interested groups in the community, the best possible advice on which the government units are to formulate their decisions.

The judiciary is independent of the executive and legislative organs of the government in the performance of its function. Judges are appointed by the governor. The courts are divided into the Supreme Court (comprising the Court of Appeals and the High Court), the District Court, the Magistrates' Court, the Coroner's Court, the Juvenile Court, the Lands Tribunal, the Labor Tribunal, and the Small Claims Tribunal.

The attorney general is the governor's legal adviser. His chambers are divided into four divisions: The Civil Advisory Division, the Prosecutions Division, the Law Drafting Division, and the Administration Division.

Generally, there is no adequate participatory democracy and self-government in Hong Kong, but people of Hong Kong are satisfied with the British administration. Numerous freedoms, especially economic freedoms, exist in Hong Kong, and human rights are respected as well. The Hong Kong judiciary enjoys a good reputation, although many complain that it deals too leniently with murderers or those who commit violent crimes.

CHINESE POLICY TOWARD HONG KONG

The three treaties through which the United Kingdom established its rule over Hong Kong were considered by the Chinese Nationalist party as "unequal treaties." One of the major goals of the Nationalist Revolution was to abrogate the "unequal treaties" and to recover Chinese territories lost to foreign countries.

After the United States and the United Kingdom (Great Britain) entered into war against Japan on December 8, 1941, the Republic of China under the leadership of Chiang Kai-shek became an ally of these two countries. In late 1942 both countries entered into negotiations with the Republic of China on the abolition of their extraterritorial and other special rights (concessions, inland navigation, stationing troops, and so on) in China. The United States' negotiations with China went very smoothly, but the negotiations between the Republic of China and the United Kingdom remained deadlocked over the Chinese demand for the return of the leased territories of Kowloon (the so-called New Territories). In order not to delay the abrogation of British extraterritorial and other special rights in China, the Chinese side finally agreed to drop the issue of the Kowloon leased territories, but it made clear that it reserved the right to reopen negotiations in the future.[4] On January 11, 1943, both countries signed treaties with the Republic of China, abrogating their extraterritorial and other special rights in China.[5]

At that time, the U.S. policy was to make China a strong and stabilizing force in East Asia after the defeat of Japan. Therefore, the United States was sympathetic to Chinese aspirations to restore its territorial integrity by regaining its lost territories. In March 1943 President Franklin D. Roosevelt proposed to T.V. Soong, Chinese representative in the United States, that if it was agreeable to the Republic of China, Roosevelt would propose to the United Kingdom a voluntary return of Hong Kong to China. At the same time, he suggested that China should designate Hong Kong and a part or the whole of Kowloon as a free port to preserve part of the British nationals' interest there. Soong reported the proposal to Chiang Kai-shek, who referred the proposal to the Supreme National Defense Council for deliberation. The council decided that if the United Kingdom returned Hong Kong to China, the Chinese government would voluntarily declare Hong Kong and the Old Kowloon area (i.e., not including the New Territories) as a customs-free port. However, the return of Hong Kong to China could not be preconditioned on this term. The designation of Hong Kong and the Kowloon area as a customs-free port had to be done voluntarily by China. Soong transmitted this message to President Roosevelt who, the Chinese side believed, did convey the message to the United Kingdom. Because the United Kingdom did not sincerely intend to return Hong Kong to China, no response was made to this message.[6]

In late 1949 the Nationalist government moved to Taiwan and on January 5–6, 1950, the United Kingdom withdrew its recognition of the Nationalist government. Therefore, the Republic of China since then has not been in a position to negotiate the Hong Kong question with the United Kingdom.

Despite its nationalistic, revolutionary, and anti-imperialist policy, the People's Republic of China (PRC) has an important stake in maintaining Hong Kong's prosperity since it acquires about 40 percent of its foreign exchange (now in the amount of about U.S. $8 billion) through its annual trade with Hong Kong.

Moreover, Hong Kong provides an outlet for Chinese political dissidents and serves to reduce the political tension at home as well as indirect contacts, such as mail and trade, with Taiwan. For these reasons, although the PRC has since 1949 considered Hong Kong as Chinese territory to be recovered, there had been no attempt to implement that goal until 1982. An editorial in the authoritative *People's Daily* (*Renmin Ribao*) of March 8, 1963, explained the PRC's policy toward Hong Kong as follows:

> At the time the People's Republic of China was inaugurated, our government declared that it would examine the treaties concluded by previous Chinese governments with foreign governments, treaties that had been left over by history, and would recognize, abrogate, revise, or renegotiate them according to their respective contents...
>
> As a matter of fact, many of these treaties concluded in the past either have lost their validity, or have been abrogated or have been replaced by new ones. With regard to the outstanding issues, which are a legacy from the past, we have always held that, when conditions are ripe, they should be settled peacefully through negotiations and that, pending a settlement, the status quo should be maintained. Within this category are the questions of Hong Kong, Kowloon, and Macao and the questions of all those boundaries which have not been formally delimited by the parties concerned in each case.[7]

The same editorial also pointed out that "there is no need for the Chinese people to prove their courage and staunchness in combating imperialism by making a show of force on the question of Hong Kong."[8]

Although the PRC was willing to maintain the status quo of Hong Kong until recently, it made clear that it would not tolerate Hong Kong becoming an independent state. In 1964 the Soviet-sponsored World Youth Forum adopted a resolution putting Hong Kong and Macao on a par with Timor Island, Papua, Oman, Aden, and South Arabia and demanded "independence" for these places in accordance with the 1960 United Nations Declaration on the Granting of Independence to Colonial Countries and People.[9] But the PRC delegates strongly protested the adoption of such a resolution.[10]

After its entry into the United Nations, when the PRC found that the General Assembly's Special Committee on Colonialism included Hong Kong and Macao in its list of colonial territories, it sent a letter to the chairman of the committee on March 10, 1972, stating that:

Hong Kong and Macao are part of Chinese territory occupied by the British and Portuguese authorities. The settlement of the questions of Hong Kong and Macao is entirely within China's sovereign right and does not at all fall under the ordinary category of colonial territories.

Consequently, they should not be included in the list of colonial territories covered by the declaration on the granting of independence to colonial countries and people.

With regard to the questions of Hong Kong and Macao, the Chinese government has consistently held that they should be settled in an appropriate way when conditions are ripe. The United Nations has no right to discuss these questions.[11]

In practice, though, the PRC tolerates Hong Kong's having a limited international status similar, to a certain extent, to that of a state. This issue is discussed in further detail in the next section.

INTERNATIONAL RELATIONS

The government of the United Kingdom is responsible for Hong Kong's international relations, but it has permitted considerable autonomy in the area of commercial and cultural relations. Hong Kong is a member of the United Nations Economic Commission on Asia and the Far East (ECAFE) and the Asian Development Bank. It is also a member of the World Meteorological Organization and an associate member of the International Maritime Organization (until 1982, the Intergovernmental Maritime Consultative Organization).[12] Hong Kong, through the United Kingdom, is in fact a party to many international conventions. It has been granted separate export quotas by its major trading partners such as the United States, the United Kingdom, Canada, and the European Economic Community. Hong Kong also maintains its own memberships in 312 international nongovernmental organizations.[13] Hong Kong has participated, through the United Kingdom, in more than 85 multilateral treaties or arrangements relating to arbitration, aviation, copyright, customs, trade, health, protection of industrial property, settlement of investment disputes, judicial assistance, maritime matters, the control of narcotics, patents, publications, satellite communications, telecommunications, and other matters.[14]

There are 61 countries that maintain consulates and eight British Commonwealth countries that maintain commissioner's offices (i.e., consulates in fact) in Hong Kong.[15] Externally, Hong Kong maintains a government office in London, Geneva (under United Kingdom Mission to the United Nations European Headquarters), and Brussels (under the British Embassy). A Hong Kong office is also maintained in the British Embassy in Washington and an Office of the Commissioner for Hong Kong Commercial Affairs in the British Consulate-General in New York. Hong Kong industrial promotion offices have been established in Tokyo, London, Stuttgart, and San Francisco. The Hong Kong Trade Development Council maintains offices in Vienna, Amsterdam, Frankfurt, Hamburg, London, Milan, Paris, Stockholm, New York, Chicago, Dallas, Los Angeles, Toronto, Miami, Panama, Osaka, and Sydney. Finally, the Hong Kong Tourist Association established branch offices in San Francisco, New York, Chicago, London, Rome, Paris, Frankfurt, Tokyo, Osaka, Singapore, and Sydney.[16] For those areas or countries in which no special offices are maintained, Hong Kong's interests are represented by British embassies or consulates. Through this comprehensive network, Hong Kong maintains extensive relations abroad and the name "Hong Kong" has become well known throughout the world.

THE SINO-BRITISH NEGOTIATION ON THE FUTURE OF HONG KONG

In the New Territories, a lease is limited to a maximum period of 15 years; thus in 1982 it was necessary to know whether after that year a lease could still be valid for another 15 years. This is because the British administrative rights in the New Territories will be terminated on July 1, 1997, the last date of the British lease of New Territories from China. Without the leased territories, Hong Kong would have virtually no agriculture or industry. It would lose its container port at Kwai Chung and thus its shipping industry. Although the runway of the airport is within the ceded territory, the incoming and outgoing aircraft have to fly over the leased territories. In other words, the leased territories are essential to the existence of the rest of Hong Kong. This fact prompted the United Kingdom to initiate discussions with the PRC on the future of Hong Kong.

In September 1982 Margaret Thatcher, the British prime minister, visited the PRC and raised the subject of Hong Kong with both Premier Zhao Ziyang and Deng Xiaoping. According to well-informed sources, Deng told Thatcher that when China recovers sovereignty, the British flag and the British governor would have to go, and China would take steps to ensure Hong Kong's prosperity. Thatcher emphasized the importance of continuing Hong Kong's links with the United Kingdom if the territory was to be preserved as a bustling commercial and financial center, but she left open the possibility that something could be worked out to satisfy China's demand that the United Kingdom recognize Chinese sovereignty over Hong Kong.[17] At the end of Thatcher's visit, a joint communique was issued stating that both countries "agreed to enter talks through diplomatic channels following the visit, with the common aim of maintaining the stability and prosperity of Hong Kong."[18]

The first stage of the negotiation, between September 1982 and September 1983, was deadlocked over the issue of sovereignty and the continued role of the United Kingdom in Hong Kong after 1997. It was reported that during the negotiation, the British undertook to explain to the Chinese the factors that accounted for Hong Kong's success, for example, Hong Kong's ability to participate, through the United Kingdom's links, in international trading arrangements such as the General Agreement on Tariffs and Trade (GATT) and the Multifiber Arrangement; the virtues of the British legal system; and the rights and freedoms guaranteed under the rule of law and the orderly administration of Hong Kong provided by the British Hong Kong government.[19] By building a case for being indispensable, the British negotiating position was based on the principle of "exchanging sovereignty for administrative power" and for "continued British administration in Hong Kong upon recognition of Chinese sovereignty."[20] In other words, the United Kingdom was willing to recognize Chinese sovereignty over the whole of Hong Kong, including those parts ceded to Great Britain in the nineteenth century, in exchange for Chinese consent to continue British administration after 1997 for a certain period such as 30 or 50 years. Under this arrangement, although the future cannot be solved once and for all, at least the issue can be shelved for a considerable period. At the beginning of the negotiations, many Hong Kong people believed that this solution would be acceptable to the PRC. This belief was strengthened by the fact that between 1974 and 1977, the PRC had rejected the Portuguese offer to return Macao to China three times.[21]

To the surprise of the people of Hong Kong, the PRC flatly denounced such a proposal. There are three major reasons why the PRC rejected this solution. First, the PRC has never recognized the legal validity of the two treaties (1842 and 1860) that ceded Hong Kong Island and the southern part of the Kowloon Peninsula.[22] By accepting the United Kingdom's proposal of "exchanging sovereignty for administrative power," the PRC would be viewed as implicitly accepting the validity of these two treaties, which is contrary to its longtime position.[23]

Second, assuming, *arguendo*, that the PRC could accept the continuation of British administration over Hong Kong under PRC sovereignty for another 30 to 50 years, how could it justify pressing its claim over unifying Taiwan with the mainland during that long period? Ironically, if there were no Taiwan problem, the PRC might tolerate the continuation of British rule in Hong Kong for an indefinite period, because at any time the PRC could ask the British to leave and restore its full sovereignty there. However, the Taiwan situation is different. Taiwan has its own defensive capability, and if the PRC leaves the island alone for another 30 to 50 years after 1997, the PRC might have to launch a costly military campaign, with wide adverse political and economic consequences to the PRC, to achieve its unification goal. In this connection, the existence of a very vocal Taiwan independence movement (albeit only a few people from Taiwan support this movement) tends only to compel the PRC to take a rigid position on both the Hong Kong and Taiwan issues.

Third, since the death of Mao Zedong in 1976, no individual in the PRC seems to be in a position to make concessions on the sensitive issue of sovereignty. If any leader or faction in the PRC were to make such a concession on Hong Kong's sovereignty, he might be attacked by other rival factions in the ongoing power struggle in China's domestic politics. On the other hand, the prestige of any leader or faction that can recover sovereignty over Hong Kong or Taiwan would be greatly enhanced.

In view of the above stated reasons, the British position was categorically rejected by China. During this period the financial and economic situation of Hong Kong deteriorated and the Hong Kong dollar steadily declined in value. Since China gets roughly a third of its annual foreign exchange from or through Hong Kong, the PRC suspected that the United Kingdom deliberately manipulated the money markets, although there is no conclusive evidence that this was the case. The chaotic economic situation did not have an influence on China's position on the sovereignty issue. It is reported that Deng Xiaoping said that even if the Hong Kong dollar should drop to 20 to 1 U.S. dollar (before the negotiation it was about 5 to 1), China would still not give in. Premier Zhao and other officials also reportedly said: "No country can put prosperity ahead of sovereignty."[24]

In the fall of 1983, China continued to put pressure on the United Kingdom by disclosing its intention to announce unilaterally its plans for the future of Hong Kong if an agreement with the United Kingdom could not be reached by September 1984.[25] Confronted with the dilemma of either reaching an agreement with China on the latter's terms or having no agreement at all, which would definitely make the Hong Kong situation worse, the United Kingdom acquiesced. Prime Minister Thatcher then informed Premier Zhao that the United Kingdom would sever all of its ties with Hong Kong after 1997, and it would concede sovereignty over all of Hong Kong, including those parts ceded to the United Kingdom.[26] Once the sovereignty issue was resolved, the negotiation continued smoothly. This Chinese negotiating style is consistent with the strategy used by China in the past—insisting on general principles while remaining flexible on concrete arrangements to implement the principles. The postsovereignty-issue negotiations were described by a reporter as follows:

> China, having won the battles on sovereignty and administration, was willing to listen as Britain detailed the complexities of Hong Kong, its international economic and financial role, the necessity for adapting rapidly to changes in its markets, the Hong Kong legal system, and the territory's obligations under a network of treaties and international organizations that it had joined by virtue of the British umbrella. The Chinese, on their part, had to spell out details of their proposal that Hong Kong would be given a "high degree of autonomy" as a special administrative region of China that would practice not the socialist system of the mainland but capitalism. In the end, the amount of detail in the final agreement was the greatest achievement of the British negotiators. The agreement and the Basic Law enshrining its principles will, after 1997, be the only buffer between Hong Kong and its Communist masters in Beijing.[27]

On September 26, 1984, the United Kingdom and the People's Republic of China initialed the Joint Declaration on the Question of Hong Kong, which was formally signed on December 19, 1984, and the instruments of ratification were exchanged on May 27, 1985.[28]

The Joint Declaration contains more than 8,000 words and is, perhaps, the second longest international agreement ever concluded by the PRC.[29] It spelled out in detail the PRC's policy toward Hong Kong, the post–1997 Hong Kong regime, and its international relations. The highlights of the declaration are as follows:

1. After 1997, Hong Kong will become a Special Administrative Region of the PRC under Article 31 of the PRC Constitution.[30] It will enjoy a "high degree of autonomy" except in foreign and defense affairs.
2. Hong Kong will be vested with executive, legislative, and independent judicial power, including that of final adjudication.
3. Hong Kong's chief executive will be appointed by the PRC after elections or consultation in Hong Kong. The government of Hong Kong will be composed of local people.
4. Hong Kong shall maintain the capitalist economic and trade systems for 50 years after 1997.
5. The existing social and economic system will remain unchanged. Freedom of speech, movement, the press, assembly, strike, and religion and other freedom will be protected by law. Similarly, private property rights will be protected.
6. Apart from displaying the national flag and national emblem of the PRC, Hong Kong may use a regional flag and emblem of its own.
7. Hong Kong may participate in relevant international organizations and international trade agreements. It may establish official and semiofficial economic and trade missions in foreign countries, using the name "Hong Kong, China" to maintain and develop relations and conclude and implement agreements with states, regions, and relevant international organizations in appropriate fields.
8. The PRC defense force stationed in Hong Kong shall not interfere in the internal affairs in Hong Kong and the expenditures for these military forces shall be borne by the PRC's Central People's Government.

The public reaction in Hong Kong was generally favorable, as observed by Frank Ching:

> Most people who took part in public discussions found the agreement much more detailed, and more reassuring, than they had expected. One feature of the Joint Declaration, however, that many Hong Kong residents are unhappy about is its reference to the stationing of Chinese troops in Hong Kong. Several Chinese leaders had said troops would not be sent, and some Hong Kong residents see China's reversal on this issue as a sign that it may also renege on other commitments.
>
> Missing from the Joint Declaration is a statement as to whether China will conscript Hong Kong youths to serve in the armed forces. The British pressed for a

declaration, and the Chinese said their policy was not to draft men from Hong Kong. But they refused to incorporate such a pledge in the Joint Declaration. Taken as a whole, however, the agreement—in all its detail and the care with which it was negotiated—signaled China's desire to reassure Hong Kong residents of its intention to abide by it.[31]

THE UNITED STATES AND THE SINO-BRITISH NEGOTIATION

Aside from the PRC and the United Kingdom, the United States maintains perhaps a closer relationship with Hong Kong than with any other country. However, until recently, the United States appeared to take a hands-off policy toward Hong Kong. It had neither committed itself to defend Hong Kong nor supported the granting of self-government or independence to Hong Kong in the United Nations. It was not until the PRC and the United Kingdom began their negotiations on the future of Hong Kong that the United States publicly renewed its concern over Hong Kong's future.[32]

The United States has an important political and economic stake in Hong Kong. Immediately after the Chinese Communists took over the Chinese mainland, the United States' interest in Hong Kong was primarily for intelligence gathering. Over the years, the role of Hong Kong as a gathering post gradually diminished. On the other hand, the spectacular economic development of Hong Kong under British laissez-faire policy transformed it into a significant economic power in East Asia and a major trading partner of the United States. At present, the United States has a significant amount of private investments and connections in Hong Kong. In 1984 Hong Kong imported US$3.1 billion worth of goods from the United States and exported US$7.9 billion of goods to the latter.[33] Hong Kong is also an important location for United States' business interests. There are approximately 14,000 American residents in Hong Kong, and approximately 500,000 U.S. nationals visit Hong Kong annually. Private investments from the United States are estimated at US$4 billion to US$5 billion, thus putting it second in Asia, after Japan, as a locale for United States' investments.[34] Moreover, the United States also has a strong interest in using Hong Kong as a base for promoting its investment and business interests in China. Finally, many of the three-quarters of a million Chinese living in the United States have family ties in Hong Kong.

Despite strong United States' interests in Hong Kong's future, the official U.S. position appeared to restrict its involvement to the role of an interested bystander during the period of the Sino-British negotiations on Hong Kong. However, it did remind the PRC on several occasions of the implications of Hong Kong's future on the Taiwan question.[35] The United States has a strong political, moral and legal interest in Taiwan under the U.S. Taiwan Relations Act of 1979.[36] Moreover, a responsible official of the U.S. State

Department did indicate U.S. support of Hong Kong's continuing participation in certain types of international organizations or agreements following restoration of Chinese sovereignty.[37] There was no indication of whether Hong Kong's 5,000 (increased from 600 in 1986) immigration quota would be maintained after the Chinese takeover.

After the United Kingdom and the PRC announced their agreement on Hong Kong on September 26, 1984, the United States made a very positive response to this agreement. Acting U.S. Department of State spokesman Alan Romberg, on behalf of Secretary Shultz, stated at the September 26, 1984, press conference that the United States "believes [that] the [Sino-British] agreement will provide a solid foundation for Hong Kong's enduring future progress," and it offered to "provide any assistance it can . . . to maintain Hong Kong's appropriate participation in international bodies" after 1997.[38] With the exception of the Republic of China on Taiwan,[39] the response from other countries was also generally favorable.[40]

TOWARD 1997 AND BEYOND: PROBLEMS AND PROSPECTS

Despite the official optimistic response to the Sino-British Declaration on Hong Kong as expressed by the United Kingdom, the PRC, and the United States, whether the future of Hong Kong will be as bright as the official expectations remains to be seen. The remaining chapters of this book attempt to analyze this issue from different angles. In Chapter 2 George Hicks assesses various problems that he believes will confront Hong Kong in the transition years before the Chinese Communist takeover in 1997. He provides a general survey of both the optimist and the pessimist and compares the two. According to Hicks, optimism over Hong Kong's future is virtually official and rather simplistic. The views that China will not kill the goose that lays the golden eggs, wants to set a good example for Taiwan, and keeps its international agreements are frequently expounded, but these reasons are also open to challenge. Despite the signing of the Sino-British Declaration on Hong Kong, China still considers the Hong Kong issue as a purely domestic affair, never to be put into the same class as China's other international agreements. The golden-goose theory and the Taiwan issue are based on a naive interpretation of China's supposed self-interests. However, a more sophisticated approach must take account of China's self-interests in a broad context, that is, in the light of Beijing's domestic political situation. A crucial issue here is: what will be the likely political cost in domestic politics for maintaining a capitalist enclave?

The remaining part of Hicks' chapter concentrates on the development in the transition period of Hong Kong between now and 1997, which will be profoundly influenced by expectations about what will happen after 1997. In his view, if China continues to liberalize, optimism about post–

1997 will rise, and events in Hong Kong during the transition period will change. With respect to the "one country, two systems" theory offered by the PRC to post–1997 Hong Kong, he believes it is essential for the PRC to induce the people of Hong Kong to have faith in this theory; otherwise there will be a high probability that as 1997 nears, most people in Hong Kong will not have sufficient faith in this theory to make them want to stay.

Apart from the question of having confidence in China, Hicks points out that the people of Hong Kong must have confidence in themselves. If the progress toward localization and self-government is unsatisfactory, self-doubt will begin to grow. The growth of effective local leadership is essential, but it is far from certain that this local leadership will emerge. This is in part because of China's reluctance to allow the British Hong Kong government to carry out this political reform. If a genuine self-government emerges before 1997, China will have difficulty in controlling Hong Kong effectively in the post–1997 period. However, the alternative is to show the people of Hong Kong that China's promise of autonomy is probably a fraud. Hicks concludes that this dilemma is going to haunt China for a long time.

The main reason why the PRC is willing to agree to let Hong Kong's capitalism continue for 50 years after 1997 is to maintain the economic prosperity of Hong Kong. Will the Sino-British Declaration achieve that goal by maintaining Hong Kong's economic prosperity toward 1997 and beyond? This issue is ably analyzed and assessed by Y.C. Jao in Chapter 3. He observes that there are three principal factors that contributed to Hong Kong's economic miracle in the post–World War II period, namely, political and social stability, economic reform, and the rule of law. During the period of the Sino-British negotiations, widespread apprehension that these factors would no longer operate once sovereignty reverted to China triggered a profound crisis of confidence in 1982–1984 that at one point nearly brought the whole financial system to the brink of total collapse. With the initialling of the Sino-British Declaration on September 24, 1984, which ostensibly embodied the three factors responsible for Hong Kong's success in the past, the situation in Hong Kong appears to be stable, at least for the foreseeable future.

Will this situation continue toward 1997 and beyond? According to Yao, the Sino-British Declaration per se does not constitute a permanent guarantee for Hong Kong's stability and prosperity. For the period from 1984 until 1987, the positive impact of the Sino-British Declaration is evident. This is because most people reasoned that the declaration brought safety and stability in the period until 1997. Given that in Hong Kong the typical pay-back period is about five to eight years, a transition period of nearly thirteen years is one that most entrepreneurs and businessmen can live with. For other nonbusiness people, the transition period is also long enough to make their plans in an orderly manner.

Moreover, the provisions of the Sino-British Declaration itself are more detailed and reassuring than expected. Although the declaration is nothing more than a piece of paper, to a frightened and insecure population, a piece of paper signed by two sovereign powers is still looked upon as something of a guarantee of their human rights and liberty. Furthermore, there is considerable evidence that China itself, concerned about the dire consequences of Hong Kong's collapse, has been trying to stabilize the local economy in various ways.

Finally, China's internal developments have important implications for Hong Kong. Although Deng's China is still far from being a liberal democracy, there is abundant evidence that it is settling down to becoming what might be called a "postrevolutionary society," the primary goals of which are now economic reconstruction and modernization, rather than class struggle and world revolution. These developments have given rise to hopes that the wide gaps in the standards of living and life-styles between China and Hong Kong will gradually diminish. Such hope might turn out to be wishful thinking, but it does have a soothing effect on the anxiety and fear of the people of Hong Kong.

With respect to the period from 1988 to 1997, Jao considers that the outlook for Hong Kong becomes much less clear and more uncertain. Any unexpected political and economic developments in either Hong Kong or China could defeat the delicate balance that the Sino-British Declaration has brought about for the time being.

In 1988 a Sino-British Joint Liaison Group will be established. Although this group does not have executive power under the Sino-British Declaration, it is feared that China's representatives in the group may gain access to sensitive or even classified information on virtually every aspect of Hong Kong life. This development, if it occurs, certainly would not contribute to the stability in Hong Kong.

Another matter of grave concern in this period is the Basic Law to be enacted by the PRC unilaterally and which is supposed to be a "miniconstitution" for post–1997 Hong Kong that will incorporate the essential features of the Sino-British Declaration. Whether this document will embody the kind of polity desired by the majority of the populace remains to be seen.

Moreover, the political and administrative structure in Hong Kong will be undergoing significant changes until 1997. The British strategy is to nurture the development of a quasi-parliamentary democracy based largely on indirect elections. Thus by 1997 a new generation of Hong Kong political leaders can take power under the terms of the Sino-British Declaration. Publicly, China has maintained silence on this development, but it is no secret that Beijing's attitude toward Hong Kong's democratization is one of distaste and displeasure. Beijing is afraid that an elected government in Hong Kong that embodies the popular will might be much less amenable to manipulation and control after 1997. More importantly, such a government might generate a "demonstration effect" on the people in the mainland with potential explosive consequences.

With this overall political outlook in context, Jao perceives that a total collapse of the economy before 1997 seems most unlikely, but the economic outlook for this period is also much more murky and uncertain than for the 1984–1987 period. In sum, much will depend on the stability of the political system, the continuity of China's pragmatic policies, and the progress of the modernization and economic reform program in China.

Jao believes that it is virtually impossible to predict the outlook of Hong Kong in the post–1997 era. In his view, the period immediately before June 30, 1997, could be very difficult for Hong Kong. The smooth transfer of power hinges on the goodwill and cooperation of the two countries. However, from Hong Kong's point of view, there will be two matters of immediate concern. One is the availability of qualified people to run the Special Administrative Region (SAR) government, which is dependent on the internal political and administrative evolution in Hong Kong to make it feel attractive and secure to remain in Hong Kong. The other is whether China would permit the chief executive of the SAR to have real power to run Hong Kong.

The real question, as perceived by Jao, is whether China will honor the Sino-British Declaration after the British withdrawal. There are two aspects to this problem. One is China's willingness and the other is its ability to honor the declaration. In this regard, Jao believes that China must be given the benefit of the doubt since it seems far-fetched to suggest that China took the trouble of negotiating an agreement (in the form of a declaration) with the United Kingdom for two years only to repudiate it deliberately. References have often been made to the previous PRC's duplicity with respect to Shanghai and Tibet. But the historical analogy is valid only if China remains the same Maoist China as it was before 1977. Therefore, the real crux of the matter is China's ability to honor the declaration. this depends on the moderates' ability to stay in power in Beijing until at least 1997 and the progress in modernization and economic reform. Finally, assuming that China is both willing and able to abide by the declaration, the question remains whether Hong Kong's status as a separate economic entity as embodied in the declaration will be accepted internationally.

In Chapter 4 Hsin-chi Kuan and Siu-kai Lau view the future of Hong Kong from another dimension: the barriers and prospects of building a consensus among the people of Hong Kong about the direction and form of political change in Hong Kong before 1997 so that it will be possible to achieve "the high degree of autonomy" for Hong Kong prescribed in the Sino-British Declaration in the post–1997 period.

Although the British government has rich experience in decolonialization, which usually follows a pattern of calculated sequential steps from the introduction of local government reforms through the localization of the bureaucracy to the granting of independence, this pattern is not applicable to Hong Kong because independence is not the ultimate goal for Hong Kong's political development. Therefore, what kind of a polity should be returned to China in 1997 becomes a taxing problem. It is apparent, according to Kuan and Lau, that Hong Kong needs a locally rooted leadership if "Hong Kong people ruling Hong Kong" after 1997 or "representative government" is to be taken seriously. This leadership will have to provide a vision for the future, to tinker at the political escapism and refugee/immigrant reflexes in society, to cultivate political efficacy and self-identity among the attentive public, and to demonstrate ability to govern before the departure of the British administration. As the present situation stands, observed by Kuan and Lau, all of these things remain less than a reality. There are several reasons contributing to this phenomenon.

The political system in Hong Kong has failed to nurture even a limited number of political leaders who can wield any moral authority. The prosperous economic sector has absorbed and will continue to draw away most of Hong Kong's talents. The dependent status of Hong Kong's post–1997 political system on an authoritarian Communist government will render the political career unattractive to some aspirants and even risky to others. The pragmatic public in Hong Kong can be mobilized for short-term benefits but can hardly be enlightened on matters of long-term principles. In other words, the political arena is too compressed for the emergence of an effective transforming leadership.

In the past, several studies have indicated that Hong Kong's political culture is of a "don't-rock-the-boat" mentality in a refugee town, which was a kind of passive acceptance of the lesser evil. Currently, according to Kuan and Lau, the people of Hong Kong are much more sophisticated. They know the limits of their power, but they are ready to resort to pressure or violence. They have not been converted to the consensus reached at the Sino-British Declaration. Political status quo is still their preference, not because it is the lesser evil, but because they are positively attached to it. It is this area that most democratic proponents in Hong Kong have failed to grasp. In contrast to them, the people of Hong Kong do not view politics in structural terms. They are much more concerned with performance. The form of government is largely irrelevant, provided they can maintain a decent living. The performance of the present Hong Kong government is evaluated highly, with a finding that bureaucrats are trusted more than politicians. After being sheltered from the trauma of Chinese politics for decades, they have become accustomed to trusting professional knowledge and administrative skills more than the advocacy of political ideals and the politicians' ability to resolve conflicts. This lack of a consensus among the public toward a democratic form of government is another barrier in building a consensus toward meaningful political reform before 1997.

With regard to the elites, the issue of 1997 is highly divisive. Those holding responsible positions in industry, commerce, banking, and the government generally tend to be conservative; those who advocate democratization in Hong Kong receive support from a number of grass-roots leaders, part of the intelligentsia, and many of the educated youth. With respect to policy options for Hong Kong's form of government, both groups of elites have avowed support for stability and prosperity and have realized that a political system rooted in Hong Kong has to be firmly established before or at the time of British departure in 1997. They differ sharply, however, on how this system should be constituted. The conservatives are afraid of too much democracy for its welfare implications and the unpredictability of the popular mood. The democratic advocates are concerned that too little democracy would be insufficient to give the future government popular legitimacy for immunity from external intervention.

The Chinese government is not interested in any significant change of the present form of government in Hong Kong, especially its democratization. This is because the present system is (1) dependent on an external force for its legitimacy, (2) relatively immune from political pressures originating from the society, (3) executive centered rather than legislature dominated, and (4) operative in a top-down policy-making mode. When Hong Kong is returned to China, it appears that it will be in China's best interest if these essential features of government are preserved. In Hong Kong's future, China is more concerned with social stability and economic prosperity than political innovation or democratization in the form of mass volatility, group activism, and partisan and adversarial politics. All of these things would make the Chinese control over post–1997 Hong Kong much more difficult than in a situation in which the bureaucratic government is stronger than the society. Therefore, China does not share the same sense of urgency for political reform before 1997.

In view of these barriers to consensus building with respect to political change in Hong Kong, a single political consensus is not likely to develop. However, there appears to be a dominant consensus in Hong Kong to favor a minimally integrated social-political system. Under those circumstances, Kuan and Lau conclude that the participants in the exercise of consensus building will eventually choose the one of familiarity, least resistance, and marginal gains. It is likely that further reforms will not depart radically from the present system. In the meantime, there will be some soul-searching activities and rhetorical games. But all of this will end in the realization that tradition is still the better mentor.

In recent discussions on the future of Hong Kong, the human rights dimension of the question has been generally ignored, despite the fact that the United Kingdom voted in favor of the adoption of the 1948 Universal Declaration of Human Rights by the General Assembly of the United Nations and its inclusion of Hong Kong in the applicable area of the two United Nations covenants on human rights.[41] Ta-ling Li analyzes this question in Chapter 5. According to him, Prime Minister Margaret Thatcher was among the first to mention the interests of the people of Hong Kong during the initial stage of the negotiations. However, Thatcher and other British officials were soon to find out that they had neither the means nor the ability to involve the people of Hong Kong in the negotiations as a third party. This is because at present there exists no formal institutions through which the people of Hong Kong can be consulted. Moreover, even if there were means to consult with the people of Hong Kong concerning their views, such as a plebiscite, the standing veto from Beijing would make them utterly unrealistic. In addition to noting these inherent difficulties, Li also observes that the British government demonstrated an attitude of calculated indifference and arrogance toward the people of Hong Kong.

One important factor for Hong Kong's phenomenal rise to its present status as one of the world's dynamic economic and financial centers is the fact that Hong Kong is a free society under the rule of law, which has made possible the release of human energy and creativity to perform wonders. Hong Kong is not a perfect society. It has the usual shortcomings associated with what is generally known as a capitalistic society, including crime, social inequities, indifference, and alienation. However, this system allows one the freedom to act and affords protection against unchecked political power in the wrong hands. As the Sino-British negotiations were underway, the people of Hong Kong were to experience a shocking and cruel awakening that they had, in fact, no control over their own destiny. The prospect of having to live again under the system from which most of them have escaped is frightening. Yet there is little they can do to avoid the fact. This crisis of confidence is not totally alleviated by the 1984 Sino-British Declaration. To the Chinese government, Li observes, the issue concerning Hong Kong is one of sovereignty, not of how the people there feel. The return of sovereignty to China is a matter of nationalism and therefore cannot be questioned. All that remains to be done is to give assurance to the people of Hong Kong that things will not change without inquiring what the people of Hong Kong are thinking. After 1997, how long will Beijing tolerate Hong Kong with its freedoms? How will Beijing keep the ideological "Hong-Kongization" from spreading to the mainland? These are fundamental questions reflecting the Hong Kong people's fear that what they have possessed now will by necessity be taken away long before the 50-year guarantee period expires. However, Chinese leaders so far have not provided convincing answers to these questions.

What can other countries, besides the United Kingdom and China, do to help the people of Hong Kong as far as their human rights are concerned?

These countries have so far provided only havens for those people of Hong Kong who can afford to leave, a small affluent minority. However, although most Western countries have no leverage on China concerning the future welfare of the people of Hong Kong, in view of their status as the major supplier of technology to China, Li suggests that they could, perhaps, insist on linking technology transfer to China with the latter's respect for human rights in Hong Kong.

The extent to which the restoration of Hong Kong to China would affect Hong Kong's economic partners and neighbors (including the People's Republic of China itself) is a main theme of Chapter 6, written by Yuan-li Wu. Whether the principal conditions under British rule that have made Hong Kong a prosperous and developing economy could continue to exist in the post–1997 period is open to doubt. One of these conditions is the British legal system. The Chinese Communist legal system and work style have never favored an independent court. Arbitrary intervention in the award and performance of contracts and in free-market operations would seem to be entirely natural and consistent with Chinese practice to date. If the Chinese system and practice are to prevail in Hong Kong, one of the basic conditions for Hong Kong's prosperity would be undermined.

A second condition for Hong Kong's prosperity is its relatively low tax burden. After the Chinese takeover, it is possible that China may increase Hong Kong's real tax burden directly or indirectly to finance its modernization program. The future Hong Kong government may also increase its social expenditures to a higher level than the British administration incurs now, thus raising the demand for revenue. Other conditions for Hong Kong's prosperity—such as a steady supply on the labor market, free currency exchange, free trade and free access to the outside world, freedom to travel, and, above all, financial privacy—are also subject to substantial change under the post–1997 PRC administration in China and in Hong Kong. In short, Wu observes that these conditions for Hong Kong's prosperity may not continue to exist after 1997 and thus may significantly affect the relations between Hong Kong and its economic partners and neighbors. However, even more important for the future of Hong Kong itself, and indirectly therefore for China, is the steady conversion of resident-owned assets in Hong Kong into foreign-owned assets before 1997. Any attempt to intervene in this ongoing quiet process is likely to trigger a crisis, a phenomenon best described as "crowding at the exit." To prevent this undesirable result from happening, Wu suggests that certain external restraints to reduce the possibility of Chinese intervention in Hong Kong could be worked out by Hong Kong's major economic partners, individually if not in concert. However, he also acknowledges that this is not likely to happen because of other countries' concern about upsetting China over this sensitive "sovereign issue" in spite of the suggested solutions being in the PRC's true economic interest. The inexorable course of a historical tragedy, foreseeable but unprevented, may therefore be developing as the parties involved stand by, with some, though by no means universal, wringing of hands. If so, how will history assign responsibility for such a future loss of freedom by 5 million people?

All optimistic assessments of Hong Kong's post–1997 development include the major argument that China wants to make the "one country, two systems" model in Hong Kong as attractive as possible to Taiwan so as to achieve "peaceful unification" with Taiwan. This argument raises an important question: Can the Hong Kong model serve as a basis for unification with Taiwan? In Chapter 7, An-chia Wu attempts to analyze this question from Taiwan's point of view. According to his analysis, the "one country, two systems" formula is a "transitional model" used by the Chinese Communists for the settlement of the Taiwan and Hong Kong issues. To transform Taiwan into a socialist society remains the ultimate goal of the Chinese Communists. Moreover, in the case of Hong Kong, the people there are helpless, and they have no way to control their own fate since Hong Kong is indefensible strategically. However, the situation of Taiwan is different. The Republic of China on Taiwan is a sovereign state with well-trained and well-equipped armed forces. Moreover, the Taiwan Straits would serve as a natural barrier to make the Chinese Communists' invasion more difficult. Furthermore, the Chinese people on Taiwan are resolutely opposed to communism. Under such circumstances, why should they place their fate in the hands of the Chinese Communists under the "one country, two systems" model?

In addition to providing the analytical chapters mentioned above, the last part of this book presents a collection of important documents on Hong Kong and a selected bibliography. Together they constitute an invaluable source of information and analysis on the future of Hong Kong that will enable readers to draw their own conclusions or to carry on further research on the subject.

NOTES

1. *1986 Britannica Book of the Year* (Chicago: Encyclopaedia Britannica, 1986), p. 695.

2. Article 3 of the Sino-British Treaty of Nanking, August 29, 1842, *Consolidated Treaty Series*, Vol. 103, p. 467; Article 6 of the Convention of Friendship between China and Great Britain, October 24, 1860, ibid., Vol. 123, pp. 73–74, and Convention between China and Great Britain respecting an Extension of Hong Kong Territory, June 9, 1898, ibid., Vol. 186, pp. 310–11.

3. This section is primarily summarized from Bill Knight, ed., *Hong Kong: 1985*

(Hong Kong: Government Publications Center, n.d.), pp. 53–69. The comments on the governmental and legal system are those of Hungdah Chiu.

4. Wang Shijie (Wang Shih-chieh) and Hu Qingyu (Hu Ching-yu), *Zhongguo Bupingteng Tiaoyue Zhi Feichu [Chung-kuo pu-p'ing-teng t'iao-yueh chih fei-ch'u, The Abolition of China's Unequal Treaties]* (Taipei: Distributed by the Central Cultural Supply Press, 1967), p. 296.

5. Text of the treaties can be found in [Republic of China] Ministry of Foreign Affairs, *Treaties between the Republic of China and Foreign States (1927–1957)* (Taipei: Taiwan Commercial Press, 1958), pp. 589–602 (Great Britain), 659–68 (U.S.).

6. Zhang Qun (Chang Chun) and Huang Shaogu (Huang Shao-ku), *Jiang Zongtong Wei Ziyou Zhengyi Yu Heping Fendou Xulue [Chiang tsung-t'ung wei tzu-yu cheng-yi yu ho-ping fen-tou shu-lueh, President Chiang's Struggle for the Cause of Freedom, Justice, and Peace]* (Taipei: Distributed by the Central Cultural Supply Press, 1968), p. 277.

7. Cited in Jerome Alan Cohen and Hungdah Chiu, *People's China and International Law: A Documentary Study*, Vol. 1, (Princeton, N.J.: Princeton University Press, 1974), p. 380.

8. Ibid.

9. United Nations General Assembly Resolution 1514 (XV) of December 14, 1960. A convenient source to find this resolution is Ian Brownlie, *Basic Documents in International Law*, 3d ed. (London: Oxford University Press, 1983), pp. 299–301. Paragraph 2 of the operative part of this declaration reads: "All peoples have the right to self-determination; by virtue of that right they freely determine their political status and freely pursue their economic, social and cultural development."

10. "Khrushchev Group Turns World Youth Forum into Anti-China Forum," New China News Agency—English, Moscow (Sept. 25, 1964), reprinted in Cohen and Chiu, *People's China and International Law*, Vol. 1, pp. 381–82.

11. Cohen and Chiu, *People's China and International Law*, Vol. 1, p. 384.

12. See list of members of World Meteorological Organization and International Maritime Organization in Department of State, *Treaties in Force: A List of Treaties and Other International Agreements of the United States in Force on January 1, 1985* (Washington, D.C.: U.S. Government Printing Office, 1985), pp. 314, 257 (hereafter cited as *Treaties in Force, 1985*).

13. *Yearbook of International Organizations, 1981*, 19th ed. (Brussels: Union of International Associations, 1981), table 4, no p.

14. For an almost complete list of these treaties or agreements, see *Treaties in Force, 1985*.

15. Knight, *Hong Kong: 1985*, p. 305.

16. Ibid., pp. 206–307.

17. Frank Ching, *Hong Kong and China: For Better or for Worse* (New York: China Council of the Asia Society and the Foreign Policy Association, 1985), p. 11.

18. Ibid., p. 12.

19. Ibid., p. 16.

20. "On Richard Luce's Recent Statement," *Beijing Review*, Vol. 26, no. 42 (Oct. 17, 1983), p. 14. See also comments in a Chinese article by Jin Fu entitled "China's Recovery of Xianggang [Hong Kong] Area Fully Accords with International Law," *Beijing Review*, Vol. 26, no. 39 (Sept. 26, 1983), p. 14. This article is translated

from Chinese version published in *Guoji wenti yanjiu* [*Journal of International Studies*], 1983, no. 4 (Oct. 1983), pp. 3–8. This publication is sponsored by the PRC's Ministry of Foreign Affairs.

21. "China rejects Portuguese colony," Associate Press dispatch from Lisbon, *The Sun* (Baltimore), Feb. 2, 1977, p. A4.

22. See the lengthy legal arguments presented in Jin Fu, "China's Recovery of Hong Kong," *Beijing Review* pp. 15–16 (English version), and *Journal of International Studies*, pp. 3–5 (Chinese version).

23. Ibid., *Beijing Review*, pp. 16–18 (English version), and *Journal of International Studies*, pp. 5–6 (Chinese version).

24. Ching, *Hong Kong and China*, p. 17.

25. Ibid., p. 20.

26. Ibid.

27. Ibid., p. 21.

28. *Facts on File, 1985*, Vol. 45, no. 2323 (May 31, 1985), pp. 412–43. For the text of the declaration and related documents, see Knight, *Hong Kong: 1985*, pp. 1–16, and *International Legal Materials*, Vol. 23, no. 6 (Nov. 1984), pp. 1366–87.

29. The longest PRC treaty is the 1962 boundary treaty with Mongolia. See *Zhonghua Renmin Gonghe guo Tiaoyue Ji* [*Collection of Treaties of the People's Republic of China*], Vol. 11 (1962), p. 19ff.

30. Article 31 provides: "The state may establish special administrative regions when necessary. The systems to be instituted in special administrative regions shall be prescribed by law enacted by the National People's Congress in the light of the specific conditions."

31. Ching, *Hong Kong and China*, p. 41. For a more dubious observation, see Barbara Crossette, "Hong Kong Sees the Future: Will It Work?" *New York Times*, Sept. 27, 1984, pp. A1, A12; and Dinah Lee, "Hong Kong Residents Cautiously Optimistic," *The Washington Post*, Sept. 27, 1984, p. A23.

32. For an analysis of this question, see Hungdah Chiu, "The Hong Kong Agreement and American Foreign Policy," *Issues & Studies*, vol. 22, no. 6 (June 1986), pp. 76–91.

33. *United States and Hong Kong, Some Important Facts*, prepared by British-Hong Kong Government Trade Department, Aug. 1985, pp. 1–2.

34. See U.S. Consul-General to Hong Kong Burton Levin's speech delivered at The Asia Society, New York, June 7, 1984, p. 3.

35. See a high U.S. State Department official's view reported in Winsome Lane, "U.S. Confident about 1997," *South China Morning Post*, Jan. 1, 1984, pp. 1, 6; and U.S. Consul-General to Hong Kong Burton Levin's speech, pp. 8–9, 11.

36. U.S. Public Law 96–8, *Statutes at Large*, Vol. 93, p. 14ff.

37. U.S. Consul-General to Hong Kong Burton Levin's speech, p. 11.

38. "U.K. and China Reach Agreement on Hong Kong," *Department of State Bulletin*, Vol. 84, no. 292 (Nov. 1984), p. 56.

39. See statement issued by the Republic of China's Foreign Ministry on September 26, 1984. *Foreign Broadcasting Information Service, Daily Report, China*, Sept. 28, 1984, p. vi.

40. Christopher Wren, "China Cuts a Hong Kong Deal with Assurances on All Sides," *New York Times*, Sept. 30, 1984, p. E3.

41. *United Nations Treaty Series*, Vol. 993, pp. 3ff. (Economic and Social) and Vol. 999, p. 171ff. (Civil and Political).

2

Hong Kong on the Eve of Communist Rule

GEORGE L. HICKS

Hong Kong on the eve of Communist rule is outwardly and officially confident but inwardly uncertain and fearful of the future: exterior calm masks internal tension. Although fears and doubts are something to be expressed in private, the pessimists quietly make arrangements to emigrate or wish they could. Intimidation, based on a fear of retribution after 1997 (or before?), and a pervasive sense of utter helplessness drives people into the seclusion of their private lives and drains the public debate of any critical spirit. Controversy takes place only at the level of the trivial; matters of substance are for governments; the powerless take no risks.

The Sino-British Agreement, imposed on Hong Kong without consultation, has decided the future; Hong Kong is to remain stable and prosperous and, above all, is to go quietly. Despite the overwhelming force of Sino-British power and the total lack of any countervailing force in Hong Kong, it is far from certain that this tidy scenario will be acted out. The overturn of the entire power structure of a great modern city and its forcible transfer to Communist rule is an unprecedented event in peacetime that may yet have a surprise ending.

Although the Sino-British alliance monopolizes political, legal, and military power and has shown how effectively it can mold world public opinion, its influence is flawed in one fatal respect: economic power.

Economic power in Hong Kong is a near monopoly of the private sector. Only business people can invest and, even more decisively, can disinvest and withdraw their funds almost in an instant and deposit them around the world. When the time comes and the screen of officially orchestrated optimism begins to crack, it will be the loss of business confidence, followed by the outflow of capital, that will expose the agreement as a pack of cards.

It is impossible to predict which cogs in the presently well-oiled machine will prove vulnerable first. High on the list of possibilities are developments such as a serious decline in civil service morale and the clear perception that the post–1997 judiciary will be neither independent nor competent. The loss of confidence in the rule of law could bring Hong Kong to its knees faster than anything short of violence. Intervention and interference by China well before 1997 cannot be ruled out either.

The possibility of the apparently invulnerable Sino-British alliance cracking before 1997 has been widely recognized. Disagreements over nationality and land sales have already emerged and have even been enshrined in the agreement. There is one other potential disagreement that is so acute that it was not even possible to refer to it in the agreement. This is the question of constitutional change before 1997: how is the goal of local autonomy to be realized? This potential problem, which has attracted little attention, is the focus of this chapter. The thesis is that this issue may prove the most intractable and will place great, perhaps fatal, strain on the alliance. The crumbling of the alliance may not be the beginning of the end, but it will be the end of the great illusion, the dream of "one country, two systems," and the hope that nothing much will change after 1997. In regard to the Hong Kong economy in the context of the 1997 issue, the thesis is that the future of Hong Kong's market economy will be essentially determined in the political arena. The economy that for so long was insulated from politics is now in the vortex of a political struggle, seeking shelter for the moment in the eye of a gigantic but slowly developing storm.

OPTIMIST AND PESSIMISTS

The Optimists

Most observers are reasonably confident that Hong Kong's free-market economy will survive until 1997 and beyond. This optimistic scenario is based on five generally held propositions:

1. *The golden-goose theory.* It is in China's economic interests to continue to allow Hong Kong to flourish because China gets about one-third of its foreign exchange from sales to Hong Kong and benefits in other ways from Hong Kong's prosperity.
2. *The Taiwan issue.* China's most important objective is the recovery of Taiwan and is therefore certain to be on its best behavior in Hong Kong. If China does not set a good example in Hong Kong, it will have no chance of ever getting Taiwan back peacefully.
3. *China always keeps it word.* Although China has a poor record in terms of keeping its word domestically, it does not break its international agreements. The agreement over Hong Kong is an international one and is the highest form of commitment between two sovereign states.
4. *China's good record in Hong Kong.* China could have easily taken over or disrupted Hong Kong at any time since 1949. Except for relatively minor and exceptional incidents in 1966–1967, China's Hong Kong record is impeccable, and there is no reason to think that it will not continue this way in the future.

5. *The China-is-becoming-capitalist thesis.* Even if it is not becoming capitalist, China is liberalizing in many ways as the revolution winds down. China's focus on modernization will help rather than harm Hong Kong.

These five propositions are widely accepted in Hong Kong as well as in the international community. The arguments all share the common feature of assuming that China will act in terms of its own interests especially its economic interests. This vision of China as an economic animal and as a politically rational actor is not without merit. There is no doubt that China's present moderate regime is basically pursuing its own economic and political interests. However, China's own history since 1949 as well as world history is strewn with examples of countries failing to pursue their own interests, however defined. A theory of narrowly and economically defined "interests" leaves little room for the role of resurgent nationalism or the dynamics of domestic politics, let alone the role of the unexpected or human and institutional failure.

The Pessimists

Even in terms of these narrowly defined "interests," there is a case for much less optimistic scenarios. The pessimists make the following points.

1. *The myths of foreign-exchange earnings.* Lucien W. Pye observed that China will earn more foreign exchange after a takeover of Hong Kong even if it half kills the golden goose.[1] This is because after the takeover, China will receive all the foreign exchange that Hong Kong earns, whereas at the moment China receives only foreign exchange for the much lower figure of its exports to Hong Kong. Hong Kong's imports from China in 1983, for example, were HK$43 billion, which represents China's foreign-exchange earnings from exports to Hong Kong. On the other hand, Hong Kong's total exports, less its exports to China, were HK$142 billion. In terms of export earnings, China would be about HK$100 billion better off if it could take over Hong Kong without causing a fall in exports. Pye argued that "a drop of nearly 70 percent in Hong Kong's earnings would still provide China with more foreign exchange than she now receives."[2]

2. *It will be in China's interests to discriminate against Hong Kong after 1997.* It will be in China's economic interests to discriminate against Hong Kong in favor of the rest of the country. This is because income and profits will accrue to private individuals and companies in Hong Kong in contrast to that of the rest of the country where they will accrue to the state. For example, it would be more beneficial for China to allocate a textile quota to Shanghai than to Hong Kong since Beijing would receive more as a state enterprise than it would as a private company in Hong Kong. It seems inevitable that this sort of decision making will occur to some degree.

3. *The concept of "one country, two systems" will not work.* A capitalist

enclave in a Communist country could not possibly survive. There are many reasons to doubt the viability of this idea. It is certain to generate acute ideological and economic tensions. China will have an irresistible temptation to interfere in Hong Kong affairs. This interference will range from low-level cadres wanting to get rich quick to requests at the highest level for donations. People in China will be jealous of the freedoms enjoyed in Hong Kong. This jealousy will eventually result in a crackdown on Hong Kong freedoms.

4. *Economic tension.* The juxtaposition of capitalism and socialism will be a source of endless economic tension. Smuggling and black-market currency transactions will be rampant. The dynamic capitalist enclave will be a constant threat to the inefficient state enterprises. Only the installation of an economic *cordon sanitaire* will resolve these problems, but that in turn will create political tensions.

5. *Ideological tension.* The implementation of "one country, two systems" will result in acute ideological tension between the two systems. The two systems are further apart than those of the Soviet Union and the United States, and who could imagine their systems coexisting within common borders? The Hong Kong model is an ideological anathema to many Chinese who have lived their lives in isolation under a regime of puritanical communism. China will find it ideologically impossible to avoid harassing the Hong Kong Chinese billionaires, who will be forced to make large contributions to prove their patriotism.

6. *Intimidation, fear, and self-censorship will cause the Hong Kong system to collapse.* There is, already, a high level of intimidation resulting in near-universal self-censorship. Almost no one dares to refer to China as a dictatorial Communist country. Few references are made in any publication to the Hong Kong Communist party, although it will probably be calling the shots after 1997. Not only has the press dramatically changed its tune, but Chinese opinion makers in government, in political circles, in business, and in the academic world, by and large, have swung around and are adopting an uncritical pro-China stance. Sycophancy often is the order of the day. In other words, Hong Kong will be unable and unwilling to resist the pressures of the Communist system. It will collapse from fear, probably before 1997.

7. *China will be unable to implement the agreement even if it tries.* Hong Kong is a ripe plum ready for the picking, and there are many thousands of cadres with sticky fingers who are waiting for their chance. The interests of individuals are different from those of Beijing or the country as a whole. Any Chinese official who is stationed in or even visits Hong Kong will be expected to enrich himself or herself; this process has already started. Natural greed and the growth of rampant corruption in the context of easy pickings and jealousy toward wealthy Hong Kong will generate unrestrainable pressures for personal enrichment.

8. *Even if Beijing does not break the terms of the agreement openly, it will find other ways of "taxing" wealthy Hong Kong Chinese.* "Voluntary donations" as a method of "taxing" the wealthy people of Hong Kong has already started. Deng Xiaoping's son visited Hong Kong and quickly and effortlessly collected US$7 million for the handicapped in China. Many other large donations to Beijing, some up to US$13 million, have followed. There will be and already is tremendous pressure for wealthy Hong Kong industrialists to invest in projects in China. This pressure is a form of arbitrary, open-ended taxation (or extortion). It is very traditional and done in the name of patriotism. Most important, it will not infringe on the agreement, and the international community is not in a position to challenge it. Other forms of pressure that have already started on a significant scale are Beijing's requests that its cadres be placed on the boards or be given management training in Hong Kong Chinese companies. All of these subtle and not-so-subtle indirect assaults on the spirit of the agreement are more likely and more dangerous than any open breaking of promises and can be done in the name of patriotism.

9. *Beijing's interpretation of the agreement will prove different from what Hong Kong and Britain expect.* The problem is that Beijing and London might interpret the same terms in the agreement differently. For example, the meanings of freedom, autonomy, democracy, political parties, representative government, and patriots are different in Beijing. Peking's interpretation of the agreement will result in a lot of unpleasant surprises. Articles 33–56 of the 1982 Chinese Constitution set out the fundamental rights of Chinese citizens. By and large, Beijing insists that these rights do exist in China. The rights in the Constitution are very similar to those in the Joint Declaration. Article 35, for example, states that "Citizens of the People's Republic of China enjoy freedom of speech, of the press, of assembly, of association, of procession and of demonstration." Clearly, Beijing will have the last word in interpreting the agreement.[3]

10. *A culture clash.* Although Hong Kong is 98 percent Chinese, its traditional culture, beliefs, attitudes, and ethics are often different from those of Communist-ruled China. This difference is not surprising after 143 years of British rule. The deep-rooted Chinese Communist way of doing things, through personal influence and "backdoorism," is generally hated in Hong Kong, which is much more of a meritocracy where regulations are followed and there is respect for the rule of law. Hong Kong culture is based on a combination of extremely hard work combined with the freedom to act in unproductive ways. Horse racing, Macao casinos, gambling in general, lotteries, nightclubs, and so on give people a zest for life and are the essential, other side of the work-ethics coin. Hong Kong's culture is "all of a piece" and has a unity that Beijing can hardly be expected to understand.

11. *The rule of law.* It will be impossible to maintain the rule of law and an independent judiciary after 1997. No one can imagine Jardines or anyone

else successfully suing the Special Administrative Region (SAR) government after 1997. China has no tradition of rule by law, and its attempts to move in this direction have met with little success. Who can imagine Deng Xiaoping, any other senior leader, or the future governor of the Hong Kong SAR agreeing that no one is above the law and then acting on it? Who will staff the judiciary that is largely expatriate? Will anyone dare to send Chinese officials to jail or even bring them to court? It is already proving necessary to hush up "incidents" involving visiting PRC officials.

12. *Hong Kong's weakened international economic status after 1997.* The agreement specifically promises that Hong Kong may participate in international trade agreements such as the General Agreement on Tariffs and Trade (GATT) and others.[4] The chances of the international community accepting Hong Kong's participation after 1997 on a reasonable basis, however, are doubtful. At the moment, it appears that Hong Kong faces a grim battle with respect to the GATT. If protectionist pressures are still strong in 1997, many countries are likely to take this opportunity to argue that as long as Hong Kong is part of China, it should not be given a separate seat in international organizations and trade agreements and therefore should not have quotas separate from those of China. If that happens, what hope would Hong Kong have of getting a fair share of China's quotas?

13. *Living standards and population movements.* Hong Kong enjoys a standard of living, in per capita terms and with access to consumer durables, that is approximately ten times higher than that of the major cities of China. This standard is sure to cause tension and pressure for equalization, which will lead China to lower Hong Kong's standards in order to achieve a certain degree of parity. Associated with this problem is the tremendous pressure of immigrants, who would seek to move to Hong Kong to raise their living standards. The colonial authorities have found it exceedingly difficult to curb the flow of both legal and illegal immigrants. Half a million or more have arrived during the last decade. Once Hong Kong is part of China, the political pressure to keep a tight rein on immigration will be relaxed. An income disparity of ten to one simply cannot be maintained. In the past, the high living standards in Hong Kong were not well known in China, but as a result of the far greater movement of people to and fro and general publicity about Hong Kong, perceptions have totally changed.

14. *Jealousy.* The jealousy of the residents of China toward Hong Kong's living standard has been contained in the past by the colonial barrier, but once that is removed and Hong Kong is part of China, who will not be jealous of the living standards and freedoms enjoyed by the people of Hong Kong? An official in Canton may well say: "They are all Chinese, all Cantonese just like us; why should their wages be ten times higher, and why do they have the freedom to travel abroad and say what they like, while we are restricted, have nothing, and cannot even travel?"

15. *The passport and nationality issue.* There is a very good possibility

that Hong Kong business people will not be able to travel with efficiency after 1997. Those who hold Hong Kong British passports will be granted a new form of British passport that will not be given a right of residence in the United Kingdom and probably will not receive widespread international acceptance. The United Kingdom cannot give the holders of this new third-rate passport (the present one is already considered second rate) the right of residence in Hong Kong after 1997 (because by then it is no longer the sovereign) nor is the United Kingdom willing to offer it in Britain. Thus third countries will probably not recognize the passport because it will not give them the right to send the holder back to any country. In fact, the people of Hong Kong have been advised to carry their identity cards when they travel to prove that they have the right of residence in Hong Kong. It is also possible that after 1997, China will look with disfavor on anyone who wants some sort of British passport, reasoning that such a person is not a true patriot. The holders of Hong Kong British Passports (BDTC) are therefore caught in a trap. If they apply for the post–1997 British Passport (BNO), they may be viewed as lacking patriotism. If they then use it, they may find that few countries will accept it. On the other hand, if they opt for a regular Chinese passport, they will be up against all of the problems that plague the Chinese passport holders. Every country demands that Chinese passports holders obtain a visa. China also demands this of all visitors. Some countries refuse to grant visas (e.g., Republic of China on Taiwan) and many others (e.g., Australia) make it difficult and time consuming to obtain one. In all, it would appear that the ability of the people of Hong Kong to travel freely after 1997 will be severely curtailed. This restriction could have crippling economic consequences since the Hong Kong economy is keyed to speed and flexibility that depends on large numbers of businesspersons traveling quickly and freely around the globe.

An Overview

The above fifteen reasons for being pessimistic about Hong Kong are all plausible. On the other hand, the five reasons for being optimistic about the future are equally strong. Neither list exhausts the possibilities, and both lists could be expanded almost indefinitely. The reasons for being pessimistic have been elaborated in greater detail because they are less well known. The reasons for optimism are conventional and are regularly discussed at tedious length (e.g., the debates in the House of Commons and House of Lords). The optimism is virtually official and is simplistic. The views that China will not kill the goose that lays the golden eggs, desires to set a good example for Taiwan, and keeps its international agreements are frequently expounded. However, they are also open to challenge. China's record with regard to keeping international agreements is far from good. Events within the past 30 years provide ample examples. China, in recent years, has broken with impunity the agreements to import wheat and the international agreements with private U.S. companies. Despite the signing of the Sino-British Agreement on Hong Kong, China still considers Hong Kong a purely domestic affair, never to be put into the same class as China's other international agreements.

The golden-goose theory and the Taiwan issue are based on a naive interpretation of China's supposed self-interests. A more sophisticated approach must take into account China's self-interests in a broader context, in the light of Beijing's domestic politics. Instead of a narrow economic approach, wider questions must be asked. For example, what will be the likely political cost in domestic politics for maintaining a capitalist enclave?

A simple listing of the arguments for and against tells us nothing about how the different factors are likely to interact with one another. What are some possible scenarios for the interaction of political and economic forces?

Any detailed scenario for 1997 and beyond would be a waste of time. For example, who in 1973 could have predicted the developments of the last 12 years in China? The rest of this chapter focuses on the transition period in which the possibilities are not so open ended.

Despite this attempt to concentrate on the transition period, it must be recognized that developments between now and 1997 will be profoundly influenced by expectations about what will happen after 1997. No doubt these expectations will range erratically, especially with each swing of the pendulum in China. If China continues to liberalize, optimism about post–1997 will rise, and events in Hong Kong during the transition period will be changed.

Nevertheless, there is a high probability that the majority opinion will become more pessimistic as 1997 nears. The modest degree of euphoria—in contrast to official euphoria—seen after the announcement of the Joint Declaration stemmed largely from relief that at least an agreement had been reached rather than from any deep-seated belief that a new future had dawned. During the period 1982–1984, there were fears that China might take over Hong Kong at any moment, and indeed, there were thinly veiled threats from China to that effect. The agreement cleared away these fears and has made Hong Kong optimistic in the near term rather than will do so after 1997. The level of mistrust of China is too high for a few pages of promises to wipe clean the bitter slate of the past. "One country, two systems" is a slogan of genius grasped by people desperate for straws, but it has an "Alice in Wonderland" quality about it that makes it a wishful dream rather than a realistic prospect.

The concept "one country, two systems" is an attempt to convince people that there will be no Communist takeover in 1997 and that Hong Kong will be an autonomous capitalist enclave for another 50 years. It is essential for Beijing to make such an extraordinary promise because it knows that unless Hong Kong can somehow be induced to believe it, most of the people who can leave will leave. However, there is a high probability that as 1997 nears, most people will not have sufficient faith in the concept to make them want to stay.

Apart from the question of having confidence in China, the people of Hong Kong must have confidence in themselves. If the progress toward localization and self-government is unsatisfactory, self-doubt will begin to grow. The growth of effective local leadership is essential, but it is far from certain that this local leadership will emerge.

To discuss these questions, it is necessary to analyze in some detail the politics of the transition period. The discussion here focuses on the central issue of political reform: how is the goal of local autonomy to be realized? Failure in this area will have fateful consequences for the economy.

THE TRANSITION PERIOD

The Basic Parameters

Little can be said about the future with much certainty, but there are three propositions that can be stated with reasonable confidence:

1. Sovereignty over Hong Kong will be transferred from London to Beijing in 1997.
2. The great majority of the population, probably about 97 percent, will be unable to leave Hong Kong no matter what happens between now and 1997.
3. Despite the uncertainty about what will happen after 1997, there will continue to be an almost unanimous agreement that the situation has no upside potential.

The first two points are self-explanatory, but the third needs elaboration. It is not easy to think of another example of a proposed change of sovereignty that does not at least promise benefits to some group. Is this really a "game in which nobody wins?"[5] The decisive evidence for this proposition is that Beijing has not promised the people of Hong Kong that their lives will be in any way improved by the takeover. The whole burden of Beijing's long list of promises in the Joint Declaration is that the status quo will be maintained after 1997. Beijing's ultimate promise is that things will be just as good as they were under the British. Beijing lays no claim to any upside potential. All it promises is that "the current social and economic systems in Hong Kong will remain unchanged and so will the lifestyle."[6]

No one else appears to have come up with any upside possibilities except of a trivial nature—for example, Hong Kong will not have to purchase British double-decker buses after 1997. (Will Chinese ones be an improvement?)

At first sight, there is another proposition that can be advocated with reasonable certainty and appears to have a similar status as a basic parameter. That is, representative government will be progressively introduced into Hong Kong. My view, as discussed below, is that reforms so far have been illusory and future changes are one of Hong Kong's great unresolved questions. Nevertheless, it is true that people will be able to elect their representatives to low and even high offices in a way that has never been possible before. For the first time, the people will have the right to voice.[7]

Although the great majority of the population will not be able to leave, a small minority, perhaps 1 percent or so of the Chinese population, will have the option of leaving, or exit.[8] Most of the non-Chinese community, some 2 percent of the population, will also be able to exit. Among the non-Chinese, only a relatively small group (10,000?) of unfortunate South Asians, Eurasians, Portuguese, and so on will have no right to exit. These holders of Hong Kong British passports appear to be caught between Beijing's racialist refusal to grant them Chinese nationality and the United Kingdom's equally racialist immigration policy.

This small minority of 3 percent or so who have the right to exit are very important. By definition, this percentage includes the entire wealthy class, since second passports can be bought from a number of countries.[9] The percentage includes the most successful entrepreneurs and many, if not most, of the top professionals as well.

These basic parameters will be among the most important determinants of developments in the transition period and beyond. In the Hong Kong case, the voice option is likely to prove a weak reed. If the democratic reforms are only a facade, people of talent and ability will refuse to participate. (This nonparticipation occurred at the District Board Elections on March 7, 1985.) Even if a genuine representative government is introduced, the high level of implicit intimidation will prevent people from speaking their minds on important issues. The intimidation stems from fear of retribution after 1997 based on what John Walden has described as "3,000 years of inherited Chinese political experience and 36 years of recent observation of the flowerings and deflowerings of the incautious and outspoken in Communist China."[10]

It is a striking, but hardly surprising, fact that those few who are fearless in expressing opinions all have the right of exit. Without exit, there can be little voice, but without voice, there can be no genuine representative government. Even if the British introduce genuine democratic reforms, they can never be effective unless candidates are free to express their opinions on sensitive issues. Only the right to exit would significantly reduce the element of intimidation. Under the shadow of China, with no right to exit, democracy can never flourish.

China is well aware that the right to exit represents a threat to China's influence. China has opposed most vociferously any proposal such as "operation lifeboat," which would have given more Hong Kong people the right to exit. China's friends such as Robert Adley, MP, have not surprisingly thundered loudest against the right to exit, calling it an intolerable insult to China.

Fortunately for Hong Kong, the 3 percent or so who have the right to exit have exercised a major restraining influence on China. If no one had the right to exit, China would have had little need to make the concessions it did in the agreement. An open voice would be totally paralyzed, and any form of democracy would be of little difference across the border.

The Hong Kong government can give people the possibility of exercising genuine voice, but this cannot be realized unless the people have the option to exit. By closing the exit option, the United Kingdom has deprived the voice of great potential significance. If other countries would grant the right of entry to significant numbers of Hong Kong people, this might profoundly affect the course of the transition.

There is also a very important interaction between exit and the lack of upside potential. Those who have the right to exit have little incentive to make long-term plans to stay when there is no upside potential. The downside possibilities are unlimited, so people with the right of exit are unwilling to take a risk when the situation offers so little in the way of a winning outcome. This situation is Chinese roulette with the status quo as the winning position. Not surprisingly, many of the people with exit options are planning to exercise them before 1997.

Exit, voice, zero upside potential, and sovereignty transfer establish a number of basic relationships for the transition period. Their interaction tends to set the possible limits rather than to indicate specific scenarios. To control the outcome further, it is necessary to introduce the major actors to clothe our model with flesh and blood. The analytical starting point must include the dominant actor on the Hong Kong political scene, the Sino-British alliance.

The Sino-British Alliance

The much publicized disagreements, disputes, and tensions that characterized the Sino-British negotiations masked a fundamental mutuality of interests. Once the British conceded the key Chinese demand for a transfer of sovereignty in November 1983, their common interests overrode their relatively minor differences. China and the United Kingdom both wanted Hong Kong to accept the agreement as enthusiastically as possible with the fewest possible questions. Both want to maintain a high level of confidence and a booming economy. China wants to inherit a thriving Hong Kong, and British interests want to do as well as possible in the years that remain. British firms (Jardines, Swire, and so on) that realize what the future holds will want to disinvest under the most favorable conditions. Whereas the British want to organize an orderly and profitable retreat before 1997, the

Chinese are more interested in the genuine long-run prosperity of Hong Kong.

The other major British interest is in trade with China. This interest requires good relations and is a strong argument for siding with China over the details of Hong Kong. Because of international strategic considerations, the United Kingdom, Japan, and the United States are extremely reluctant to offend Beijing over Hong Kong.

Whereas the United Kingdom has these strong reasons for supporting China, the latter in turn has every reason to support the British authorities in Hong Kong. This support is even written into the Joint Declaration. Article 4 states that "during the transitional period between the date of the entry into force of this Joint Declaration and 30 June, 1997, the Government of the United Kingdom will be responsible for the administration of Hong Kong with the object of maintaining and preserving its economic prosperity and social stability; and that the Government of the People's Republic of China will give its cooperation in this connection."

This article not only ensures the United Kingdom of Chinese support but also legitimizes British rule for the first time. Far from being a lameduck government, the colonial authorities are ruling for the first time not just with the acquiescence of Beijing but with its firm authorization and promised support. China is not ready to take over Hong Kong; it needs the United Kingdom during the transition period and is willing to give its full support. Just how far China is willing to go to support the colonial authorities, only time will tell.

Traditionally, the Hong Kong government has had to share power with the big British banks and trading companies, the hongs. But the hongs are in retreat with a succession of large British companies being taken over by Chinese interests. These commercial interests were the only serious countervailing power. But as this influence wanes, the Hong Kong government is left dominating the scene and being further strengthened with new Beijing support.

The lack of any countervailing power centers is the most striking feature of the local scene. The leading Chinese business and professional groups are potential centers of independent power, but the colonial authorities have always successfully coopted their leadership. A skillful combination of dispensing patronage, flattery, and general trading on the pervasive colonial mentality is more than enough to win the loyalty of the leading lights. The Sino-British alliance is thus joined by the leading local worthies collectively known as UMELCO. (They are the unofficial members of the Executive and Legislative councils who advise the governor.)

The loyalty of the local influentials was severely tested when they had to accept the Joint Declaration wholeheartedly. Most proved their loyalty with their support. Two or three, however, refused to support it, and one actually resigned (Lo Tak-shing). Despite their loyalty, the UMELCO leg of the alliance is weak since it possesses no independent power. Its power is derived from the government, which appoints the members and, more effectively, may even fail to reappoint them.

Whether the Sino-British alliance can remain united throughout the transition period is one of the key questions that will determine the fate of Hong Kong. An open break would be disastrous. Fear of this break will help to keep it together. Although held together by common interests, it is very much a marriage of convenience, a union of strange bedfellows lacking any ideological common ground and with many potential conflicts.

An exceedingly complex and difficult problem that the alliance has to face is the question of political reform. This issue is certain to place a great strain on the union and could even tear it apart. Just how is Hong Kong going to make itself "democratic" and what will be the role of China?

The Democratic Mirage

John Walden, a former director of home affairs, argued that Hong Kong is being "piped along the democratic road by misleading government publicity, in pursuit of the mirage of a strong, representative and autonomous government."[11]

The rationale behind the British use of illusions and democratic facades does not arise from a natural deviousness but from the cruel dilemma they face. S.K. Lau recently pointed out that "any reform measures, which purport to give real and ultimate political power to the Hong Kong people without the explicit permission of the Chinese government, would mean that Britain, in contravention of the Sino-British Agreement, would be able to hand over only a *nominal* sovereignty to China in 1997. This cannot be allowed to take place."[12]

The British have to introduce the form of democracy in Hong Kong, but they cannot allow the substance. They are caught on the horns of what Lau called a "difficult dilemma" that can be "resolved" only through the creation of a convincing illusion: the democratic mirage.

The democratic mirage is essentially a British concept expounded in the *White Paper: The Further Development of Representative Government in Hong Kong* published in November 1984 and is reflected in the "high degree of autonomy" promised by China in the Joint Declaration.[13] These documents project two complementary illusions and are essentially two sides of the same coin. Each draws strength from the other, although neither would be convincing alone. The Chinese document promises autonomy for Hong Kong, whereas the British *White Paper* shows how a representative government will be developed enabling Hong Kong to function democratically and autonomously. A British representative government would be useless without the Chinese promise of autonomy. Autonomy would hardly be plausible without the British plan for democratic development in the transition period. Taken as a whole, the democracy-autonomy mirage represents the finest achievement of the Sino-British alliance, but it is also its Achilles' heel.

Walden asked why the United Kingdom started to introduce democratic reforms in Hong Kong in 1980 when there was no public pressure for it. The reason was that the previous governor, Sir Murray MacLehose, had been told during a visit to Beijing in 1979 that British administration could not continue after 1997.[14] This information was kept secret in 1979 to give the United Kingdom government time to tighten restrictions against immigration from Hong Kong that resulted in the Nationality Act of 1980. These restrictions enabled the United Kingdom to keep the people of Hong Kong out of the United Kingdom, but it left the government exposed to potential criticism that it had been "failing in its moral responsibilities by handing over British subjects to a Communist regime against their will."[15] Walden implied that this exposure was virtually the sole reason for the introduction of democratic reforms since there was no public pressure in Hong Kong for any change. The 1980 *Green Paper on Local Administration* had to be forced into policy "with public support for it drummed up by a massive government propaganda campaign."[16]

Having established the reason for introducing democracy, Walden asked the key question about its content: "What hope do Hong Kong people have of exercising firm control over the government of Hong Kong [Special Administrative Region (SAR)] after 1997? No hope at all under the reforms now under way."[17] The reason is that the elections of representatives are to bodies that have no real power. "In baiting their democratic trap with the offer of an elected Legislative Council, the Hong Kong Government is giving the misleading impression that it is actually handing over positive power to the people."[18] Walden pointed out that power lies not in the Legislative Council but in the civil service and in particular in its secretarial posts.

Stressing the power of the civil service, Walden said that "virtually the entire process of formulating policies for Hong Kong, seeing them carried out and making decisions affecting Hong Kong's internal and external affairs, is under the direct control of secretaries. The Hong Kong Government's political reforms make no provision at all for this monopoly of executive power to be shared with members of a representative legislature."[19]

Walden argued that it is absolutely essential for the government to devolve real power upon the institutions it is supposed to be democratizing or at least to subject the all-powerful civil service to other forms of public surveillance. If this is not done, the "outcome of the government's political reforms can only be an illusion of representative government. This is because the Sino-British Agreement on Hong Kong gives the Chinese Government the right to appoint all secretaries."[20] It therefore follows that "it would be self-delusion of the highest order for Hong Kong people to assume that the promises repeatedly made to them of 'representative' and 'autonomous' government after 1997 can have any meaning at all unless the monopoly of power now exercised by Hong Kong's most senior civil servants is brought under public control."[21]

This is a masterly exposure of the democratic facade but is incomplete in various ways. Although it is undoubtedly true that the main reason for the British erecting the democratic facade is to satisfy the United Kingdom's public conscience that British subjects are not being delivered to the Communists against their will, the motives are more complex, as Lau made clear.

The most important weakness or at least incompleteness of Walden's thesis is that he thinks the United Kingdom could make Hong Kong's democracy genuine, if only London had the will. Walden sees it as a lack of will, whereas Lau more convincingly interprets it as a lack of power. Lau would argue that the devolution of power Walden demands would be simply unacceptable to China. China wants to inherit the United Kingdom's real power, not a watered down, etiolated version. Since genuine democracy involves the devolution of real power, the United Kingdom has no choice but to opt for the facade.

Lau's analysis starts with the proposition that because of the weakness of the local political forces, the direction of political development will be determined by the ruling elites, the United Kingdom and China. Although there will be differences between the two countries, Lau argued that their mutual interests will prevail and that they will structure the course and content of political reform in Hong Kong. They will shape the nature and composition of Hong Kong's emerging political elite. Political development will be planned and exhibit a top-down pattern.

Lau then discussed the reasons for introducing political reform. "From the standpoint of the government, in order to govern in a difficult time and with diminished authority, political reform with the purposes of increasing popular participation and power sharing has to be introduced fairly speedily. In addition, the imperatives to exit in glory and to sweeten the Sino-British deal to be 'sold' to the British people by a package of liberal political reforms are also powerful pro-reform factors."[22] Of these reasons, the need to satisfy British public opinion is probably the most important. The colonial authorities must appear to be handing over power to the autonomous Hong Kong government and not to Beijing.

This is the main dilemma faced by the British. When all previous colonies were being brought to independence, power was devolved on local organizations and their representatives, but in Hong Kong's case, full sovereignty has to be handed over to China.

Lau pointed out that this is not the only dilemma faced by the British. He listed nine dilemmas of which the most important is the interests and response of the Chinese government. It is reasonable to argue that China is insisting that the United Kingdom transfer real and not nominal sovereignty in 1997, but apart from this overriding consideration, what are Chinese attitudes toward political reform? China has promised Hong Kong autonomy in 1997, but if this promise is to carry any conviction, it cannot oppose some democratic reforms before 1997. If China does not support the British reforms, the people will realize that they will be dismantled after 1997, and the whole effort will quickly fail.

Lau argued that from the Chinese viewpoint, "the existing institutional structure is doing well and should not be changed unnecessarily. The political system can remain intact and operate smoothly after its mentors—the British—are gone."[23] Because of the great concentration of power in the hands of the governor and secretaries, the present system must be almost ideal from a Chinese viewpoint. China, on the other hand, has the need to "give the strategic elites a feeling that they will have a stake in the system and the need to demonstrate to the outside world that the Hong Kong SAR is truly autonomous."[24]

It is in China's interests to have no significant change in the reality of the system but to create the appearance of a democratic reform. There is thus a fairly close alliance of British and Chinese interests, but China "does not share with the British the sense of urgency in political reform."[25] China will oppose any reforms that "will establish a virtually independent political entity in Hong Kong beyond Chinese control" that may "produce forces antagonistic to China" or "create undesirable political aspirations within China through their demonstration effects."[26] On balance, it is clear that China does not want any real political reform or any meaningful steps toward a representative government and that the United Kingdom is fully aware of this position. China wants the appearance of democracy, but it has its own reasons for being much more nervous about it. This is a temporary alliance of interests with a democratic facade suiting both parties.

It is not, however, a genuine expression of independent interests. It is the supposed Chinese veto on real reform that compels the United Kingdom to opt for the facade that is needed by both sides to appease world opinion. What does the United Kingdom get in return for playing the Chinese tune and introducing this democratic charade that carries appalling risks? The answer is the Joint Declaration, which is essentially a document whereby the United Kingdom agrees to transfer real sovereignty in return for China's promise of autonomy and preservation of Hong Kong's life-styles. The United Kingdom's concession is to allow China to appoint the governor and the secretaries. This would be meaningless unless the United Kingdom had not also agreed to leave unchanged the governmental power structure. The governor and the secretaries cannot have their power reduced without China's permission. Once China had been ensured of unconditional real sovereignty, it was willing to guarantee a long list of freedoms to keep Hong Kong happy. Many of these freedoms are already guaranteed in the 1982

Chinese Constitution and therefore cost little and meant less. Others represent a real concession on China's part.

China's promise of autonomy and the long list of guaranteed rights and freedoms need the support of the British *White Paper* to appear credible. Unless the British have a plan for developing a representative government before 1997, no one is going to place much faith in the Chinese promise of a "high degree of autonomy" for Hong Kong. Equally, the *White Paper* would have been a transparent fraud and an instant disaster unless China had promised Hong Kong an autonomous status after 1997. They are complementary sets of promises, two expressions of the same illusion. The fact is that the coin is a clever forgery and has not caused many problems so far, but the future may be another matter.

Autonomy is likely to prove every bit as illusory as democracy. China's appointment of the key figures who monopolize power will be enough to ensure that. A passing acquaintance with Chinese history or even the definition of autonomy in the Chinese political lexicon should be sufficient to remove doubts on this score. But if 1997 and after is a foregone conclusion, the same cannot be said of the transition period. The key question is whether the Sino-British alliance that has spawned the autonomy-democracy mirage can continue to carry it off. As powerful as this alliance is, it is asking a lot for people to believe in a mirage when they are very close to it, as they will be in the years just before 1997.

A single illusion in isolation has a short life span; it is too easily contradicted by facts. A network of mutually reinforcing illusions is something different. The official philosophy of a Hong Kong in Wonderland has an eerie logic of its own that has so far proved immune to attack. Without a doubt, this is the high spot to date of the Sino-British alliance. Although neither the agreement nor the *White Paper* would carry any conviction alone, together they stand almost beyond challenge. The British define the path to democracy and the Chinese promise an environment where it can be practiced.

The Alliance under Strain

Despite the stunning success of the autonomy/democracy illusions, the relationship between China and the United Kingdom over the issue of democratic reform is likely to prove difficult, perhaps disastrously so. This is the real Achilles' heel of the alliance rather than the issues of the Sino-British Joint Liaison Group or land leases. Any alliance has conflicts of interests, but these two much feared areas of disagreement are relatively clear-cut and have been dealt with out in the open. The conflict of interests that underlies the superficial alliance with respect to democratic reform is much more threatening. It could tear the alliance apart.

Before proceeding further with this line of thought, it might be helpful to reflect first on the special circumstances of Hong Kong that have made it possible to promote successfully such an inherently implausible idea as democracy for Hong Kong. Simply on general grounds, Hong Kong must appear to be one of the most unlikely places for the development of a functioning democracy. For 143 years, it has been run as a classic nineteenth-century British colony, which is sometimes described as an authoritarian bureaucracy. As a result, people have had no political experience. In another 12 years, this British colony will be handed over to China, where it is hoped the newly formed democracy will continue to operate with a high degree of autonomy as a special administrative region of China. The plan and expectation is that this new democracy will have filled the vacuum left by the departing British and, one hopes, will be successfully resisting any unwanted interference from China.

The entire scenario is so implausible that its popular acceptance requires some special explanation.

1. As Lau pointed out, "the political atmosphere of the late 20th century is suffused with democratic and populist rhetoric," which is sufficient to ensure that the idea of democracy is accepted without question, regardless of the situation. For example, the possibility of autonomy without democracy as an objective is not considered.
2. The role of wishful, escapist thinking in the Hong Kong context can hardly be exaggerated. With 12 years to go, optimism is almost essential for sanity.
3. The demand for democracy within Hong Kong is feeble. The pressure comes largely from the government, which uses its dominance of the media to drum up support. By and large, people do as they are told, both to vote and stand as candidates. The recent district board elections held on March 7, 1985, strikingly illustrated the effectiveness of traditional paternalism. The day after the elections, one popular newspaper ran the headline "Top government men all praise for voters." It was reported that the governor "gave a pat on the back for the people who cast their ballots and said that he was very pleased with the voter turnout."
4. The love of symbols and the power of government patronage exist. The trappings of power such as the possibility of making it to the queen's honor list still has enormous appeal.
5. Political innocence is the mesmerizing force of the government's propaganda machine.
6. There is increased authoritarianism of the government. Lau noted the apparent paradox of a fervent drive toward political reform associated with an underlying trend of increasing authoritarianism.[27] There are plenty of recent examples to confirm this trend since Lau wrote: the government's ruthless overriding of the bar association and legal opinion in general on the issue of juries for complex commercial cases, dismissal of the Urban council members of the Housing Authority, steamrolling of electronic road pricing despite near unanimous opposition of the district boards, and so on. Perhaps this new no-nonsense trend stems from

> the feeling that a more powerful and effective government is needed to oversee the transition period. Perhaps the new support from Beijing makes it possible, through the elimination of the danger of anticolonial protests.

However explained, this new wave of authoritarianism and official intimidation is effective in getting out the vote and the candidates and in compelling an apparent consensus and approval of the government's plans.

These reasons go far to explain why the government's proposals for political reform receive such an uncritical acceptance. But as the already large gap between official rhetoric and reality continues to grow, will this passive acceptance of the government's line continue, perhaps until 1997?

As time goes on, the United Kingdom will come under increasing pressure to allow substantive rather than illusory reforms. At the same time it must be eager to get the open support of China for its plans. Unless China supports the United Kingdom's reform plans, confidence will rapidly ebb.

All of this is not to suggest that the United Kingdom is straining at the Chinese leash in a desire to introduce substantive reforms. Far from it, the United Kingdom has its own reasons for wanting to proceed slowly. A major reason is the desire to avoid demoralizing both the civil service and its faithful appointed advisers to the Legislative and Executive councils. Both the higher levels of the civil service and the corps of loyal advisers are highly conservative and basically opposed to political reform. The local elites are interested in some reform, however, to the extent that it will help them to protect their own interests after 1997. The higher civil servants have what Lau called an "intolerant, contemptuous, and condescending attitude towards 'politicians' in general, 'radicals' and 'troublemakers' in particular."[28] Too rapid reforms run the danger of detracting from the "prestige and reputation of the bureaucracy while the status and reputation of the budding politicians have yet to be built up."[29] Fear of antagonizing the civil service is undoubtedly one reason why the suggested reforms have not promised to touch the power of the civil service. China, too, would not like the United Kingdom to take any steps that adversely affect stability and prosperity through the weakening of the bureaucracy.

There is, therefore, a delicate balance not only between the United Kingdom and China but also involving the higher levels of the civil service, which is still mainly British, and the traditional local elites, who play a vital role, even though it is essentially advisory. Their frustration and withdrawal from the political process would be a severe blow, for it will be a long time (if ever) before the electoral process generates qualified leaders who can replace them.

Another group that has to be considered is the growing number of political activists, reformers, and pressure groups who are pushing for democratization and autonomy. This group, however, lacks genuine popular support as the masses remain apathetic. They also suffer from a feeling of futility in the face of "combined" Sino-British power.

The government's insistence on indirect elections and functional constituencies helps to ensure that the political activists will remain divided and powerless. The chances of mass-based political parties evolving in Hong Kong must be considered practically nil. For the government, political parties are anathema. They conjure up the vision of dreaded "adversarial politics." The hope of the government seems to be that leadership will emerge on an individual basis. With one hand, the government encourages politicization through its massive promotion of elections, but with the other it practically guarantees apathy by ensuring that those elected are little more than powerless puppets. Nevertheless, these activists, who are willing to stand for elections, are, officially at least, the hope of the side. They are the elected, who, it is hoped, will fill the vacuum left when the British depart. This vacuum theory of Hong Kong politics is very popular and not surprisingly most popular with the activists themselves. If the government fails to make substantive reforms in the coming years, the activists, perhaps with limited public support, will protest energetically, and the government will find it more and more difficult to ignore them.

This situation is fundamentally unstable. There is no way that a democratic mirage of this order can be sustained all the way to 1997. The government will come under increasing pressure from the activists who will have members on the Legislative Council in the near future. The public opinion in the United Kingdom will also become involved if the government does not introduce meaningful reforms.

Caught between the Scylla of genuine reform and the Charybdis of a democratic mirage, sooner or later the government will have to take the risk of genuine reform and take its chances not only with its own civil service but with the loyal elites. There are hints that this is already happening. The Hong Kong bill, which was recently passed by the United Kingdom Parliament, makes it possible for London to increase greatly the power of the Hong Kong Legislative Council. The bill gives the right to the British government to transfer its responsibilities to the Legislative Council on any date it chooses.

The powers in this bill, when combined with the fact that 24 out of the 56 members of the Legislative Council will soon be elected, will make possible the start of a real power shift away from the executive to an elected legislature. The United Kingdom would hardly dare implement this election without getting China's advance approval since such a devolution of power away from the colonial government to the elected legislature is a threat to China's future sovereignty.

The United Kingdom and Hong Kong could argue that China should have no objection because the Joint Declaration promises Hong Kong a high degree of autonomy, and London is only preparing Hong Kong for such an autonomous status. China is unlikely to agree. China's interpretation of "autonomy" is different from that of the British. But China still wants to get the credit for any major political reform. China, however, will have to recognize that some British preparation of Hong Kong for its new autonomous status is imperative. The alternative is a loss of British credibility as the demand for real reform gains ground and a fatal loss of China's own credibility when it is seen to be blocking reform.

This issue is more likely to place a great strain on the Sino-British alliance than any other issue. It will test China's willingness to support the British. Will China be willing to see the United Kingdom carry out real reforms and devolve real power on an elected legislature? Will China be satisfied with anything less than full sovereignty in 1997?

As the years go by, the Sino-British alliance will come under increasing strain as the United Kingdom will require more and more support from China. Will China be willing to help the United Kingdom? Will China be able to continue to swallow its ideology and even nationalism in the interests of *Realpolitik*? Much will depend on internal developments in China. It is possible that the period of the negotiations saw China at its most flexible, and in the future China will be less willing to suppress the ideological element in its policies.

This issue of political reform is an extraordinarily interesting test of China's pragmatism. China, unsurprisingly, wants to have it both ways. China wants the United Kingdom to transfer unencumbered sovereignty. At the same time, China wants Hong Kong and the world public opinion to believe that genuine autonomy is just around the 1997 corner. Without preparation during the transition period, autonomy will carry no conviction. If China is to make the autonomy promise convincing, it must allow the United Kingdom to devolve real power on Hong Kong. China cannot prevent this, and an attempt to do so could place an unbearable strain on the alliance.

THE HONG KONG ECONOMY IN THE CONTEXT OF 1997

Growth in Historical Perspective

A strong case could be made for the argument that Hong Kong is the most successful example of rapid economic development that the world has ever seen. In the heyday of capitalism between 1850 and 1913, output per head in the advanced countries grew by not more than 1.5 to 2 percent per year. In this period, Japan had the fastest growing economy with output per head rising by about 2.5 percent per year from 1874 to 1914.[30]

In the 1950–1973 period output per head in the same advanced European nations grew by 3 to 4 percent per year, or twice as fast as it had before 1914. It was much the same story for the growth in world trade, which had expanded by 3.5 to 4 percent per year before 1914 but in the post–1950 period grew at 7 to 8 percent in constant prices.[31]

In the decades after 1950, a small group of East Asian countries, led initially by Japan, achieved rates of growth of output and trade that were roughly twice that of the rest of the world and four times those held in the years before 1914. Japan, followed by Hong Kong, Singapore, the Republic of China on Taiwan, and Korea, experienced rates of growth in per capita output of 6 to 8 percent and of trade from 15 to 25 percent. Japan's growth rate in the decades before 1914 was only one-fifth of what it achieved from 1952 to 1967.

This is the background against which to view Hong Kong's extraordinarily swift transition from poverty to prosperity. Despite the influx of refugees that helped to triple the population, Hong Kong was able to maintain a growth in per capita income of about 7 percent a year, giving it a tenfold increase in real income per head in 35 years. It took the United Kingdom two centuries from 1750 to 1950 to achieve a tenfold increase in per capita income.[32]

Table 2.1 compares Hong Kong's performance with other East Asian high performers. Hong Kong had the highest average annual rate of growth of Gross Domestic Products (GDP) despite the influx of refugees. Singapore, which does not have refugee problem, did slightly better in per capita terms.

Aggregate growth rates, however, do not tell the whole story. Hong Kong's performance in the other vital areas was equally impressive, although often more difficult to document.

The distribution of income in Hong Kong is always a difficult area in statistical terms. For what the figures are worth, the distribution of income by 1980 was considerably more equitable than it had been in 1960. World Bank figures indicate that income in Hong Kong was more evenly distributed than in the United States. In the United States, the lowest 20 percent of the population received 4.6 percent of total income compared with 5.4 percent in Hong Kong. The top 10 percent in the United States took 33.4 percent compared with 31.3 percent in Hong Kong.[33]

Life expectancy at birth is higher in Hong Kong than in the United States (74 years for females versus 71 for males), and the infant mortality rate is lower. In most other areas, Hong Kong's achievements have been similarly impressive.

Many of the standard explanations for Hong Kong's success give excessive credit to the policy of laissez-faire. With a very similar economic structure, Singapore has been able to grow just as fast despite much more government intervention.

Writing nearly 30 years ago, at the dawn of Hong Kong's industrial revolution, Edward Szczepanik said that

> Laissez-faire capitalism . . . is of the utmost importance for understanding the recent growth of Hong Kong. The colony was founded as a free port and this idea has

Table 2.1
Growth Rates of East Asian Countries, 1960–1982

Country	Population (Millions)	GNP per capita Dollars 1982	GNP per capita Growth Rate 1960-82	G.D.P. Growth Rate 1960-70	G.D.P. Growth Rate 1970-82
Hong Kong	5.2	6,173	7.0	10.0	9.9
Singapore	2.5	5,910	7.4	8.8	8.5
Taiwan (Republic of China)	18.4	2,500	6.3	9.6	8.7
South Korea	39.3	1,910	6.6	8.6	8.6
Japan	118.4	10,080	6.1	10.4	4.6

Source: World Bank: World Development Report, 1984, pp. 218-221.

remained almost unchanged. Economic liberalism extends, of course, not only to foreign trade but also to all internal economic activities: production, transport, exchange and finance. The economic development of Hong Kong has not been directed by any over-all national plans. Instead of appeals to national pride or imposition of overriding national aims to benefit future generations, self-interest has been the prime mover of Hong Kong's economic growth.[34]

Writing 20 years after Szczepanik, Alvin Rabushka, a leading U.S. authority on Hong Kong, claimed that "Hong Kong among the world's more than 130 countries, most closely resembles the textbook model of a competitive market economy, encumbered only with the barest overlay of government."[35] In an earlier book, Rabushka claimed that "Hong Kong is the industrial world's least regulated and lowest taxed economy." It is said to be a "Gladstonian paradise."[36]

Not to be outdone by Rabushka, Jon Woronoff entitled his book *Hong Kong: Capitalist Paradise.* His paean to Hong Kong capitalism occupies more than 300 pages and ends with a rephrasing of Lincoln Steffans' statement "I have spent some time in the past and it works."[37]

The government's role in the Hong Kong economy is of much greater significance than has been implied previously. The government is a major actor in fields such as housing, education, health, and transport. Approximately 40 percent of the population live in government-subsidized public housing, and the government controls rents for part of the private sector. In the field of education, the great majority of pupils at both the primary and secondary levels enjoy government subsidies. Health services are highly subsidized with only nominal charges at government hospitals. The government also plays an influential role in the transport field either through direct responsibility as with the railway, airport, and port or through the regulation of fares and so on for transport facilities that it does not itself control.

Perhaps the most important contribution of the government is the maintenance of the rule of law. The stability and certainty of laws in Hong Kong underpin the business confidence that is so crucial. The loss of this certainty after 1997 would deal a devastating blow to the free-market economy. An economy that moved from poverty to prosperity in 35 years could regress even more spectacularly.

The Hong Kong economy is resilient in the face of economic batterings, but it is potentially fragile when confronted with political changes that introduce noneconomic uncertainties such as that associated with a breakdown of the rule of law. In this respect, it is unlike the large, closed, semisubsistence economy. The economy of China was unable to survive great leaps and cultural revolutions, partially because of the large agricultural sector that was relatively unaffected and partially because the capital and labor were essentially locked into the economy. In Hong Kong, much of

Table 2.2
Merchandise Trade of Selected Asian and Pacific Countries (Billions of Dollars)

	Exports	Imports
Hong Kong	21	24
China	22	19
India	8	14
Japan	139	132
Australia	22	24
U.S.A.	212	255

Source: The World Bank, World Development Report, 1984, pp. 234-239.

the capital and the entrepreneurs and even some of the skilled labor are free to relocate and will do so in response to a relatively minor deterioration of the situation. Knowledge of this factor of Hong Kong's success is a constraint on China's policy toward Hong Kong, but it will not be easy for it to understand the delicate combination of factors that lies behind Hong Kong's success.

Hong Kong and the East Asian Miracle

Hong Kong is widely reputed to be the world's third largest financial center, and the serious disruption of it either before or after 1997 would have serious financial implications both for the region and the world. Except for Japan, in most of the East and Southeast Asian areas the financial sector is seriously underdeveloped and Hong Kong banks and insurance companies play a crucial role.

Apart from its importance as a financial center, Hong Kong plays a major and pivotal role in a variety of other ways. As a major world trading country, Hong Kong's exports are important for some products and some countries. As an importer, it is an important market for some suppliers.

The significance of Hong Kong as a trading nation is indicated by Table 2.2. Although China, Hong Kong, and Australia are of almost equal importance, Hong Kong's total trade is about one-tenth of that of the United States, which has 40 times Hong Kong's population.

Hong Kong plays a vital role in the transport and communication field throughout the region. The airlines and shipping of countries such as the Republic of China on Taiwan and the Phillipines are partially dependent on the use of Hong Kong. Hong Kong is also a major center for tourism in the area.

Apart from the areas of trade and services, Hong Kong's role is perhaps even more vital in less tangible ways. There are more international companies with head offices in Hong Kong than anywhere else in the region. Although Hong Kong's exports could perhaps be supplied by other East Asian countries, some of Hong Kong's other advantages are not so easily replaced. Geographically, Hong Kong lies in the center of the region halfway between Korea and Japan to the north and Singapore and Indonesia to the south. Hong Kong's infrastructure is second to none in the area. Frequency and convenience of airline flights, good telephones, telex, hotels, restaurants, and shopping make up an infrastructure that gives the best value for money. English is widely spoken, and the international press is available and never censored.

Consequently, these assets make Hong Kong a unique and irreplaceable center for doing business in East Asia. China will continue to need Hong Kong after 1997, and no other city in the area could possibly perform its functions. Hong Kong performs a vital integrating role for the area as a whole. Unlike Japan, which is inward looking in so many ways, Hong Kong is oriented to the outside world.

Many scholars recognize the importance of Hong Kong to the region as a whole. Chalmers Johnson, for example, stated that "the ending of Hong Kong's ability to perform its true functions will have enormous consequences not just for the people of Hong Kong but for all the nations of the Pacific Basin."[38]

A detailed study of the role of Hong Kong in the economies of the East Asian region is something that urgently requires research. Much is known about the economic relationship between Hong Kong and China and the role of Hong Kong in China's economy. The importance of Hong Kong to the other countries of the region remains largely unexplored. What little that is known indicates that Hong Kong's greatest importance is in terms of finance and general services and as a base for international companies.[39] Its importance in the field of air transport and shipping is especially difficult to estimate. The airlines of Taiwan and the Philippines depend heavily on Hong Kong for passengers proceeding to Europe. These airlines lack the long-distance aircraft that would be required if Hong Kong was not available. The dependence of neighbouring countries on the transshipment of goods through Hong Kong is also considerable but difficult to document.

The Hong Kong and China Trade

How significant is trade with Hong Kong and China for the main actors in this drama? The United Kingdom's trade with Hong Kong and China is shown in Table 2.3. The United Kingdom's trade with Hong Kong is far

Table 2.3
The United Kingdom's Trade with Hong Kong and China (£ Million Sterling)

	1981		1982		1983	
	Hong Kong	China	Hong Kong	China	Hong Kong	China
Exports	618	120	732	103	726	159
Imports	899	184	873	193	1,178	231

Source: The Statesman's Yearbook, 1985-86, London: Macmillan, 1985, pp. 1317-1318.

more important than its trade with China. Although United Kingdom's exports to China increased by more than 50 percent in 1983, its sales to Hong Kong were still nearly five times greater than its sales to China. The United Kingdom also buys from Hong Kong five times as much as it buys from China.

In 1983 the United Kingdom's total exports were £60,500 million, so the exports to China of £159 million accounted for only 0.26 percent of the total. Exports to Hong Kong of £726 million were 1.2 percent of the total and China and Hong Kong combined, less than 1.5 percent of the United Kingdom's exports. The United Kingdom's imports in 1983 were £65,993 million. China supplied only 0.35 percent of these imports whereas Hong Kong's share was 1.8 percent. Of the United Kingdom's total trade, only 1.8 percent is with Hong Kong and China combined.

It is clear that both Hong Kong and China are insignificant trading partners for the United Kingdom. Despite the fact that the United Kingdom-Hong Kong trade is nearly five times greater than United Kingdom-China trade, this figure is insignificant from the viewpoint of the United Kingdom's total trade.

China may be thought to have more growth potential than Hong Kong, but it can never be much in terms of the United Kingdom's overall trade. Since trade with Hong Kong is so much more important than the China trade, it is unlikely that the United Kingdom would be tempted to sacrifice Hong Kong for the sake of future China trade. The significance of trade with both countries suggests that this was not a major issue at the Hong Kong talks. The lure of future China business could hardly have swayed the United Kingdom significantly.

In view of the fact that Hong Kong is a British colony, it is interesting to note how little of Hong Kong's trade is with the United Kingdom. This lack of trade demonstrates that Hong Kong is not a colony in the traditional sense; economically, it functions as an independent state. Table 2.4 gives Hong Kong's foreign trade by country.

In 1984 only 5.3 percent of Hong Kong's total trade was with the United

Table 2.4
Hong Kong's Foreign Trade, 1984 (HK$ Billions)

	Exports	%	Imports	%
U.S.A.	61.4	44.5	24.3	10.9
China	11.3	8.2	55.8	24.9
U.K.	10.5	7.6	8.7	3.9
Japan	5.1	3.7	52.6	23.6
Singapore	2.6	1.9	12.2	5.4
TOTAL	90.9		153.6	

Source: Hong Kong 1985: A Review of 1984, p. 308.

Table 2.5
Hong Kong's China Trade, 1974–1984 (HK$ Billions)

	1974	1978	1982	1983	1984
Total Imports	34.1	63.0	142.9	175.4	223.3
From China	6.0	10.6	32.9	42.8	55.8
%	17.6%	16.8%	23.0%	24.4%	25.0%
Total Exports	22.9	40.7	83.0	104.4	137.9
To China	0.1	0.1	3.8	6.2	11.3
%	0.4%	0.2%	4.5%	5.9%	8.2%
Total Re-exports	7.1	13.2	44.3	56.3	83.5
To China	0.2	0.2	8.0	12.1	28.7
%	2.8%	1.5%	18.0%	21.5%	34.0%

Source: Census and Statistics Department, Hong Kong Review of Overseas Trade, pp. 24-26.

Kingdom, down from 6.7 percent in 1980. Table 2.4 shows how modest United Kingdom's Hong Kong trade is, compared with that of the United States, China, and Japan. Thus Tables 2.3 and 2.4 demonstrate that the United Kingdom and Hong Kong are insignificant to each other in terms of trade.

The fact that the United Kingdom rules Hong Kong but basically does not trade with it is in contrast with China, whose share of Hong Kong's trade has grown enormously in recent years. Table 2.5 shows that in a

Table 2.6
The Role of Hong Kong in China's Trade (US$ Billions)

	1982	1983	1984
China's Exports (Total)	21.9	22.1	24.0
H.K.'s Imports from China	5.0	5.5	7.1
% of China's Exports going to Hong Kong	22.8	24.9	29.6
China's Imports (Total)	16.6	19.6	21.2
H.K.'s Exports to China (including re-exports)	1.8	2.4	5.0
% of China's Imports supplied by Hong Kong	10.8	12.2	23.8

Source: Far Eastern Economic Review, Asia 1985 Yearbook, pp. 136-140, 151-152.

decade China doubled its share of Hong Kong's trade from about 9 percent to about 18 percent. Particularly remarkable has been the growth of exports and reexports. Exports and reexports to China were negligible until 1979, when they began to grow rapidly.

The growth of reexports to China indicates that Hong Kong has recovered its traditional entrepôt role. Because of ideological considerations, China had once artificially suppressed its purchases from Hong Kong. But when economic considerations were once again allowed to dominate, Hong Kong's exports and reexports to China boomed. The growth in both exports and imports is also a sign of the increasing integration of the two economies. Unlike the United Kingdom, China is a large and growing factor of Hong Kong's trade. Does the same hold true for Hong Kong's role in China's trade?

According to the figures in Table 2.6, Hong Kong took nearly 30.0 percent of China's exports in 1984, up 7 percentage points since 1982. Hong Kong supplied 23.8 percent of China's imports in 1984, a huge increase over the 12.2 percent of 1983. Close to 27 percent of China's total trade was with Hong Kong in 1984, up from less than 18 percent in 1982.

By 1984 about 18 percent of Hong Kong's total trade was with China compared with the 27 percent of China's total trade with Hong Kong. Both China and Hong Kong are extremely important to each other, and the mutual trade dependence is growing rapidly. The character of the trade is becoming better balanced with the dramatic growth of Hong Kong's exports to China. Traditionally, China has run a very large balance of payments surplus with Hong Kong. In 1982 this surplus was US$3.2 billion and US$3.1 billion in 1983. Although Hong Kong's imports from China grew

Table 2.7
Expenditures on the Gross Domestic Product, Constant 1983 Prices

	Total GDP		Per Capita GDP	
	$ Billion	% Change	$ Thousand	% Change
1978	110	9.5	24	7.4
1979	124	11.7	25	5.2
1980	137	11.0	27	7.4
1981	150	9.4	29	7.0
1982	155	2.9	29	1.4
1983	162	5.1	31	3.6
1984	178	9.6	33	8.5

Source: Estimates of Gross Domestic Product 19966-1984, Hong Kong: Census and Statistics Department, pp. 7-12.

rapidly in 1984, the sensational increase in Hong Kong's exports to China reduced China's 1984 balance of trade surplus to US$2.1 billion. Another similar increase in Hong Kong's exports might eliminate China's trade surplus with Hong Kong.

The continued prosperity of Hong Kong during the transition period is of great importance to China. As a market that takes about 30 percent of China's exports and the source of a large, though declining, trade surplus, Hong Kong must be considered important, if not indispensible, for China's modernization. Of great significance is the trend that both Hong Kong and China are becoming increasingly dependent on each other.

Recent Trends and Outlook for the Future

Despite the acute political uncertainty, the Hong Kong economy continued to perform strongly in 1984. Table 2.7 gives the bottom line: total and per capita GDP in constant prices.

The political crisis caused a fall in investment and capital flight, but the performance of the economy in 1984 was stronger than at any time since the boom years of 1979 and 1980.

The years 1982 and 1983 had been comparatively poor, but during the seven years from 1977 to 1984, the growth of per capita incomes in constant prices averaged a high 5.8 percent. GDP in constant prices grew at an average rate of 8.4 percent.

The growth surge in 1984 was export driven, with rising exports to the United States and China being the major factors. Domestic exports grew by about 17 percent in 1984 in real terms, compared with a 1983 growth of 14 percent. The value of exports to the United States exploded in 1984 by an incredible 40 percent. Domestic exports to China in 1984 grew by an even more remarkable 81 percent, and exports to China defied all adjectives with a 130 percent growth. As a result, China became Hong Kong's second largest export market.

It is doubtful whether the Hong Kong economy can continue to grow at this rate in 1985 and beyond. The rate of growth of exports is virtually certain to slow, which in turn will slow the rate of growth of the economy. The growth of protectionism in the United States, Hong Kong's largest market, has already produced an adverse impact on Hong Kong and will continue to do so.

Perhaps the darkest cloud ahead is noneconomic and is much closer to home. The Joint Declaration appears to have "solved" Hong Kong's political problems, but the analysis in the previous parts of this chapter suggests that Hong Kong's apparent return to its traditional "no-politics" state may not last. There is no imminent crisis, rather a slow buildup of political tension because of unresolved problems, including how to introduce "democracy" into Hong Kong.

The future of the Hong Kong economy over the next few years is likely to be primarily influenced by the interaction of two factors: the worldwide growth of protectionism and the relationship of London and Beijing over Hong Kong. The outlook is ominous on both counts.

CONCLUSION

Although the issue of democratic reform has appeared as the United Kingdom's problem, it is ultimately China who faces this as a true dilemma. The Hong Kong bill indicates the United Kingdom's intention eventually to devolve real power on the elected legislature, but the refusal to plan beyond 1985 in the *White Paper* on legislative government signals the United Kingdom's aim of securing an early commitment from China.

How will China react? To sustain confidence in its promises and keep Hong Kong stable and prosperous, China dares not openly oppose democratic reform. On the other hand, China can hardly agree to genuine reforms because they must involve the devolution of real power, which will prevent the transfer of full sovereignty in 1997. To allow the United Kingdom rather than China itself to carry out the reforms requires the suppression of ideology and nationalism as well as the acceptance of less than full sovereignty in 1997. This will be a hard pill to swallow, but the alternative is to show the people of Hong Kong that China's promise of autonomy is probably a fraud. If the people of Hong Kong are not allowed to prepare for autonomy before 1997, they will have no confidence that they will be allowed to enjoy it after 1997. This dilemma is going to haunt China for a long time.

NOTES

1. Lucien W. Pye, "The International Position of Hong Kong," *China Quarterly*, no. 95 (Sept. 1983), pp. 456–68. This is a stimulating early article noteworthy for the controversial argument that Peking is likely to gain, rather than lose, foreign exchange through the takeover of Hong Kong.

2. Ibid., p. 462.

3. Cf. Hungdah Chiu, "The 1982 Chinese Constitution and the Rule of Law," *Review of Socialist Law*, Vol. 11, no. 2 (1985), pp. 143–60.

4. Section 3, paragraph 10, of the Joint Declaration.

5. Chalmers Johnson, "The Mousetrapping of Hong Kong: A Game in Which Nobody Wins," *Asian Survey*, Vol. 24, no. 9 (Sept. 1984), pp. 887–909. This is a highly influential article much quoted by those who relish extreme arguments.

6. See Section 3, paragraph 5, of the Joint Declaration.

7. The term is borrowed from A.O. Hirschmann, *Exit, Voice and Loyalty: Responses to Decline in Firms, Organizations and States* (Cambridge: Harvard University Press, 1970), pp. 3–5, where the author discusses in detail the conditions under which the exit option of an organization's members will prevail over the voice option, and vice-versa.

8. Ibid.

9. Mark Tier, *How to Get a Second Passport* (Hong Kong: WMA Publishing Co., 1984).

10. John Walden, "Hong Kong Chases a Democratic Mirage," *Asian Wall Street Journal*, March 7, 1985, p. 12.

11. Ibid., p. 12.

12. Siu-kai Lau, "Political Reform and Political Development in Hong Kong: Dilemmas and Choices," in *Hong Kong and 1997: Strategies for the Future*, ed. Y.C. Jao et al. (Hong Kong: Center of Asian Studies, University of Hong Kong, 1985), pp. 25–26.

13. Hong Kong Government, *White Paper: The Further Development of Representative Government in Hong Kong* (Nov., 1984).

14. Walden, "Hong Kong Chases a Democratic Mirage," p. 12. Walden's argument that Deng told Sir Murray in 1979 that China would reassert sovereignty in 1997 cannot be definitely confirmed, but it is supported by a variety of evidence. For example, Sir S.Y. Chung said that high officials in China told him that Peking did tell MacLehose in 1979 that China would regain sovereignty in 1997. See interview with Sir S.Y. Chung, *Asiaweek*, June 1, 1984. Even the Sino-British Declaration hints at this when it states that the attempt by the governor in Beijing in 1979 to solve the question of land leases expiring in 1997 did not result in measures to solve the problem (Introduction, paragraph 6). Peking could hardly have left the issue in the air at that point.

15. Walden, "Hong Kong Chases a Democratic Mirage," p. 12.

16. Ibid.

17. Ibid.

18. Ibid.

19. Ibid.

20. Ibid.

21. Ibid.
22. Lau, "Political Reform and Political Development," p. 25.
23. Ibid., p. 33.
24. Ibid., p. 34.
25. Ibid., p. 33.
26. Ibid., p. 34.
27. Ibid., p. 27.
28. Ibid., p. 33.
29. Ibid.
30. Simon Kuznets, *Economic Growth of Nations* (Cambridge, Mass.: Harvard University Press, 1971), pp. 38–39.
31. W.A. Lewis, *The Evolution of the International Economic Order* (Princeton, N.J.: Princeton University Press, 1978), p. 33.
32. J.G. Williamson, "Why Was British Growth So Slow during the Industrial Revolution?" *Journal of Economic History*, Vol. 44 (1984), pp. 687–712.
33. World Bank, *World Development Report, 1984* (New York: Oxford University Press, 1984), pp. 263–73.
34. E. Szczepanik, *The Economic Growth of Hong Kong* (London: Royal Institute of International Affairs, 1958), p. 7.
35. Alvin Rabushka, *Hong Kong: A Study in Economic Freedom* (Chicago: University of Chicago Press, 1979), Chapter 1, p. 1.
36. Alvin Rabushka, *Value for Money: The Hong Kong Budgetary Process* (Stanford, Calif.: Hoover University Press, 1976), p. 1.
37. Jon Woronoff, *Hong Kong: Capitalist Paradise* (Hong Kong: Heinemann Educational books, 1980), p. 253.
38. Johnson, "The Mousetrapping of Hong Kong," p. 889.
39. Only Hong Kong's importance in international trade is easily documented. About one-fourth of Hong Kong's trade is with the United States, which means that about 2.25 percent of United States trade is with Hong Kong. About 3 percent of Japan's total trade is with Hong Kong, which is 18 percent of Hong Kong's trade. Hong Kong's role as a trading partner is modest compared to its other functions.

3

Hong Kong's Economic Prospects after the Sino-British Agreement: A Preliminary Assessment

Y.C. JAO

After two years of protracted, and at times acrimonious, negotiations, the People's Republic of China and the United Kingdom initialed an agreement on September 26, 1984, on the future of Hong Kong. Under the agreement, sovereignty over the whole Hong Kong area (Hong Kong Island, Kowloon Peninsula, and the New Territories) will revert to China on July 1, 1997, and Hong Kong itself will become a Special Administrative Region (SAR) of China that will be allowed a high degree of autonomy, with its existing socioeconomic system preserved for 50 years after the transfer of sovereignty.[1] Subsequently, the legislatures of both countries ratified the agreement, and it was formally signed on December 19, 1984. Thus in 12 years Hong Kong, widely regarded as the last bastion of laissez-faire capitalism, will fall under the rule of a totalitarian state.

The purpose of this chapter is to assess objectively Hong Kong's economic prospects in the light of the Sino-British Agreement. Economic forecasting can often be a frustrating and thankless task in today's complex world.[2] In Hong Kong's case the difficulties are compounded immeasurably by the fundamental change in the territory's political status. Nevertheless, such an attempt must somehow be made, however great the margin of error might be. Accordingly, this chapter proposes to discuss Hong Kong's economic prospects from three time perspectives. Given the many imponderables surrounding the Hong Kong situation, some of the discussions, especially those relating to the distant future, can be regarded as no more than informed conjectures.

RECENT BACKGROUND

Before one can make any meaningful prognosis, a brief review of the recent background is necessary.[3] Before 1982 Hong Kong enjoyed the reputation of being one of the fastest growing economies in the world, a member of the famed "four little dragons" of Asia. From a relatively poor and obscure entrepôt before World War II, Hong Kong, by the mid–1960s, had transformed itself into an export-oriented industrial city-state. Since the late sixties, it has been further emerging as a leading financial center in the Asian-Pacific region. Hong Kong's per capita gross domestic product (GDP), measured at current prices and exchange rates, increased by 23 times from HK$1,250 (US$243) in 1947 to HK$32,080 (US$5,638) in 1981, the third highest in Asia after Japan and Singapore. This had been achieved during a period when population had tripled to 5.15 million. From 1947 to 1981 the average annual growth rate of the economy in real terms was 8.68 percent. In the more recent period of 1976–1981, it was an incredible 11.9 percent, arguably one of the highest in the world.

Hopes that this brilliant record of economic growth and prosperity could be sustained on a long-term basis were disappointed in 1982. The severe world economic recession finally caught up with Hong Kong. Domestic exports, which used to provide the main impetus to growth, actually declined in volume in that year. But a much more portentous development came from the political front. China's demand for sovereignty over the whole Hong Kong area, officially confirmed during Prime Minister Margaret Thatcher's visit to Beijing in September 1982, dealt a shattering blow to public confidence in Hong Kong's future. The diplomatic negotiations between China and Britain that began after Thatcher's trip dragged on slowly under the shadow of China's threat that it would announce a unilateral "solution" for Hong Kong if the bilateral talks failed to produce an agreement by the end of September 1984. In the wake of these shocks, the stock market and the property market collapsed; the prices of shares, land, and real properties in 1982 fell by 50–70 percent from their peaks in 1981. The erosion in asset values and the escalation of bad debts in turn caused a severe liquidity squeeze for many property firms and financial institutions, particularly the less prudent deposit-taking companies (DTCs) that resulted in many failures and bankruptcies. The fiscal system, which used to enjoy almost unbroken annual budgetary surpluses, also fell on hard times. The 1982–1983 fiscal year ushered in three consecutive years of sizeable fiscal deficits, unprecedented for Hong Kong, largely because of plummeting land sales as a result of the depression in the real estate sector. The real growth rate of the economy dropped sharply to 1.1 percent from 9.4 percent a year earlier. Finally, the Hong Kong dollar came under heavy pressure from two sources: outright capital flight and internal portfolio shift from domestic-currency to foreign-currency-denominated deposits. The exchange rate against the U.S. dollar fell relentlessly from US$1.00 = HK$5.69 at the end of 1981 to US$1.00 = HK$8.00 on September 17, 1983. The next few days saw wild and seemingly uncontrollable speculation against the Hong Kong dollar. The final crunch came on Saturday, September 24, 1983. As news was received that the Beijing talks ended in a stalemate, panic selling of the Hong Kong dollar pushed the exchange rate to US$1.00 = HK$9.60, a record for Hong Kong. Many shops began to quote prices in U.S. dollars and refused to accept Hong Kong legal-tender notes. Panic buying of staples and imported items also broke out. More ominously, rumors spread quickly about the solvency of banks and DTCs.

In retrospect, the financial crisis of September 1983, caused largely by the anxiety and apprehension over 1997, marked a turning point in Hong Kong's recent history.[4] The Hong Kong government, faced with the impending breakdown of the financial system, reversed its previous laissez-faire stance and took active steps to stabilize the financial sector. On September 25, 1983, the day after the "Black Saturday," the government announced that it was actively considering a currency stabilization plan based on full convertibility. Within the next week, it took over Hang Lung Bank, which was unable to meet its obligations due to heavy deposit withdrawals and loan losses, and participated in a joint rescue operation for Sun Hung Kai Bank, another local institution faced with severe liquidity problems. On October 15, 1983, the government proclaimed a two-point stabilization plan that local economists had been advocating for some time. The first measure of overriding importance was the replacement of the previous floating-exchange-rate system with a "linked-exchange-rate" system, under which the issue of banknotes must be backed 100 percent by U.S. dollars at a fixed rate of US$1.00 = HK$7.80. The other measure was the abolition of the 10 percent withholding tax on interest income from Hong Kong-dollar-denominated deposits with financial institutions, thereby removing the tax advantage from holding foreign-currency-denominated deposits.

Despite initial confusion and skepticism, the linked-rate system has proved highly successful. With the exception of a brief speculative attack in July 1984, the Hong Kong dollar has held remarkably steady against the U.S. dollar at HK$7.80, even though the latter had risen strongly against virtually all major currencies during the period October 1983 to March 1985. Hong Kong's new monetary system depends for its stability on full convertibility and the process of "arbitrage and competition," whereby any deviation from the officially predetermined rate can generate automatic market forces to restore equilibrium.[5] Equally important, the improved political atmosphere has also helped. Apparently shaken by the near collapse of Hong Kong, both China and Britain took a more accommodating attitude in the negotiations, and from October 1983 onwards, steady progress was made. As Table 3.1 shows, the weighted exchange-rate index, which measures the external value of the Hong Kong dollars against 15 major currencies, rose steadily both before and after the Sino-British settlement, although there has been some moderate fall since March 1985 in conjunction with the U.S. dollar. The latest reading of 72.0 on October 4, 1985, represents a 25.8 percent appreciation over the nadir of 57.2 reached on September 24, 1983.

Another sensitive, though volatile, indicator of public confidence is the

Table 3.1
Hong Kong Dollar Exchange-Rate Index (December 18, 1971 = 100)

End of Month	1981	1982	1983	1984	1985
January	87.6	85.8	79.0	69.1	76.9
February	88.5	86.3	78.7	68.9	78.2
March	88.8	88.7	78.3	67.8	76.2
April	89.2	87.7	76.2	68.0	76.6
May	90.1	89.5	73.9	69.4	76.7
June	89.6	89.7	73.8	69.9	76.4
July	88.3	89.1	73.7	71.4	74.4
August	85.1	88.2	71.3	71.9	74.2
September	81.5	86.9	65.3	73.4	72.6
October	84.2	79.8	67.8	74.5	
November	85.3	80.5	68.2	75.2	
December	85.9	80.1	68.3	75.4	

Source: Hong Kong Monthly Digest of Statistics

Hang Seng index of stock prices. It reached an all-time high of 1,810.20 on July 17, 1981, during the speculative frenzy that marked the years of "overheating" in 1978–1981. Since then, the market had retreated under the double pressure of recession and spiraling interest rates, but the decline in stock prices accelerated after the 1997 issue surfaced as a formal diplomatic issue. By December 2, 1982, the stock index had fallen to 676.3, off 63 percent from its 1981 peak. There was a mild recovery in the first seven months of 1983, but the financial crisis in September again drove the index down to 690.06 on October 4. After the successful implementation of the currency stabilization scheme on October 17, 1983, the stock market staged another mild recovery until May 1984, when Deng Xiaoping's televised outburst on the stationing of troops in Hong Kong after 1997 and his proposal of a joint liaison group to monitor the implementation of any agreement again undermined public confidence to such an extent that the index fell to a low of 746.02 on July 13. It was only after British Foreign Secretary Sir Geoffrey Howe's second visit to Beijing at the end of July did a publicly perceived breakthrough occur when he obtained reassurances from Deng that the liaison group would not be "an organ of power." In anticipation of a settlement, the market staged another recovery from August 1984 onwards. This time, however, the recovery was sustained. As indicated by Table 3.2, at the end of September 1985, the index stood at 1,511.80, about 102.60 percent higher than its low in July 1984.

Indeed, in the first three months of 1985, the market was much excited by spectacular takeover bids, which had not been seen in Hong Kong for many years. On January 22, 1985, Li Ka-shing, Hong Kong's top property tycoon, bought a 34 percent stake in Hong Kong Electric Holdings from Hong Kong Land Co. Ltd., a subsidiary of the old-line British conglomerate Jardine Matheson & Co. Li paid HK$2.9 billion (US$372 million). Then in February, another British-owned conglomerate, Wheelock Marden, be-

Table 3.2
Hang Seng Index of Stock Prices (July 31, 1964 = 100)

End of Year/Month	High	Low	Closing
1981	1,810.20	1,113.77	1,405.82
1982	1,445.32	676.30	783.82
1983	1,102.64	690.06	874.94
1984			
January	1,102.38	871.06	1,102.38
February	1,134.12	1,022.85	1,059.29
March	1,170.35	1,014.38	1,014.38
April	1,115.85	1,023.96	1,037.06
May	1,034.73	893.01	915.30
June	966.12	901.07	901.07
July	868.63	746.02	800.15
August	926.78	826.74	926.78
September	1,014.98	911.78	1,002.50
October	1,056.84	963.50	1,015.13
November	1,136.11	1,027.48	1,128.10
December	1,206.83	1,115.01	1,200.38
1985			
January	1,388.42	1,220.74	1,365.02
February	1,435.17	1,312.43	1,375.25
March	1,401.15	1,300.97	1,382.04
April	1,521.30	1,389.13	1,520.56
May	1,647.88	1,516.21	1,613.87
June	1,643.35	1,427.08	1,570.61
July	1,692.06	1,565.04	1,680.62
August	1,711.51	1,652.19	1,656.10
September	1,616.17	1,511.80	1,511.80

Source: Hang Seng Bank Economic Research Department

came the object of a takeover battle between Hong Kong's shipping tycoon Sir Yue-kong Pao (reputedly the largest shipowner in the world) and a Singaporean Chinese businessman, Khoo Teck Paut. Eventually, Pao won the battle, paying HK$2.5 billion (US$320 million) for the company. On March 19 the Bahrain-based Arab Banking Corporation acquired control of Sun Hung Kai Bank, a subsidiary of Sun Hung Kai & Co., a financial services groups listed on the stock exchange. The Arab Banking Corporation paid HK$360 million (US$46.2 million) for the acquisition and injected another HK$372 million (US$47.7 million) into the bank.

The real economy actually rebounded somewhat earlier than the financial sector. Responding characteristically to the U.S.-led world economic recovery, Hong Kong's domestic exports rose by 14.7 percent in real terms in 1983, against a decline of 1.78 percent a year earlier. As a result, the growth rate of the whole economy quintupled to 5.9 percent from the depressed 1982 level. In 1984 the export-propelled mechanism gathered momentum, with the real growth rate of domestic exports rising to 17 percent. The growth rate of the real GDP shot up to 9.6 percent, which was about one percentage point higher than the trend growth rate in 1946–1981. Other macroeconomic indicators also showed a generally healthy pattern. The annual inflation rate, measured by consumer price indexes, declined to 8.1 percent in 1984 from 9.9 percent a year earlier and from double-digit figures in the early eighties.[6] The unemployment rate fell from 5.1 percent in the first quarter of 1983 to 3.8 percent in the fourth quarter of 1984. The underemployment rate declined from 1.5 percent to 0.8 percent during the same period.[7] Tourism, another major pillar of the Hong Kong economy, also had a booming year. The number of visitors increased by 11.7 percent to 3.1 million, and their estimated expenditures rose by 25.7 percent to HK$14.3 billion (US$1.83 billion).[8] Even the real estate sector, generally regarded as the hardest hit by the recent economic recession and political uncertainty, has shown signs of revival from the final quarter of 1984. For instance, between October and November 1984 the number of sale and purchase agreements registered with the Land Office rose sharply by 80 percent over the same period last year. In the first five months of 1985, the total number of real estate transactions increased by more than 30 percent, and the value of the transactions increased by 70 percent.[9] Prices of land at public auctions, a sensitive indicator of the property market, were 10 to 20 percent higher than expected in late 1984 and early 1985.[10] Demand for residential housing, particularly the smaller units, improved considerably with the overall vacancy rate falling to 4 percent in 1984 from 9.9 percent of the previous year and prices rising falling by up to 20 percent.[11]

Until the end of May 1985, most macroeconomic indicators, except exports, appeared to suggest that Hong Kong was enjoying a steady recovery. A renewed euphoria in the first eight months after the Sino-British accord seemed to contradict the pessimism that prevailed barely a year ago.[12] Then, on June 6, the Overseas Trust Bank (OTB), a large local bank founded by overseas Chinese, suddenly declared insolvency. Although the bank's collapse is shrouded in mystery, criminal fraud is probably the principal cause. Four senior executives have been arrested and are facing trial. On June 7, the Hong Kong government, fearing a domino effect on the banking system, took over the bank by using HK$2 billion (US$257 million) from the Exchange Fund. Four days later, the government took over a subsidiary of OTB, the Hong Kong Industrial and Commercial Bank, when an agreement to purchase it by the Hong Leong Group of Malaysia fell through. Rumors began to spread quickly about the soundness of other small independent banks. On June 17 the Hong Kong and Shanghai Banking Corporation and the Bank of China announced that they had jointly extended a "substantial standby secured credit facility" to Ka Wah Bank. At the height of the crisis, the Hang Seng Index dropped by 12 percent in three trading sessions from 1629.50 to 1427.08. The banking crisis of June 1985 once again exposed the seamy side of Hong Kong's banking system.

ECONOMIC PERFORMANCE AFTER THE SETTLEMENT AND FUTURE PROSPECTS

For a situation as complex and fluid as Hong Kong's a precise prognosis of the indefinite future is virtually impossible. A more feasible exercise is to survey Hong Kong's economic performance right after the settlement, 1985–1987, and to then assess its economic prospects in broad terms from a two-stage time perspective: the period from 1988 to 1997, and the post–1997 future.

Hong Kong's Economic Performance from 1985–1987

To predict the performance of the economy in the short run until 1987 is not easy but is not impossible. This is the period in which the positive impact of the Sino-British Agreement appears to be dominant. The strong economic recovery that began in late 1983 lasted for about 18 months but began to falter in mid–1985.

When the Hong Kong government presented its budget on February 27, 1985, it recognized that the previous year's extraordinary real growth rate of 9.6 percent could not be sustained because of the visible slowdown of the U.S. economy. However, it still predicted a real growth rate of the GDP of 7.2 percent on the reasoning that although export growth would decline from 17 percent to 11 percent, the resulting decrease could be offset to a large extent by a vigorous pickup in domestic demand. However, in actual fact, exports not only did not grow but actually declined in real terms, so that real GDP growth plummeted sharply to only 0.8 percent in 1985.

In hindsight, neither the Hong Kong government (which has better access to current and confidential information) nor economists in the private sector did well in predicting the performance of the government.

In a report written for the Economist Intelligence Unit (EIU) of London in the summer of 1983, I made forecasts of the real GDP growth for 1984–1987, which for the first year (1984) has now been shown to have been greatly underestimated. The Hong Kong government, which confines itself to an annual forecast made at the beginning of each year, has not fared much better for 1983 and 1984, as may be readily seen from Table 3.3.

My report was written at a time of great crisis, when the whole financial system teetered on the brink of total collapse. Moreover, the forecast for Hong Kong is constrained by the EIU's own "international assumptions" for the world economy, which predicted low growth of world trade and rising nominal oil prices from 1985 onward. Although the latter scenario has not materialized, the slowdown in the United States has been sufficiently severe to cause unfavorable repercussions for Hong Kong. For 1985, the Hong Kong government's original prediction turned out to be excessively

Table 3.3
Real Growth Rate of Hong Kong's Gross Domestic Product (Percent)

	1983	1984	1985	1986	1987
Projected:					
EIU	---	5.0	3.6	3.7	4.4
Hong Kong Government	3.7	6.3	7.2		
Actual:	5.9	9.6			

Source: Hong Kong: Economic Prospects to 1987, EIU Special Report No. 156, London, 1983; Budget Speech by the Financial Secretary of Hong Kong, various years.

optimistic as compared to the actual outcome, whereas my estimate, though also erring on the optimistic side, was less wide off the mark.

As a small, open economy, the external trading environment largely dictates Hong Kong's economic prospects. From the vantage point of 1986, the world economy appeared to be in a state of flux. On the one hand, with oil prices falling and stabilizing at a lower level and inflation winding down perceptibly in the major industrialized countries, one great original cause of the prolonged "stagflation" since the early 1970s has been removed, at least in the near future. Thus there is somewhat more room for maneuver in these countries in considering expansionary fiscal and monetary policies. On the other hand, the recovery that began in late 1983 has been highly erratic and uneven. The levels of real interest rates, unemployment, and fiscal deficit have also still been distressingly high. Past excesses and subsequent deflationary adjustments have given rise to severe strains in the banking system of many countries. "Financial fragility" for instance, is now an issue for real concern in both the United States and Hong Kong. Worse still, structural maladjustments and trade imbalances have exacerbated frictions in international economic relations. Any escalation of protectionist measures resulting in worldwide trade war could spell disaster for a trade-dependent economy like Hong Kong.

With these cross-currents in mind, even a short-run forecasting exercise, as indicated in Table 3.3, can be somewhat equivocal. If a trade war can be avoided, and the United States, Western Europe, Japan, and other industrialized countries can somehow maintain steady positive growth, it should not be beyond Hong Kong to maintain a 5 to 6 percent growth rate in 1986 and 1987. If, on the other hand, the trading environment deteriorates, and the major industrialized countries continue to be plagued by "growth recession," my original "pessimistic" estimates of 3.7 percent for 1986 and 4.4 percent for 1987 may turn out to be more realistic.

However, an average annual real growth rate of 4 percent in 1985–1987, although less than half of Hong Kong's trend growth rate in 1946–1981, is still fairly respectable by world standards. For example, Hong Kong's rival, Singapore, had a negative growth for 1985 and at least two more stagnant years afterward. Since the currency reform of October 1983, Hong Kong's inflation rate has fallen dramatically from more than 10 percent to around 4 percent in 1985 and 1986. Meanwhile, the unemployment and underemployment rates in mid–1986 remained low and stable at 3 and 1 percent, respectively. Thus, as of late 1986, the economy of Hong Kong, although not buoyant, is not in a despondent state. Since Hong Kong's imminent collapse was widely predicted as late as 1984, an explanation is called for.

To understand the present situation, one must first analyze the state of mind in Hong Kong between July 1982 and September 1984, which was extremely nervous and jittery. Especially in the summer of 1983, when China launched a strident anti-British propaganda campaign, there was real possibility that the Beijing negotiations might end in failure. In that event, many people feared that China would unilaterally take over Hong Kong before 1997, as it had threatened to do. Prohibitions on the movement of money and capital, restrictions on personal freedom, and socialization of private enterprises might follow immediately. With an agreement that is de facto an international treaty, most people reasoned that the period until at least 1997 would be fairly safe. Since successive Chinese governments from the 1920s onward, Nationalist or Communist, have denounced Hong Kong's colonial status as being based on "unequal treaties," a phrase that Sun Yat-Sen coined, it is ironic that the Sino-British accord formally legitimatizes British rule until 1997. It is expressly stated in the 1984 accord that the United Kingdom will be responsible for the administration of Hong Kong until June 30, 1997. Given that in Hong Kong the typical payback period is about 5 to 8 years, a transition period of nearly 13 years is one that most entrepreneurs and business people can live with. For other nonbusiness people, the transition period is also long enough for them to make their plans in an orderly manner. Thus the postaccord calm or even euphoria basically reflects confidence in the status quo under the British administration.

Second, the provisions of the Sino-British Agreement itself are more detailed and reassuring than expected. Apart from the preservation of the existing socioeconomic system for 50 years after 1997, which was already known before the accord, one surprising feature is that "the provisions of the International Covenant on Civil and Political Rights and the International Covenant on Economic, Social, and Cultural Rights as applied to Hong Kong shall remain in force."[13] Admittedly, the agreement is nothing more than a piece of paper, but to a frightened and insecure population, a piece of paper signed by two sovereign powers is still looked upon as something of a guarantee of their human rights and liberties. Also, although it is widely realized that the post–1997 Special Administrative Region (SAR)

Table 3.4
Net Financial Transactions between Hong Kong and China (HK$ Millions)

	End of Quarter	Licensed Banks	Deposit-taking Companies	Total
1979	Q1	+4,725	+96	+4,821
	Q2	+5,231	+102	+5,333
	Q3	+5,266	+116	+5,382
	Q4	+5,701	+32	+5,733
1980	Q1	+5,386	+190	+5,576
	Q2	+4,676	+445	+5,121
	Q3	+4,617	+390	+5,007
	Q4	+5,352	+445	+5,797
1981	Q1	+5,984	+588	+6,572
	Q2	+4,291	+487	+4,778
	Q3	+3,343	+64	+3,407
	Q4	+2,567	-597	+1,970
1982	Q1	-100	-613	-713
	Q2	-2,010	-641	-2,651
	Q3	-2,677	-404	-3,081
	Q4	-4,933	-525	-5,458
1983	Q1	-5,468	-1,446	-6,914
	Q2	-5,366	-1,803	-7,169
	Q3	-7,001	-1,868	-8,869
	Q4	-7,333	-1,822	-9,155
1984	Q1	-9,710	-694	-10,404
	Q2	-12,473	-1,235	-13,708
	Q3	-12,670	-1,114	-13,784
	Q4	-10,020	-659	-10,679
1985	Q1	-5,022	-1,222	-6,244
	Q2	-2,204	-306	-2,510

*A negative sign denotes net liabilities to China, while a positive sign denotes net claims on China.

Source: Banking Commissioner's Office, Hong Kong.

government will be subject to Beijing's manipulation and control, it is still much more preferable than direct rule by Communist cadres sent from the mainland.

Third, there is considerable evidence that China itself, concerned about the dire consequences of Hong Kong's collapse, has been trying to stabilize the local economy in various ways. One manifestation, which is fully documented, is the shift from debtor to creditor status, vis-à-vis Hong Kong's financial institutions. As shown in Table 3.4, between the first quarter of 1982 and the third quarter of 1984, China's net claims on Hong Kong's financial institutions (or Hong Kong's net liabilities to China) increased sharply to HK$13,784 million (US$1,758 million), which was not an inconsiderable sum. As I have argued elsewhere, there can be various plausible interpretations of why China became a net lender to Hong Kong, but the fact that this change occurred at a time when Hong Kong was experiencing great strains and stresses is suggestive.[14] Moreover, from the end of 1984 onward, after the accord was signed, China's net claims on Hong Kong fell sharply to only HK$2,510 million (US$322 million) in the second quarter of 1985. It is also known that China has invested heavily in all sectors of the Hong Kong economy in recent years, although there is no official documentation of the amount involved. According to Wang Guangying, chairman of the Beijing-owned Everbright Industrial Corporation, China has in recent years invested some US$4 billion in Hong Kong through 50 Chinese representative and trade offices in more than 300 projects.[15] An estimate by the Industry Department of the Hong Kong government reveals that at the end of March 1985, Beijing owned or controlled 124 firms in trade and industrial promotion, 44 in banking and finance, 5 in insurance, 19 in manufacturing, 4 in publishing and printing, 53 in transportation and tourism, and 26 in real estate and construction.[16] These firms do not, however, include hundreds of department stores and retail outlets selling Chinese products.

During Hong Kong's currency crisis of 1982–1983, China lost, according to my estimate, about US$1.1 billion as a result of the sharp depreciation of the Hong Kong dollar. Yet it has refrained so far from passing on the loss to Hong Kong consumers by raising sharply the supply prices of Chinese goods. It may be that the depreciation of *renminbi* against the Hong Kong dollar by 36 percent since October 1983 has rendered such a move unnecessary. But given that Hong Kong's demand for Chinese goods is generally inelastic, China could have exploited the price mechanism if it so desired. Two other examples of China's concern for Hong Kong's stability are the takeover of two large Hong Kong industrial firms in 1984 that nearly went bankrupt and the Bank of China's support to Ka Wah Bank in June 1985 as mentioned earlier.[17]

Finally, for obvious reasons, China's internal developments have important implications for Hong Kong. Western economists' studies indicate that the post-Mao leadership's adoption of a more pragmatic and outward-looking economic policy has resulted in substantial gains in output, particularly in agriculture, and some improvement in the standard of living of the population.[18] Since 1978, to attract foreign investment and technology, China has set up four Special Economic Zones (SEZs) on the southern coast, opened 14 coastal cities and the whole coastal areas to foreign investment, and enacted various forms of "economic legislation." In October 1984 the Communist party's Central Committee decided that the reform program so successfully applied to the rural sector would be extended to the urban areas with emphasis on freeing prices and wages from rigid state control and giving greater autonomy to the enterprises. In social, cultural, and intellectual life, there has also been a noticeable depoliticization or loosening of the total regimentation so characteristic of the Maoist era. Except for a short-lived "antispiritual pollution campaign" in 1983, political "mass movements," which in the past have caused so much turmoil, have basically ceased since 1977. Deng's China is still far from being a liberal democracy, but there is abundant evidence that it is settling down to becoming what might be called a "postrevolutionary society," the primary goals of which are now economic reconstruction and modernization, rather than class struggle and world revolution.[19] These developments have given rise to hopes that the wide discrepancies in standard of living and life-style between mainland China and Hong Kong will gradually diminish over time. Such hopes might turn out to be wishful thinking, but they do have some soothing effect on the anxiety and fear of the people of Hong Kong.

Outlook for the period from 1988–1997

The outlook for Hong Kong in this period is much less clear and more uncertain. Any unexpected political and economic development in both Hong Kong and China could upset the delicate balance and cause uneasiness, which the Sino-British Agreement seems to have brought about for the time being.

Under the terms of the Sino-British Agreement, a Joint Liaison Group will establish its principal base in Hong Kong on July 1, 1988. When China first broached the idea of the group in July 1984, a minor currency crisis was triggered in Hong Kong.[20] The panic, though short-lived, reflected two fundamental concerns: one was whether the liaison group might not become a "shadow government" through which China could manipulate or control the British administration even before 1997; the other was that the very idea of the group suggested Chinese distrust of Britain's sincerity in implementing the agreement. Although subsequent consultations have resulted in a clause in the agreement that the group is not an organ of power and will not play any administrative or supervisory role, widespread unease and suspicion about that real purpose of the group still persisted. For instance, one of the functions of the group is expressly stated in the agreement as follows: "to exchange information and conduct consultations on such subjects as may be agreed by the two sides."[21] Thus even though the group may not have executive powers, it is feared that China's representatives in the group can gain access to sensitive or even classified information on virtually every aspect of Hong Kong life.

The other matter of grave concern is the Basic Law that is supposed to be a constitutional document for the post–1997 Hong Kong that incorporates the essential features of the Sino-British Agreement. During the period of 1988–1997, the Basic Law will be drafted and promulgated. Some 23 Hong Kong representatives have already been invited to participate in the drafting process. But whether the future "miniconstitution" will embody the kind of polity desired by the majority of the populace remains to be seen. Moreover, China regards the enactment of the Basic Law, unlike the Sino-British Agreement, as a strictly internal affair. As Yuan-li Wu aptly points out in Chapter 6, the Basic Law is predicated on the People's Republic of China's (PRC's) Constitution, which has been rewritten three times during a single decade and can be changed again by a rubber-stamp National

People's Congress.[22] Whatever one's view on this matter, the modus operandi of the liaison group and the Basic Law will provide a litmus test of China's sincerity in promising Hong Kong a high degree of autonomy.

Meanwhile in Hong Kong, the political and administrative structure will be undergoing significant changes in the runup to 1997. In anticipation of their withdrawal, the British have published two official papers—the *Green Paper* and the *White Paper*—in quick succession after British Foreign Secretary Sir Geoffrey Howe announced the abandonment of sovereignty in April 1984.[23] The British strategy is to nurture the development of a quasi-parliamentary democracy based largely on indirect elections. Thus by 1997 a new generation of Hong Kong political leaders can take over power under the terms of the Sino-British Agreement.[24]

Pursuant to this objective, fairly successful elections to the district boards (roughly equivalent to local councils in the United Kingdom) and the Legislative Council (roughly equivalent to Parliament) were held in March and September 1985, respectively. Publicly, China has maintained silence on Hong Kong's internal political development, but it is no secret that Beijing's attitude toward Hong Kong's democratization is one of distaste and displeasure. Xu Jiatun, director of the Hong Kong Xinhua News Agency (New China News Agency, China's de facto diplomatic mission in Hong Kong) has publicly warned against any hasty change in Hong Kong's governmental structure before 1997.[25] Meanwhile, the Communist press in Hong Kong has reminded the British, in none too subtle terms, that sovereignty is to be transferred to the PRC, not Hong Kong. However cautious and timid Hong Kong's move toward representative government may be, it has already aroused fears in Beijing that an elected government in Hong Kong that embodies the popular will may be much less amenable to manipulation and control after 1997. More importantly, such a government might generate a "demonstration effect" on the people in mainland China with potentially explosive consequences. To the Chinese Communists, democracy is more of an anathema than capitalism.

Given that the ultimate source of power rests with China, it is doubtful whether Hong Kong can ever evolve into a truly independent and democratic polity. The parameters are already set by the Sino-British Agreement and will be reaffirmed by the Basic Law. Moreover, in terms of the likely impact, changes in Hong Kong's domestic administrative machinery are insignificant compared to political changes in China.

The two questions that concern Hong Kong most are leadership succession and policy continuity. Unless there is a biological miracle, the death of Deng Xiaoping will most probably occur sometime during this period. Recent developments suggest that Deng and his followers have achieved a considerable victory in enlarging and consolidating their political power. In June 1985 Deng announced the demobilization of 1 million soldiers and a long list of reshuffles of key military personnel. Later in September, at a meeting of the Communist party's Central Committee and a specially convened National Conference, some 131 old guards were retired. Younger and better educated cadres, known to be Deng's protégés, were promoted to the Politburo and Central Committee. A new Five Year Plan for 1986–1990 was also announced that stressed the continuation of Deng's modernization and economic reform program. It is true that Deng still has to contend with a powerful group of conservatives under the leadership of Chen Yun, a senior party veteran and former economic planner who has been highly critical of what he regards as overhasty liberalization that leads to inflation, widespread corruption, and other undesirable capitalistic influences and practices. However, Chen was also an opponent of Mao's irrational and irresponsible policies in the late fifties. Hence his current strictures should not be interpreted as a fundamental opposition to the current pragmatic modernization and reform policies.

The implications of the above analysis are that as long as there is no repetition of another Cultural Revolution and moderate pragmatists are in power in Beijing, Hong Kong in the remaining years of British rule should be able to weather the political vicissitudes in China as it has done during the past 36 years. It is also in China's own interests to preserve Hong Kong's stability for reasons well documented.[26] Apart from regularly providing about one-third of China's hard-currency earnings, Hong Kong also serves as an unexcelled offshore financial center, entrepôt, and information center for China. If Beijing plays its cards wisely, it will be able to acquire from Britain in 1997 with virtually no expenditures all of these first-rate facilities, which it knows can never be replicated elsewhere in China.

With this overall political outlook in mind, a total collapse of the economy before 1997 seems most unlikely. But the medium-term economic outlook is also much more murky and uncertain than the short-term one. Since a numerical projection for the period 1988–1997 is impossible, we will instead discuss certain broad trends and major issues of concern.

The first is the stability of the financial sector. We have observed how the financial crisis of 1982–1983, comprised of the currency crisis, banking crisis, and fiscal crisis, shook the Hong Kong economy to its very foundation. We also have observed how the linked-exchange-rate system introduced in October 1983 saved Hong Kong from financial ruin by restoring confidence in the Hong Kong dollar. Indeed, from January 5, 1985 to October 1985, the Hong Kong dollar was so stable against the U.S. dollar that the three-month forward rate on the U.S. dollar, a sensitive indicator of currency confidence, dropped below the official rate of 7.8. The spot rate also fell below par after May 6, 1985. But whether the strength of the Hong Kong dollar is a temporary or permanent phenomenon remains an open question. In normal times, the present system relies on the automatic mechanism of "arbitrage and competition" for its efficacy. In an emergency, however, the decisive factor is the resources of the Exchange Fund. The accounts of the fund have never been published, but the financial secretary, Sir John Bremridge, in an interview with *Fortune* in October 1983, hinted that the size of the fund was at least US$4.3 billion.[27] This fund amounted to about 2.2 times the outstanding currency in circulation at that time. The stated multiplier is unlikely to diminish because of the 100 percent requirement under the new linked-rate system. Applying it to the latest monetary statistics, the fund's assets are estimated to cover about 101.4 percent of M1, 21.6 percent of M2, and 17.9 percent of M3, all denominated in Hong Kong dollars as of July 1985.[28] In normal circumstances, such a cover should be more than enough to ensure convertibility into foreign currencies, but in a general panic, it is doubtful whether the fund can indefinitely withstand a persistent flight from the Hong Kong dollar. Although we have ruled out a recurrence of Maoist turmoils in China, some pressure on the currency can be expected on Deng's death or other events that might be perceived as signs of instability, given Hong Kong's ultrasensitivity to political developments in China. If China is serious about Hong Kong's stability, it should instruct its powerful Bank of China Group in Hong Kong to cooperate with the Hong Kong monetary authorities to forestall any currency crisis. On several occasions some top officials of China's banking institutions have made statements that they are prepared to do so.[29]

Much speculation has been made about the outflow of capital from Hong Kong since 1982, but there is hardly any quantification, because Hong Kong does not yet have a comprehensive balance-of-payments accounting system.[30] Only a trade account, including invisibles, is now available. As may be seen from Table 3.5, Hong Kong's trade account has improved considerably in recent years, resulting in a surplus of HK$11.64 billion (US$1.49 billion) in 1984. But the trade account, unlike the capital account, is more a function of economic performance than other intangibles like political uncertainty and confidence. Before October 1983, net outflow of capital showed up in the rapid depreciation of the domestic currency. After the implementation of the linked-rate system, the remarkable stability of the Hong Kong dollar would seem to suggest that net outflow has become less of a problem. Indeed, the success of the scheme may have attracted considerable inflow of capital, tending to offset any outflow due to other reasons.

Another element of the financial crisis, illiquidity or insolvency of depository institutions, may arise not only from political uncertainty but also from mismanagement or even fraud. Hong Kong's regulatory record in this respect is, to say the least, less than perfect. In early 1985, at the advice of the Bank of England, the regulatory authorities prepared a series of reforms, including a minimum capital to risk assets ratio, to tighten prudential supervision. Before these measures could be implemented, however, the Overseas Trust Bank crisis erupted. The government had to bail out the bank by injecting HK$2 billion in the first instance. This rescue operation and the government's decision to inject HK$1.5 billion of capital into the loss-

Table 3.5
The Visible and Invisible Trade Account (HK$ Millions)

	1979	1980	1981	1982	1983	1984
Visible Trade						
Domestic Exports	55,912	68,171	80,423	83,032	104,405	137,936
Re-exports	20,022	30,072	41,739	44,353	56,291	83,504
Total Exports of Goods	75,934	98,242	122,163	127,385	160,699	221,441
Imports of Goods	85,908	111,651	138,375	142,893	175,442	223,370
Visible Trade Balance	-9,974	-13,408	-16,212	-15,508	-14,743	-1,929
Visible Trade Gap (%) (*)	11.6	12.0	11.7	10.9	8.4	0.9
Imports of Goods Adjusted (**)	86,339	111,794	139,246	143,769	176,574	224,812
Visible Trade Balance Adjusted (**)	-10,405	-13,552	-17,083	-16,384	-15,875	-3,371
Visible Trade Gap Adjusted (%) (**)	12.1	12.1	12.3	11.4	9.0	1.5
Invisible Trade						
Exports of Services	19,258	22,203	27,218	30,671	36,922	44,455
Imports of Services	11,968	14,912	19,234	20,889	25,081	29,440
Invisible Trade Balance	7,290	7,291	7,984	9,782	11,841	15,015
Visible and Invisible Trade						
Exports of Goods and Services	95,192	120,445	149,381	158,056	197,621	265,896
Imports of Goods and Services (**)	98,307	126,706	158,480	164,658	201,655	254,252
Visible and Invisible Trade Balance	-3,115	-6,261	-9,099	-6,602	-4,034	11,644
Visible and Invisible Trade Gap (%) (***)	3.2	4.9	5.7	4.0	2.0	(4.6)

Notes

(*) Visible trade gap, that is, the proportion of the value of imports of goods not covered by the value of total export of goods.

(**) Adjusted to take account of imports of gold for industrial and commercial use.

(***) Visible and invisible trade gap, that is, the proportion of the value of imports of goods and services not covered by the value of exports of goods and services. The figures in brackets denote a visible and invisible trade surplus expressed as a percentage of the value of imports of goods and services.

Source: Hong Kong Government

making Mass Transit Railway Corporation (MTRC) have grave fiscal implications.

After three consecutive years of deficits, Hong Kong's fiscal reserves had fallen from HK$23 billion in April 1982 to HK$15.3 billion in April 1985, with the net contingent liabilities reduced from HK$16.5 billion to HK$8.7 billion.[31] These reserves will be further diminished by the commitments to OTB and MTRC. In the past three fiscal years, the government therefore has had to raise the direct tax rate by 2 percentage points (the standard rate from 15 percent to 17 percent and the corporation profits tax from 16.5 percent to 18.5 percent) and also to increase a wide range of indirect taxes. Inevitably, Hong Kong's attractions as a low-tax financial center have suffered, especially as Singapore, Hong Kong's arch rival, has steadily cut its taxes to lure financial institutions and banking business away from Hong Kong.[32]

The second major concern is the rate of capital formation. In 1982–1984, largely due to the confidence crisis, the growth rate of capital formation in real terms was −2.4 percent, against an average rate of 8.7 percent in 1966–1981. The fall in real capital formation was accounted for mostly by the sharp decline in private sector building and construction and private investment in plant, machinery, and equipment. Traditionally, capital formation is the most volatile component of Hong Kong's GDP and is also highly sensitive to political developments. For example, in 1967–1968, when the Cultural Revolution spilled over to Hong Kong, real capital formation declined by 17 percent and 9 percent, respectively. For the year 1985, real capital formation was forecast to recover modestly to 3 percent, with private investment in plant and machinery rising by about 6 percent. Private building and construction would grow by 5 percent.

Over the long term, it is almost impossible to predict how this vital component of GDP will behave. Public sector capital formation is presumably more stable, being under the direct control of the government. To avoid being labeled a "lame duck," the Hong Kong government, supported by the United Kingdom, has repeatedly proclaimed that it will invest vigorously in Hong Kong's future. But government investment in Hong Kong is a function of government revenue, with large-scale and persistent deficit financing not considered. Some public projects, such as the MTRC, will be completed shortly and cannot serve as a permanent source of capital formation. Private sector capital formation is governed not only by the prospective yield on real investment but also by long-term expectations about political stability, personal freedom, and property rights. Admittedly in the past, speculative activities in building and construction had produced unhealthy and distorting effects on capital formation. The deep depression in the property market has, however, largely wiped out speculators. Private investments in housing will therefore be more in line with demographic trends and final demand. If the tourist sector can maintain its present bullish trend, the construction of hotels should also provide some stimulus to gross capital formation.

Private investment in plant, machinery, and equipment is more promising for two reasons. First, it is largely a function of exports, and barring a prolonged worldwide depression, it should be able to maintain a reasonable rate of positive growth. Second, industrial investment is an area where there is a high overseas interest. According to a recent survey by the Industry Department of the Hong Kong government, foreign investment in Hong Kong's manufacturing industries did not seem to have been much affected by the political uncertainty in 1982–1984. The total amount of overseas investment increased by 63 percent from HK$7,013 million in August 1981 to HK$11,448 million in September 1984. The three largest source countries are the United States (53.7 percent), Japan (21.1 percent), and the United Kingdom (6.9 percent). The three largest industries are electronics (35.5 percent), textiles and garments (9.9 percent), and electrical products (8 percent). The average investment per worker also increased by 79 percent from HK$89,000 to HK$159,400 during the same period. It should be stressed, however, that the official report uses the Hong Kong dollar as the unit of account. During the same period, the Hong Kong dollar underwent substantial devaluation. In terms of the U.S. dollar, the growth rates became much less impressive: total investment increased by 19.3 percent from US$1,230 million to US$1,468 million, while investment per worker increased by 30.9 percent from US$15,614 to US$20,436. The devaluation and subsequent stabilization of the Hong Kong dollar did, however, provide an additional attraction to foreign investors. In the same report, nearly half of the 442 respondents disclosed plans to expand their operations in Hong Kong, whereas only 2 indicated intention of leaving.[33]

The currency factor is one reason why foreign firms, particularly multinational corporations from strong-currency countries like the United States and Japan, are generally more sanguine about Hong Kong's future than indigenous firms, both before and after the Sino-British Agreement. But there are other good economic reasons. Typically, a multinational firm's investment in Hong Kong is a calculated risk quantitatively trivial relative to the firm's global assets, which nevertheless forms an integral part of the firm's global strategy. The firm also has reason to believe that it will command more respect from China after 1997, as it is backed by its home government. Furthermore, if the firm is prestigious enough, it can use its name to tap the local capital market. Thus the Security Pacific Bank of California made a HK$500 million commercial paper issue in November 1984 to finance its takeover of minority interests in a Hong Kong bank, the Bank of Canton. By contrast, given the uncertainty over the future, it is entirely rational for an indigenous firm with most of its assets concentrated in Hong Kong to diversify its assets away from Hong Kong as much as possible.

Unlike a foreign firm, a local firm after 1997 can expect protection only from the Hong Kong SAR government, which is ultimately responsible to the Central People's Government in China.

One does not have to subscribe to the theory of "rational expectations" to agree that economic agents process information efficiently and act accordingly to protect or promote their own interests. We can therefore expect that local firms in Hong Kong will increasingly follow the strategy of what might be called "precautionary diversification" or "precautionary internationalization." This strategy may take many forms, but the principal elements are: (a) transfer of liquid assets abroad, leaving only money balances enough for transactions purposes in Hong Kong; (b) establishment of branches or offices in foreign countries or acquisition of foreign firms in whole or in part; (c) sale of the firm's equity to a foreign firm or formation of a joint venture entity with a foreign firm in Hong Kong; and (d) removal of the registered head office from Hong Kong to a foreign country, especially a tax haven.

It should be emphasized that this strategy does not necessarily imply outright withdrawal. Unless conditions become utterly intolerable, very few firms will actually abandon Hong Kong even after 1997 because the attractions of doing business in Hong Kong and the lure of the China market are considerable. As an illustration, the decision of Jardine Matheson, the oldest British conglomerate in Hong Kong, to move its legal domicile to Bermuda in 1984 has not resulted in the winding down of its operations. Instead, the company is expanding its business with China, having reportedly explained its corporate policy to Beijing's satisfaction. It is also well known that virtually all of Hong Kong's shipping companies are incorporated in countries like Liberia and Panama for tax purposes.

The most prominent case of "precautionary diversification" is the Hong Kong and Shanghai Banking Corporation (HSBC), a British bank founded and incorporated in Hong Kong in 1865. Because it is also Hong Kong's de facto central bank, it cannot move its head office elsewhere without causing immediately a financial panic and banking crisis. This caution, however, has not prevented it from embarking on a global diversification program long before 1997 became a diplomatic issue. In 1980 it completed the acquisition of Marine Midland Bank of the United States, a coup that catapulted its global ranking to the 17th largest commercial bank in the world. However, the British Monopoly and Merger Commission thwarted its attempt to take over the Royal Bank of Scotland in 1981. According to the commission, which had access to the bank's full financial data, even in 1980 Hong Kong accounted for only 28.6 percent of the bank's global assets. In May 1984 the HSBC sold its subsidiary, the Mercantile Bank, which operates mainly in India and Thailand and is shrinking in size to Citibank. It is widely known that the HSBC is mainly interested in the United States, United Kingdom, Europe, and Australia for expansion. In early 1985 the bank was granted a license in Australia, following liberalization of the banking system there. It also acquired a substantial stake in James Capel, a leading London brokerage house. On June 26, 1985, it purchased four New York City branches of the failed Golden Pacific National Bank for about US$6.35 million.[34] In October 1985 the bank acquired the branches of the failed Canadian Commercial Bank.[35] There is widespread speculation that the HSBC is looking for another major acquisition either in the United Kingdom or Europe. Nevertheless, according to chairman Michael Sandberg, the bank, probably the 20th largest in the world in 1985, will continue to be based in Hong Kong. Moreover, the bank is said to be involved in some 200 projects in China, and its China Area Office will be one of the fastest growing departments over the next few years.[36] Another recent example of "precautionary diversification" was the decision by the giant Sing Tao publishing group to transfer its ownership to Australia in May 1985.[37]

Precautionary outflow of capital, as long as it is effected in an orderly manner or is not accompanied by the physical departure or emigration of the owner, is not necessarily detrimental to Hong Kong. Indeed, if the outflow of capital takes the form of investment in foreign assets of all kinds, the income stream generated by these assets can become a significant factor in sustaining Hong Kong's aggregate economic activity. We can predict that Hong Kong's Gross National Product (GNP) will henceforth grow more rapidly than its GDP. Emigration, especially a reduction of human resources, can be a potentially serious problem. But emigration is constrained by the immigration policies of a small number of desirable countries of destination. The United Kingdom has already, through its Nationality Act, slammed the door to Hong Kong holders of British passports, although it is understood that a small number of the Hong Kong elite, including top civil servants, will be granted residence in the United Kingdom after 1997 as a secret morale-boosting deal. Other countries like the United States, Canada, and Australia all have strictly enforced quotas for Hong Kong. Unless the immigration regulations and quotas of these countries are significantly liberalized, emigration will not be a viable option for the vast majority of the Hong Kong population.[38]

The third major aspect of the economy that warrants close monitoring and study is the evolving economic relationship between Hong Kong and China. One salient feature of the post-Mao era is the rapidly growing trade and investment flows between the two. China replaced Japan as Hong Kong's largest supplier in 1982. It also became Hong Kong's fourth largest export market in the same year and then the second largest in 1984. As for entrepôt trade, China became Hong Kong's largest country of destination in 1980 and the largest country of origin as early as 1969. Tables 3.6 and 3.7 summarize merchandise and entrepôt trade between Hong Kong and China for the period 1977 until the first eight months of 1985. Several

Table 3.6
Merchandise Trade between Hong Kong and China (HK$ Millions)

Year	Domestic Exports to China	Total Exports to China	Imports from China	Trade Balance for Hong Kong
1977	31	206	8,115	-7,909
1978	11 (-64.5)	225 (+9.2)	10,597 (+30.6)	-10,302 (+30.3)
1979	603 (+5381.8)	1,918 (+752.4)	15,201 (+43.5)	-13,283 (+28.9)
1980	1,605 (+166.2)	6,247 (+225.7)	21,948 (+44.4)	-15,701 (+18.2)
1981	2,924 (+82.2)	10,968 (+75.6)	29,510 (+34.5)	-18,542 (+18.1)
1982	3,806 (+30.2)	11,798 (+7.6)	32,935 (+11.6)	-21,137 (+14.0)
1983	6,223 (+63.5)	18,406 (+56.0)	42,821 (+30.0)	-24,415 (+15.5)
1984	11,283 (+81.3)	39,347 (+113.8)	55,753 (+30.2)	-16,406 (-32.8)
1985 (first 8 months)	10,416 (+60.7)	42,742 (+99.4)	35,687 (-2.5)	+7,055 (-146.5)

Source: Census and Statistics Department, Hong Kong

Note: Total exports = domestic exports + re-exports. Figures in brackets are year-on-year percentage growth.

Table 3.7
Entrepôt Trade between Hong Kong and China (HK$ Million)

Year	Re-exports to China	Re-exports from China through Hong Kong
1977	175	2,492
1978	214 (+22.3)	3,659 (+46.8)
1979	1,315 (+514.5)	5,663 (+54.8)
1980	4,642 (+253.0)	8,394 (+48.2)
1981	8,044 (+73.3)	12,834 (+52.9)
1982	7,992 (-0.005)	14,694 (+14.5)
1983	12,183 (+52.4)	19,680 (+33.9)
1984	28,064 (+130.4)	28,107 (+42.8)
1985 (first 8 months)	32,326 (+116.2)	21,739 (+19.0)

Source: As for Table 6.

Note: Figures in brackets are year-on-year percentage growth.

important features may be noted. One is the impressive year-on-year growth rates in all trade categories. Although they are expressed in value terms in the tables, the growth rates in real terms are also very high. The growth rate of domestic exports to China in 1984, for example, was as high as 60 percent, faster than the 50 percent recorded in 1983. Second, the phenomenal growth of domestic exports to China is perhaps the most surprising and exciting development in the post-Mao era. During a period of less than eight years, such exports had increased by nearly 40 times from almost nothing to more than HK$11.3 billion (US$1.45 billion). When such exports began to shoot up in 1979–1980, most economists tended to dismiss them as raw materials or semiproduced goods for processing in the Shenzhen special economic zone, to be shipped back to Hong Kong for finishing and reexporting. However, a more careful study of six-digit-commodity composition suggests that in recent years, finished consumer and producers goods, such as watches and clocks, transport and telecommunications equipment, and metal manufactures, have accounted for 51 to 55 percent of Hong Kong's domestic exports to China. Therefore, the value-added contribution to Hong Kong's GDP is not insignificant.[39] China's purchase of Hong Kong goods partially reflects modernization requirements, pent-up consumer demand, and a much-improved foreign-exchange position. The country's total foreign-exchange reserves have increased from US$2,345 million in 1977 to US$17,302 million in September 1984.[40] Third, the equally phenomenal growth of reexports to and reexports from China in the post-Mao years have unequivocally confirmed Hong Kong's reemergence as the leading entrepôt for China and the whole Pacific Basin. However, unlike the pre–1950 entrepôt, Hong Kong today is a highly sophisticated financial and trading center with a respectable manufacturing base in which entrepôt trade is a nice complement but not a key pillar of the economy.

What these data show is that China's modernization program and outward-looking development strategy has produced significant and positive impacts on the already close trading relationship between Hong Kong and China. Hong Kong's importance as an export market and an entrepôt for China has been further enhanced. At the same time, China itself is opening up as an export market for Hong Kong, which has been desperately trying to diversify its markets for some time due to protectionist pressures elsewhere. Provided that there is no undue political interference, the symbiotic relationship between the two could develop into a powerful mutually interactive engine of economic growth.

But although Hong Kong should do everything possible to nurture this relationship, it should also guard itself against any unrealistic expectations or any politically motivated scheme of "coprosperity." Although the growth rates in various trade categories have been gratifyingly high in recent years, they cannot be expected to continue indefinitely because there is a finite limit to China's demand for Hong Kong products, which basically require relatively low levels of technology. It will not be long before China catches up and produces in sufficient quantity the kinds of goods it now imports from Hong Kong. Furthermore, despite stunning increases to the end of 1984, China's foreign reserves are still small compared to the country's size and development needs. Indeed, in May 1985 China once again had to curtail imports as its foreign-exchange reserves fell sharply from US$17,302 million in September 1984 to US$11,978 million in March 1985.[41] It should be noted from Table 3.6 that China's trade surplus against Hong Kong, declined in 1984, mainly due to the sharp increase in Hong Kong's exports to China. In the first eight months of 1985, China's traditional surplus actually turned into a deficit. Although an isolated abberation can be tolerated, it is doubtful whether China can afford to let the trade surplus disappear indefinitely, because it is China's long-term strategy to maximize its hard-currency earnings from Hong Kong to pay for the import of capital equipment and high technology.

From Hong Kong's point of view, exports to China hardly help it to "trade up." Only the advanced industrialized countries of the West can provide a permanent source of foreign exchange, management skill, and high technology. Protectionist restrictions on certain products, notably textiles, garments, footwear, and watches, do not invalidate the general correctness of the strategy that, without cutting itself off from China, Hong Kong should continue to orient its trade and economic development toward the affluent and sophisticated markets of the West.[42] As to the booming entrepôt trade, it is a tribute to Hong Kong's excellent infrastructure and nonpolitical status; yet entrepôt trade per se contains relatively little value added to the economy.

This chapter has discussed China's injection of funds into Hong Kong through state corporations or pro-Beijing private firms. Although there can be no doubt about Beijing's genuine desire to maintain Hong Kong's stability, it is doubtful whether Beijing can afford to pour money into Hong Kong indefinitely, given China's huge demand for scarce capital funds for its modernization program. Moreover, the investment flow is by no means unidirectional. Since China opened its door to foreign investment in 1979, Hong Kong interests have topped all foreign investors in either joint ventures or wholly-owned enterprises. According to a high official of the China Resources Co., Beijing's largest state trading corporation in Hong Kong, Hong Kong business people since 1979 have invested about US$4.5 billion in China's cities and provinces, or about 60 percent of total foreign investment.[43] In the special economic zone of Shenzhen, Hong Kong's position is particularly predominant, accounting for about 80 percent of total investment. Indeed, it is not an exaggeration to say that Shenzhen has become virtually Hong Kong's satellite town.[44]

Although Hong Kong's projects are mostly small, such as housing, hotels, commerce, and light industries, with short pay-back periods, there are also giant projects such as the US$3.5 billion Daya Bay nuclear plant in Guangdong Province, which is a joint venture between a Hong Kong utility firm and China Light and Power Co. Projects also include the US$900 million highway project linking Hong Kong with Shenzhen, Canton, and Zhuhai in which a Hong Kong firm, Hopewell Holdings, is heavily involved. In March 1985 a new investment company, the Hong Kong Macau International Investment Co., was formed with a registered capital of HK$500 million. It is a joint venture between the Bank of China and leading businessmen from Hong Kong, Macau, and Southeast Asia. One of the projects now being considered is a regional airline linking Hong Kong with China.[45] Hong Kong's investment behavior in China is by no means inconsistent with the thesis of "precautionary diversification" stated earlier. Our hypothesis says only that a rational Hong Kong businessperson or investor will diversify his or her assets globally without forsaking Hong Kong and China.

The final issue of concern during the transitional period is macroeconomic policy and structural change. A topic like this warrants a separate chapter, so it can be treated only cursorily here. The Hong Kong government traditionally espouses a policy of "positive nonintervention," which roughly means that the government will not interfere with the market economy unless there is a clear case of market failure that calls for action to protect the public. To a large measure, the brilliant record of Hong Kong's economic growth after World War II, the benefits of which filter down to a large section of the population, has vindicated the policy. In recent years, however, there has been mounting criticism of this policy of which three major points may be singled out for discussion. The first is that the laissez-faire attitude toward the depository institutions has resulted in a spate of crises involving both banks and DTCs that inflicted great losses on the public. This criticism was much more valid for the banking crises of the early sixties than for the crisis of 1982–1983, because in the latter case, the important factor of political uncertainty was beyond the control of the regulatory authorities. Nevertheless, it remains true that Hong Kong's approach to the banking crisis and irregularities in the financial markets has been depressingly ad hoc and ex post, never having any far-sighted and comprehensive plan to forestall the liquidity crisis and to check fraudulent practices. However, as already mentioned, the problem is being tackled again with a view to tightening prudential supervision. The challenge and dilemma is how to protect the ordinary depositors and investors without throttling initiatives and innovations in the banking and financial-services industries.

The second major criticism concerns the poor conduct of monetary policy, especially during the "overheating" of 1978–1981. Again, this issue is too complex and technical a subject to be discussed in full here. Suffice it to say that Hong Kong did not need a discretionary monetary policy before June 1972 when it was on the sterling exchange standard. As long as the Hong Kong dollar was pegged to sterling at a fixed rate, money supply was automatically determined by the amount of sterling or the state of the balance of payments. After the floating of sterling, Hong Kong left the Sterling area, and the Hong Kong dollar was pegged to the U.S. dollar until November 26, 1974, when a massive speculation against the U.S. dollar forced Hong Kong to float its own currency. The conventional wisdom in economic theory until then was that under a floating exchange-rate regime, a small open economy would be more able to pursue an independent monetary policy. The presumption in this hypothesis is that the institutional framework or instruments of monetary control are already in place. In Hong Kong, however, neither condition is satisfied. There is neither a central bank nor a large government debt in which open-market operations can be made. From November 1974 to October 1983 the Hong Kong monetary authorities could control neither the quantity nor the price of money (the external exchange rate). Instead, makeshift experiments such as moral suasion, a 100 percent liquidity requirement against the Exchange Fund's short-term balances with the banking system, the three-tier financial structure, government borrowing on the interbank market to twist the yield curve, and the statutory incorporation of the Hong Kong Association of Banks all had been to no avail. Money stock and bank credit, however, continued to grow at excessive rates, and the Hong Kong dollar degenerated from a strong to a weak currency.[46]

Admittedly, the 1997 issue further aggravated the monetary situation after July 1982, but seeds of the decay were sown in 1972 when the note-issuing banks were no longer required to surrender foreign-currency assets for their Certificates of Indebtedness in advance as backing for issuing notes. Instead, they merely credited the account of the Exchange Fund with Hong Kong dollar proceeds, which would then be used by the fund to acquire the necessary foreign currencies on the open market. The reform of October 1983 reimposed the pre–1972 constraint of 100 percent foreign-currency backing on the note-issuing banks. In essence, both the pre–1972 and post–1983 systems are variants of the colonial currency-board system, which in turn was basically a gold exchange standard. The reform of October 1983 not only saved Hong Kong from an imminent collapse of the whole financial system but also solved the money-supply problem through the traditional automatic mechanism and external constraint. In other words, under the present system, the exchange rate is predetermined, but the money supply is endogenously determined by the balance of payments.

Under the pre–1972 Bretton Woods system, the Exchange Fund was obligated to intervene if the market rate diverged from the official rate by more than 2.25 percent either way, but under the post–1983 system the Exchange fund is not supposed to intervene at all while convergence between the market rate and the linked rate is attained by "arbitrage and competition" or the threat of such a process. Although the palpable benefits such as lower inflation, greater stability of the currency, and so on are substantial, an objection may be made concerning the linked-rate system for tying Hong Kong inexorably to the changing fortunes of the U.S. economy. This observation is indeed a compelling critique, which the current robustness of the U.S. economy can conceal only temporarily. Nevertheless, notwithstanding the long-term problem of U.S.-transmitted cyclical fluctuations, the present system is still much better than that of 1974–1983 in which neither the money stock nor the exchange rate was under control. Consequently, the floating-exchange-rate regime did not afford any protective insulation from fluctuations emanating from abroad. Since currency stability is the overriding concern, most economists still strongly favor the retention of the linked-rate system.[47]

The third criticism is directed at the lack of an industrial policy in an age of rapid technological innovations and structural changes in the economy. Critics especially point out the heavy involvement of governments in guiding and establishing "strategic industries" and various forms of direct and indirect subsidies to industrial development in Singapore, South Korea, and Taiwan—Hong Kong's main rivals in international trade. However, recent studies have shown that state-sponsored projects in heavy industries, refineries, petrochemicals, and so on in these countries have turned out to be financial losers and a serious policy error. By contrast, Hong Kong's policy of avoiding government intervention and grandiose schemes, reliance on the flexibility of private entrepreneurs, and the law of comparative advantage has generally served Hong Kong well.[48] This argument is not to suggest that Hong Kong can afford to be complacent. A number of government-subverted organizations, such as the Trade Development Council, Productivity Center, Vocational Training Center, and Management Association, are doing useful work in promoting Hong Kong products abroad, disseminating information on technological innovations and management skills, training personnel and so on. These bodies, which can generate substantial external economies, should be strengthened and subsidized with public revenue. Indeed, the government's advisory committee on diversification has recommended such subsidization.[49] The government has wisely avoided direct subsidy to individual firms and industries. Moreover, the fiscal crisis of 1982–1983 and subsequent deficits have rendered any proposal about large-scale government assistance to industrial development irrelevant. However, pressure groups, eager to win popular support and perhaps curry favor with Beijing, continue to clamor for governmental aid to industries. To resist such demands, as well as demands for higher spending on social welfare, would be difficult for any government, particularly a government with only a limited horizon. But it must resist if Hong Kong's long-term interests are to be served.

In general, the government should do its utmost to provide a stable and conducive environment for investment and economic activity and assist nonprofit-making organizations that generate substantial externalities in research, knowledge, and development as well. It should, however, refrain from directly subsidizing any individual firm or industry. Concerning the provision of venture capital for new and innovative firms or industries, again the answer lies not with the government but with the private capital market. There are complaints that the stock-market-listing rules are biased against the small, unestablished, but innovative and promising firms. In the United States and United Kingdom the over-the-counter markets and private placements partially tackled this problem. It is strange that Hong Kong, reputedly the third largest financial center in the world, has not yet thought of these new techniques.[50]

In-depth study of the structural change in the economy is hampered by the fact that not only did official GDP estimates begin only in 1973 but also the time series had been revised twice for the period between 1966 and 1982. Based on the "production" method of GDP estimation, the contribution of the primary sector of the economy of Hong Kong in the period of 1980–1983 is negligible, and the share of manufacturing declined during this period from 23.9 percent to 21.9 percent. The combined share of the sector, including manufacturing, public utilities, and construction, declined from 31 percent to 29.9 percent. One mystery concerns the behavior of the sector, comprising financing, insurance, real estate, and business services. This sector formerly was a high performer, but after advancing to 23.8

percent in 1981, its share dropped sharply during the next two years to 18.8 percent. The most plausible cause of this reversal was the financial crisis and real estate slump in 1982–1983. Whether this decline is only a temporary aberration or a permanent trend remains to be seen.[51]

Comparison of structural changes over a longer period is difficult because the time series on GDP by industrial origin for 1970–1980 was computed by another method. The data before 1970 is even more sketchy and unreliable. It appears that the share of manufacturing in GDP rose from 24.7 percent in 1960 to 30.9 percent in 1970 and then declined steadily to 21.9 percent in 1983. The financial-services sector, broadly defined to include banking, finance, insurance, real estate, and business services, rose sharply from 9.7 percent in 1960 to 23.8 percent in 1981 and then declined to 18.8 percent in 1983. The primary sector showed a long-term decline from 3.6 percent to less than 1 percent during the same period.[52] Although there are year-to-year fluctuations, the general pattern is that the tertiary sector has gained at the expense of the primary and secondary sectors, a pattern more or less consistent with the experiences of most industrialized countries. The relative decline of manufacturing, the growing protectionism in industrialized countries, and the revival of China trade have given rise to a view that Hong Kong should phase out its manufacturing activities and concentrate on promoting its status as a financial center, information center, and entrepôt. This argument ignores the problem of labor absorption during structural adjustment.[53] Manufacturing industries remain the largest employing sector. From 1961 to 1984, employment in manufacturing industries increased from 512,438 to 904,709, although its relative share in the labor force fell from 43 percent to 37 percent. The retraining and relocation of these workers to the tertiary industries, even if desirable and feasible, will take generations to accomplish.

The Post–1997 Outlook

If the period from 1988–1997 is already hard to forecast, the post–1997 outlook is virtually impossible to predict. The period immediately before June 30, 1997, could be very difficult for Hong Kong. The smooth transfer of power hinges on the goodwill and cooperation of the two signatories. From Hong Kong's point of view, there will be two matters of immediate concern. One is the availability of qualified people to run the SAR government. As previously suggested, this availability depends on the internal political and administrative evolution in Hong Kong. The other concern is the chief executive, who, under the terms of the agreement, "will be appointed by the Central People's Government on the basis of the results of elections or consultations to be held locally." The chief executive then nominates the principal officials that the Central People's Government appoints.

In the end, the composition of the SAR government will most probably be a ritualistic and stage-managed affair. There can be no illusion about the SAR government exercising any real independent power over major policy decisions. The best we can hope for is that China will be content with its final veto, leaving Hong Kong alone in the administration of day-to-day affairs.

The real question therefore is whether China will honor the Sino-British Agreement after the British withdrawal. This is a subject on which there can be endless controversy. As suggested in the previous section, the behavior of China's representatives on the Joint Liaison Group and the drafting process and contents of the Basic Law can give important clues to, but not necessarily conclusive evidence on, China's intention. Only time will tell whether the pessimists or the optimists are right. My view is that there are two aspects to this problem. One aspect is China's willingness and the other aspect is its ability to honor the agreement.

Regarding the willingness to observe the agreement, I believe that China must be given the benefit of the doubt. Given that Hong Kong is indefensible either militarily or politically, China could have taken over the territory at any time during the past 36 years, either by force, much as India did to Goa, or simply by cutting off the water supply from Shenzhen. But even during the most xenophobic years of the Maoist era, China had correctly observed the existing treaties on which British rule is based, although they have never been formally recognized. It seems far-fetched to suggest that China took the trouble of negotiating with Britain for two years, signing an agreement that is effectively an international treaty, only to repudiate it deliberately. References have often been made to the previous duplicity in respect of Shanghai and Tibet. But although the historical fact is indisputable, the historical analogy is valid only if China remains the same Maoist China as it was before 1977. Therefore, the real crux of the matter is China's ability to honor the agreement. It will be able to do so if the moderates are still in power in Beijing by 1997 and substantial progress in modernization and economic reform has occurred. Our remarks about the "postrevolutionary society" in the previous section are therefore still applicable.

Assuming that China is both willing and able to observe the agreement, the question remains whether Hong Kong's status as a separate economic entity, enshrined in the agreement, will be internationally accepted. Although most of Hong Kong's major partners have welcomed the settlement, the goodwill is couched in vague terms and can be taken no more than as a diplomatic gesture.

One issue of critical concern is Hong Kong's quota under the Multifibre Arrangement (MFA). The textiles and clothing industries still account for about 41 percent of Hong Kong's total industrial workforce and 40 percent of its total domestic exports. Any attempt by an importing country to abolish Hong Kong's independent quota and to merge it with that of China's would deal a severe blow to Hong Kong. It could be a disaster for Hong Kong if such a tactic were widely copied.[54] Similar considerations can apply to other international organizations and institutions such as the General Agreement on Tariffs and Trade (GATT), the Coordinating Committee on Export Controls (COCOM), the Most-Favored-Nation Treatment (MFN), and the Asian Development Bank (ADB). In short, there is considerable uncertainty about whether individual countries as well as international institutions will in fact recognize and accept Hong Kong as an independent economic entity after 1997. Given Hong Kong's heavy dependence on external trade, the uncertainty is not conducive to its future prospects. Another thorny problem concerns those countries that have no diplomatic relations with China. Because Hong Kong is apolitical or politically neutral, it has been able to maintain normal and even thriving economic and financial ties with these countries and also serve as an intermediary between the particular country and China. Both aspects may be jeopardized when China absorbs Hong Kong. The Republic of China on Taiwan is the most conspicuous example. Taiwan has publicly denounced the Sino-British Agreement as "invalid," although it has stopped short of declaring that it will sever all ties with Hong Kong after 1997. Taiwan has always enjoyed a trade surplus against Hong Kong. In 1983 this surplus amounted to some US$982 million. It is also an open secret that Taiwan has been trading with mainland China via Hong Kong. If Taiwan insists on not trading with any part of Communist China, it could, in theory, divert all its trade with Hong Kong to a third country, most likely Japan or Singapore. South Korea and Indonesia are also in a similar position, although their attitude is likely to be more flexible.

The transfer of sovereignty may also affect Hong Kong's position as a financial center. For example, at present, Taiwan is a considerable borrower from Hong Kong-based international banks, its net indebtedness to them amounting to some US$432.0 million at the end of 1984. After 1997 Taiwan may insist that all such loans be syndicated elsewhere, perhaps in Taipei's offshore banking center, established in July 1984, which claims total assets of US$5.2 billion as of May 31, 1985. South Korea and Indonesia are also heavy borrowers. Should both of them also demand that syndicated loans be arranged elsewhere (e.g., Tokyo or Singapore), Hong Kong's attractiveness as a financial center to international banks will be greatly diminished. The same may also be true for other financial institutions like insurance companies, mutual funds, unit trusts, and securities houses.[55] A compensating factor is the lure of the China market. But this lure depends on China's political stability and economic performance.

There are also countries that are eager to trade with both Hong Kong and China, but China regards them as "untouchables" on political and ideological grounds. Israel and South Africa are the most prominent examples. Presently, they maintain good trading relations with Hong Kong, but whether these relations can continue after 1997 without interference from China is an open question.

Although the international attitude toward the post–1997 Hong Kong may create problems, there is a positive side to it. If China really wants to maintain Hong Kong's stability and prosperity, it must respect Hong Kong's status as a separate economic entity; otherwise international recognition will be withheld. In the case of Taiwan, the implications for Hong Kong are more than economic. The existence of a strong and stable Taiwan will exert a restraining influence on Beijing's behavior toward Hong Kong. Thus China does face some external constraints, even if they are implicit. In this sense, the Sino-British Agreement will not be just a piece of paper. It has to be stressed, however, that the constraint must be exercised with care and tact, for Hong Kong may well be ruined if it becomes a "political football" in any confrontation between China and third countries.

Finally, one question that has not received the attention it deserves is the enormous gap in income and civil liberties between China and Hong Kong. Confining ourselves to relative incomes, in 1984, Hong Kong's GDP, per capita, measured at current prices and exchange rate, was US$5,951. China's Gross Social Product, (GSP), the nearest equivalent to GDP, was about US$443.[56] This means China's nominal income per head is only one-thirteenth of Hong Kong's. This difference does not necessarily measure the gap in real income, because there must be an allowance for purchasing power discrepancies. The requisite quantitative exercise is not feasible for this occasion because of the lack of reliable price data and the well-known phenomenon of "repressed inflation" in China. It is reasonable to infer, however, that even after purchasing-power adjustments on assumptions most favorable to China, an extremely wide gap will remain. Ideally, China's economy should grow at a higher rate than Hong Kong's; thus over time the gap would eventually diminish. Yet so far the empirical record has shown the reverse. For example, according to the World Bank, the average annual growth rate of China's GNP per capita, at constant prices, was 3.5 percent in the period 1957–1979.[57] By contrast, in 1961–1979, the average annual growth rate of Hong Kong's GDP per capita, at constant prices, was about 6.9 percent, according to Hong Kong government estimates. That was nearly twice that of China's in roughly the same period.[58] Another World Bank study gives the GNP per capita growth rate of China and Hong Kong in real terms at 4.5 percent and 6.8 percent, respectively, for the period 1973–1982.[59] In 1984 China's nominal GSP per capita is reported to have grown by 12 percent. There is no information about the deflator, but the retail price index is said to have risen by 2.8 percent.[60] However, China's price index is widely regarded as an unreliable indicator of inflation.[61] I estimated that the true inflation rate for 1984 was at least 7 percent. Real income per head, therefore, grew at most by 5 percent. Hong Kong's growth rate of real GDP per capita in the same year was 8.5 percent. As the Hong Kong economy becomes more mature, its growth rate will slow down, even in the absence of any catastrophic development. China's growth rate will accelerate with the progress in modernization and reform. But even assuming that China will eventually grow at a higher rate than Hong Kong, it may still take several generations before China can catch up with Hong Kong.

The huge gap in income, personal freedom, and other benefits of an open society is the major reason why Hong Kong is such an irresistible magnet for the people of China, particularly those living in the southern province of Guangdong (Kwangtung). From 1977 to 1980 at least 211,900 illegal immigrants entered Hong Kong from China and were allowed to remain having "reached base." This large influx was in addition to some 55,000 legal immigrants from the mainland.[62] Faced with this avalanche, the Hong Kong government was forced to abandon the so-called reached-base policy in October 1980 and repatriate all illegal immigrants on capture or detection.[63] Whether immigration can be effectively controlled will be a severe test for the future SAR government. Moreover, many party cadres and government officials in China are likely to fight among themselves for getting posted to Hong Kong because of its many attractions—a process that has probably started already.

Another vexing problem for China is the black market activities involving China's currency, the *renminbi* (RMB, people's currency), and the Hong Kong dollar. The RMB has been devalued by 36 percent since October 1983 against the Hong Kong dollar when the latter was stabilized by the link to the U.S. dollar. (From 1981 to 1984, the RMB was devalued by 40 percent against the U.S. dollar.) Devaluation is not necessarily bad. Indeed, most economists would agree that for a developing country whose currency is overvalued, a suitable devaluation, coupled with tight monetary-fiscal policy and gradual liberalization of the financial sector, will be conducive to long-term growth. It is embarrassing, however, that the black market rate in China for the Hong Kong dollar is always a step ahead of the official rate. The situation is particularly chaotic in the SEZs. In Shenzhen, for example, there are three currencies in circulation: The Hong Kong dollar, the Foreign Exchange Certificate (FEC), and the RMB. But because the Hong Kong dollar is the preferred means of payment as well as the store of value, prices quoted in Hong Kong dollar are the lowest, whereas those quoted in RMB are the highest. Moreover, whereas the official rate of exchange is 1 yuan equaling 2.75 Hong Kong dollars, the black market rate was 1 yuan equaling 1 Hong Kong dollar in March 1985.[64] The root cause of this phenomenon is that the RMB is not convertible, whereas the Hong Kong dollar is freely convertible and therefore represents real purchasing power over all goods. The problem is not unique to China but common to all centrally planned economies and mixed economies where there is an exchange control.

The dilemma for China is this: In 1997 Hong Kong will become China's responsibility. After the British era of economic progress and prosperity, China's authority and prestige would be severely damaged if Hong Kong should stagnate and decline under Chinese rule. Purely from the political and psychological point of view, China will be compelled to do everything possible to promote the Hong Kong economy. To do so, however, will mean diverting scarce investible resources to Hong Kong and, paradoxically, will perpetuate the wide gap in income and wealth that is the source of so many difficulties. Resentment against the "special policy" toward Hong Kong will no doubt grow among the populace, the political and social consequences of which cannot be lightly dismissed. The real "Hong Kong Question" therefore will not be solved for China until real income and civil liberties on the mainland have shown a significant and sustained improvement over their present abysmal level.

CONCLUSIONS

After two years of excruciating anxiety and uncertainty, the Sino-British Agreement has brought a sense of relief to the people of Hong Kong, not because it embodies their free choice but because there is no other viable alternative.[65] To the extent that it has produced a calming effect on public confidence, the agreement is at least partially responsible for the recent economic recovery in Hong Kong and a reasonably stable outlook for the near term. But it is not a permanent guarantee of stability and prosperity for Hong Kong. The prospects for the intermediate and distant future from 1988 onward are uncertain. Much will depend on the stability of the political system, the continuity of pragmatic policies, and the progress of the modernization and economic reform program in China. In the final analysis, Hong Kong's future as a free-market economy is a function of China's goodwill, good conduct, and good performance. However, China also cannot act with impunity over Hong Kong. Apart from its own rational interests, it also faces some explicit external constraints. Moreover, as a domestic issue after 1997, Hong Kong is bound to create tensions and dilemmas within China. The Sino-British Agreement therefore does not represent a final solution of the "Hong Kong Question."

NOTES

1. See *A Draft Agreement between the Government of the United Kingdom of Great Britain and Northern Ireland and the Government of the People's Republic of China on the Future of Hong Kong*, Hong Kong, Government Printer, September 26, 1984, hereafter cited as *Sino-British Agreement.*

2. Even in a society without any fear of loss of freedom, economic agents' behavior patterns are profoundly affected by what they perceive to be a change in policy regime, rendering econometric forecasts largely irrelevant. This effect is known

in economic theory as the "Lucas Critique." See Robert F. Lucas, "Econometric Policy Evaluation: A Critique," in *The Phillips Curve and Labor Markets*, ed. Karl Brunner and Alan H. Meltzer (Amsterdam: North Holland, 1976), pp. 19–46.

3. This section draws on *Hong Kong: Economic Prospects to 1986*, Economist Intelligence Unit Special Report 156, London, Nov. 1983, which I wrote for the Economist Intelligence Unit.

4. For a detailed analysis of the crisis, see Y.C. Jao, "The 1997 Issue and Hong Kong's Financial Crisis," *Journal of Chinese Studies*, Vol. 2, no. 1 (1985), pp. 113–53. For an earlier analysis that avoids the 1997 issue, see John G. Greenwood, "Hong Kong's Financial Crisis: History, Analysis, Prescription," *Asian Monetary Monitor*, Vol. 6, no. 6 (1982), pp. 2–69.

5. For an exposition of the new monetary arrangement, see John Greenwood, "The Monetary Framework Underlying the Hong Kong Dollar Stabilization Scheme," *China Quarterly*, no. 99 (Sept. 1984), pp. 631–36; Y.C. Jao, "The Monetary System and the Future of Hong Kong," in Y.C. Jao, et al., eds., *Hong Kong and 1997: Strategies for the Future* (Hong Kong: Centre of Asian Studies, University of Hong Kong, 1985).

6. *The 1985–86 Budget: Speech by the Financial Secretary, moving the Second Reading of the Appropriation Bill*, Hong Kong: Feb. 27, 1985, parag. 25.

7. Full employment in Hong Kong is represented approximately by an unemployment rate of between 3 percent and 3.5 percent. The *unemployment population* is defined in the General Household Survey as all persons aged 15 and over who during the week before enumeration had no work at all and were seeking work. The *underemployed population* is defined as employed persons who worked less than 35 hours during the week before enumeration and were seeking more work.

8. Information supplied by the Hong Kong Tourist Association.

9. *Hang Seng Economic Monthly*, (Dec. 1984), pp. 1–4; *Registrar-General's Annual Report*, 1984–1985, Statistic Appendix Tables V, "Land Office Instruments Registered and Crown Leases Issued," and Table VI, "Land Office Statistics."

10. "Consortium Pays $190 million for Prime Kowloon Site," *South China Morning Post*, Nov. 29, 1984, p. BN1; "Barracks Site Goes to Swire for $703 million," *South China Morning Post*, Apr. 19, 1985, p. 1; "Hong Kong's Residential Boom Spreads," *Asian Wall Street Journal*, Apr. 19, 1985, Section 2.

11. Rating and Valuation Department, Property Review, 1984; *Far Eastern Economic Review* (Feb. 28, 1985), pp. 48–50; "Strong Recovery in the Property Market," *Hong Kong Bank Economic Report* (June 1985), pp. 1–2.

12. For instance, Chalmers Johnson described Hong Kong as a "cric"—a "collapsing recently industrialized country." See his "Mousetrapping of Hong Kong: A Game in Which Nobody Wins," *Asian Survey*, Vol. 24, no. 9 (Sept. 1984), pp. 887–909.

13. *Sino-British Agreement*, Annex I, Section XIII.

14. Y.C. Jao, "The Enigma of Hong Kong's Financial Transactions with China," *Asian Monetary Monitor*, Vol. 8, no. 3 (May 1984), pp. 26–31.

15. "China Pours US$4 billion into Here," *South China Morning Post*, Apr. 26, 1984, p. BN1. Wang is the brother-in-law of Liu Shaoqi, the late president of the People's Republic of China. Assigned to Hong Kong in 1983, Wang's mission was to calm the jittery colony. P.E. Johnson, an assistant director of the Industry Department of the Hong Kong government, also mentioned the US$4 billion figure in

a speech to the Arizona World Trade Association on March 19, 1985. However, according to the general manager of the Bank of China in Hong Kong, the figure is close to US$5 billion. See Zhang Xueyao's speech entitled "China-Hong Kong Economic Relationships," given at the symposium The New Economic Challenges and Opportunities: Hong Kong Moving into the 90s and Beyond, sponsored by the Hong Kong Affairs Society, March 31, 1985.

16. Information from private correspondence.

17. The two companies are Conic Investments Ltd., an electronics firm, and China Cement (H.K.) Ltd., a cement company.

18. See for example, the following articles in no. 100 (Dec. 1984) issue of *The China Quarterly*: K.C. Yeh, "Macroeconomic Changes in the Chinese Economy during the Readjustment," pp. 691–716; R.M. Field, "Changes in Chinese Industry Since 1978," pp. 742–61; K.R. Walker, "Chinese Agriculture during the Period of the Readjustment, 1978–83," pp. 783–812; Y.Y. Kueh and C. Howe, "China's International Trade," pp. 813–49; N.R. Lardy, "Consumption and Living Standards in China, 1978–83," pp. 849–65. See also Nai-ruenn Chen and Jeffrey Lee, *China's Economy and Foreign Trade, 1981–85* (U.S. Department of Commerce, Sept. 1984); Chu-yuan Cheng, "China's Economy: Advances and Dilemmas," *Current History*, Vol. 83, no. 492 (Sept. 1984), pp. 257–74.

19. For perceptive studies of China's political and social changes, see Harry Harding, "The Transformation of China," *The Brookings Review* (Spring 1984), pp. 3–7; Kenneth Lieberthal, "China's Political Reforms: A Net Assessment," *The Annuals of the American Academy* (1984), pp. 19–33.

20. Y.C. Jao, "Hong Kong Dollar Looking for Political Parity," *Asian Banking* (Sept. 1984), pp. 47–55.

21. *Sino-British Agreement*, Annex II, parag. 3c.

22. Yuan-li Wu, "The Future of Hong Kong before and after 1997," *The American Asian Review* (Winter 1984), pp. 13–23.

23. *Green Paper: The Further Development of Representative Government in Hong Kong* (Hong Kong: Hong Kong Government Printer, July 1984); *White Paper: The Further Development of Representative Government in Hong Kong* (Hong Kong: Hong Kong Government Printer, Nov. 1984).

24. According to John Walden, former director of home affairs in Hong Kong, after being told by Deng Xiaoping in Peking in March 1979 that British rule could not continue after 1997, Sir Murray MacLehose, a former governor, initiated the process of representative government in 1980 by creating popularly elected district boards, or local councils. See John Walden, "Hong Kong Chases a Democratic Mirage," *The Asian Wall Street Journal*, March 7, 1985. It is now known that MacLehose never told the Hong Kong people the whole truth, relaying only Deng's message that investors could "put their hearts at ease." The 1980 initiative is embodied in an earlier green paper entitled *A Pattern of District Administration in Hong Kong* (Hong Kong: Hong Kong Government Printer, 1980).

25. "Facing the Future: Speech by Xu Jiatun to the Hong Kong Chinese Chamber of Commerce," *Ta Kung Pao* (Hong Kong), Aug. 6, 1985, Section 1, p. 4.

26. Y.C. Jao, "Hong Kong's Role in Financing China's Modernization," in *China and Hong Kong: The Economic Nexus*, ed. A.J. Youngson (Hong Kong: Oxford University Press, 1983), Chapter 1.

27. "Interview: Damping Down Hong Kong's Rising Panic," *Fortune* (Oct. 31, 1983), pp. 74–75.

28. M1, M2, and M3 are alternative definitions of the money supply. M1 is the sum of currency in circulation with the public plus demand deposits with licensed banks. M2 is the sum of M1, savings, and time deposits with licensed banks plus certificates of deposit issued by licensed banks and held outside the monetary sector. M3 is the sum of M2 and deposits with deposit-taking companies plus certificates of deposit issued by DTCs and held outside the monetary sector.

29. For this issue and other related monetary issues, see Jao, "The Monetary System and the Future of Hong Kong."

30. According to Hong Kong's deputy secretary of monetary affairs, "there is sufficient evidence to support the view that there has been an increased outflow of certain types of capital" in 1982–84, although he did not quantify it. See A.R. Latter, "Changing Patterns of External Flows," paper presented to the Hong Kong Management Association, Aug. 22, 1984. According to Robert F. Emery of the Division of International Finance and Board of Governors of the Federal Reserve System, official data in *Treasury Bulletin* and *Survey of Current Business* show that "there has generally been an outflow of capital from the United States to Hong Kong, rather than an inflow." Cited from Emery's letter to the author dated Feb. 21, 1985.

31. *The 1982–83 Budget*, parag. 41; *The 1985–86 Budget*, parag. 41.

32. For a fuller discussion, see Y.C. Jao, "Hong Kong's Revenue Proposals and Their Implications," *Bulletin for International Fiscal Documentation*, Vol. 38 (1984), pp. 298–301.

33. *Report on the Survey of Overseas Investment in Hong Kong's Manufacturing Industry*, Industry Department, Nov. 1984, mimeo.

34. "HK Bank to Acquire Four US Branches," *South China Morning Post*, June 8, 1985, p. BN1.

35. "Canada Deal a Boost for Bank," *South China Morning Post*, Oct. 6, 1985, Sunday Business, p. 1.

36. Michael Sandberg, "Hong Kong, China, and Hong Kong Bank," speech to the Foreign Correspondents' Club, March 8, 1985.

37. "Sing Tao's Assets Set to Go Down Under," *South China Morning Post*, May 23, 1985, p. BN1.

38. The U.S. Congress has recently (September 1985) passed legislation increasing the immigration quota for Hong Kong from 600 to 5,000 a year.

39. Computed from *Hong Kong Trade Statistics Annual Supplement 1983*, Census and Statistics Department, Hong Kong.

40. *International Financial Statistics*, International Monetary Fund, Dec. 1984. The figure is higher than the official Chinese government figure by the amount of SDRs and reserve position in the IMF.

41. *International Financial Statistics*, International Monetary Fund, Aug. 1985.

42. A good discussion of this issue is given in Victor Mok, "Hong Kong's External Trade at the Crossroads," in Jao et al., *Hong Kong and 1997*.

43. "Hong Kong Invests US$4.5b in China," *Ta Kung Pao* (Hong Kong), Oct. 5, 1984, Section 3, p. 12.

44. This is discussed in various studies in Y.C. Jao and C.K. Leung, eds., *China's*

Special Economic Zones: Policies, Problems and Prospects (Hong Kong: Oxford University Press, 1986).

45. "HK, Macau Group Plans Airline," *South China Morning Post*, March 12, 1985, p. BN1.

46. For a fuller analysis, see J.G. Greenwood, "Hong Kong's Financial Crisis: History, Analysis, Prescription," *Asian Monetary Monitor*, Vol. 6 (1982), pp. 2–69; Y.C. Jao, "The Financial Structure," in *The Business Environment in Hong Kong*, ed. D. Lethbridge (Hong Kong: Oxford University Press, 1984), pp. 124–79.

47. See J.G. Greenwood, "Why the HK$/US$ Linked Rate System Should Not Be Changed," *Asian Monetary Monitor* (1984), pp. 2–17; Jao, "The Monetary System and the Future of Hong Kong."

48. Y.W. Sung, "The Role of the Government in the Future Industrial Development of Hong Kong," in Jao et al., *Hong Kong and 1997.*

49. *Report of the Advisory Committee on Diversification*, Hong Kong Government, 1979.

50. For a discussion of the placement method as a device to encourage the smaller company seeking venture capital, see E. Ancrum, "Placements—A Halfway House," *The Hong Kong Manager* (Aug. 1984), pp. 16–18.

51. *Estimates of Gross Domestic Product, 1966–1984*, Census and Statistics Department, Hong Kong, 1985.

52. *Report on the National Income Survey of Hong Kong*, Hong Kong Government Printer, 1969; *Estimates of Gross Domestic Product.*

53. For a careful quantitative study of this problem, see Tzong-biau Lin, Victor Mok, and Yin-pin Ho, *Manufactured Exports and Employment in Hong Kong*, Hong Kong: The Chinese University Press, 1980.

54. This is discussed in detail in Kayser Sung, "Trading on from 1997, with Special Reference to Hong Kong's Textile Agreements," Jao et al., *Hong Kong and 1997.*

55. For a more detailed analysis of the prospects of Hong Kong's financial sector, see Y.C. Jao, "Hong Kong's Future as a Financial Center," *Three Banks Review*, Vol. 145 (1985), pp. 35–53. The asset figure for the Taipei offshore banking center was reported in *South China Morning Post*, July 3, 1985, p. 2.

56. Computed from data contained in "Statistical Bulletin on the National Economy and Social Development in 1984," *Renmin Ribao* (People's Daily), March 10, 1985, p. 2.

57. *China: Socialist Economic Development*, Vol. 1, Washington, D.C.: The World Bank, 1983, p. 77.

58. *Estimates of the Gross Domestic Product*, various years.

59. *The World Bank Atlas 1985*, Washington, D.C., The World Bank.

60. "Bulletin of the Statistical Bureau," *Renmin Ribao* (People's Daily), March 10, 1985.

61. For an interesting analysis of the true inflation rate in China, see G. Peebles, "Inflation in the People's Republic of China, 1950–1982," *Three Banks Review*, Vol. 142 (1984), pp. 37–57.

62. *Hong Kong Annual Report 1981*, Hong Kong Government Printer, 1981, Chapter 11. According to Tao Siju, China's deputy minister of public security, in August 1985 there was a backlog of 600,000 applications by Chinese citizens to

immigrate to or visit Hong Kong. See Shu Ge, "China Relaxes Regulations on Entry and Exit," *Liaowang* [*Outlook*], Vol. 2 (Oct. 1985), pp. 15–16.

63. The "reached-base" policy means that once an illegal immigrant escaped capture at the border and reached the urban area, he would be allowed to stay.

64. For a more detailed analysis, see Y.C. Jao, "Banking and Currency in the Special Economic Zones: Problems and Prospects," in *China's Special Economic Zones: Policies, Problems and Prospects*, ed. Jao and Leung; S.Y. Ma, "Is Gresham's Law Taking Place in China's Foreign Exchange Market?" Discussion Paper No. 51, Department of Economics, University of Hong Kong, March 1985. The black market quotations for the Hong Kong dollar are admitted in the Communist press of Hong Kong. "RMB Falls to 1:1 Against HK$: Rampant Black Market Activity in Guangdong and Fujian," *Wen Wei Pao* (Hong Kong), March 25, 1985, Special Feature on the People's Congress and People's Political Consultative Conference, p. 2. The FEC is a kind of convertible RMB issued to foreign visitors against their foreign currencies.

65. Before the Sino-British Agreement was initialed, public opinion polls taken in Hong Kong showed that the majority of the respondents favored the status quo. See Joseph Y.S. Cheng, ed., *Hong Kong: In Search of a Future* (Hong Kong: Oxford University Press, 1984), Chapter 3.

4

Hong Kong's Search for a Consensus: Barriers and Prospects

HSIN-CHI KUAN and SIU-KAI LAU

After two years of tortuous and agonizing negotiations, the government of the People's Republic of China (PRC) and the government of the United Kingdom signed a Joint Declaration on the Question of Hong Kong on December 21, 1984.[1] The declaration provides that Hong Kong will be restored to the People's Republic of China beginning July 1, 1997. Thereafter Hong Kong shall become a Special Administrative Region of the PRC enjoying a high degree of autonomy with executive, legislative, and independent judicial power, including that of final adjudication. The laws currently in force and the current social and economic systems in Hong Kong will remain unchanged. Its status as a free port and an international financial center also will remain unchanged. An impressive array of rights and freedoms, including the respect for private property, ownership of enterprises, and legitimate right of inheritance, is to be protected by the Special Administrative Region government. The Chinese government pledges that the above basic policies shall be valid for 50 years beyond 1997.

Concerning the political system of the future Special Administrative Region, the Joint Declaration and its Annexes contain the following major provisions:

1. The chief executive shall be appointed by the Central People's Government on the basis of the results of elections or consultations to be held locally.
2. The legislature shall be constituted by elections.
3. The executive authorities shall abide by the law and shall be accountable to the legislature.

These provisions offer little guidance for the design and implementation of the necessary changes in the political institutions to ensure a smooth transfer of sovereignty in 1997.[2] As a result, Hong Kong was drawn into a whirlpool of political overtures for constitutional development. A social convention was ushered in as if John Locke's theory of social contract was being put to test.

The search for a political future for Hong Kong can be fruitfully regarded as a process of consensus building that involves the Chinese government, the British government, the Hong Kong government, and the people of Hong Kong as participants. A consensus is a "state of agreement, which varies in intensity and scope over time, incorporating the goals for society, the procedures for decision making, and the particular policies."[3] This concept is useful for its theoretical fertility, linking shared agreements to political stability and legitimacy, two issues that are dominating the political agenda in Hong Kong.

This process of consensus building can be divided into two phases, with the Joint Declaration as the line of demarcation. The two phases differ from each other in terms of the principal actors, the kinds of referents, and the parameters within which issues are debated further down the value scale.

The first phase, which has already passed, consisted of the negotiations between the Chinese and the British government. It concerned arguments about fundamental goals and values. Under the objectives of stability and prosperity, both parties achieved swift agreement in the beginning. Debates then ensued over whether these objectives could be maintained better with or without the British administration. After the British government retreated from its original position for a British presence in Hong Kong after 1997, the negotiations were brought to an end with the proposition of autonomy for Hong Kong under Chinese sovereignty.

This proposition has become a parameter for the discussion to be conducted in the second phase. The issues have to do with what kinds of political institutions and procedures are compatible with a high degree of autonomy for Hong Kong under Chinese sovereignty. It is primarily a tug-of-war among the Chinese government, the Hong Kong government, and the people of Hong Kong. The British government has adopted a low profile. In the words of Timothy Renton, foreign office minister responsible for Hong Kong affairs: "What I think our job . . . is with and through your government, the Hong Kong Government, to advise if our advice is asked and to help you develop the sort of system that suits Hong Kong and reflects the wishes of the people of Hong Kong."[4]

This chapter is concerned with the second phase, namely, the question of whether a consensus about the direction and form of political change in Hong Kong may arise. We need to identify the barriers to consensus building and to analyze the value preferences of the principal participants before anything definite can be said of the prospects.

BARRIERS TO CONSENSUS BUILDING

The problem of Hong Kong knows no historical precedent. In groping for its solution, everyone is a novice. However, the British government does have rich experience in decolonialization, which usually takes a pattern of calculated sequential steps from the introduction of local government reforms through the establishment of a representative assembly and localization of bureaucracy to the granting of independence. This strategy does not, however, apply to Hong Kong simply because independence is not the ultimate goal. What kind of a polity should be returned to China in 1997 thus becomes a taxing problem.

For the Chinese government, the idea of "one country, two systems" also represents an innovative attempt at national unification. As the stakes involve not only Hong Kong but also the Republic of China in Taiwan, the experiment mapped out for Hong Kong must demonstrate a kind of treatment intrinsically different from past records of unification policies in Tibet. It is precisely the uncharacteristic promise of keeping the capitalist system and the bourgeois freedoms intact in Hong Kong that needs more than a verbal assurance of credibility. The chartered cities in feudal Europe in the eleventh century is a successful kindred example mentioned in the Chinese press. As a political "charter" for Hong Kong is developing, interaction problems will occur between the ex-colonial transmigration and its socialist hinterland.

The challenge to the Hong Kong people is no less novel. They are economically not politically oriented. Even when politicization has reached a point of no return, there are genuine concerns about its economic implications. David K.P. Li, a banker who serves as a member of the Basic Law Drafting Committee and an unofficial member of the Legislative Council of Hong Kong, stated: "I have no views on direct election. But I am worried about the people of Hong Kong being more and more politicized so that they no longer concentrate on production. I think this is no good."[5] Whether or not they are involved in politics against their will, they are required to serve two masters simultaneously, one outgoing and one incoming.

As never before, there exists a novel situation of political engineering, in which a satisfactory outcome hinges on the wisdom and consent of all. The strength of the Hong Kong government lies in its ability to implement immediately any necessary political reform. However, in carrying out such reforms, the consent of the Chinese government is needed to bestow upon such reforms the status of permanence. Moreover, the resilient people of Hong Kong have to ultimately give vitality to those reforms. Before any consensus can be reached among them, certain barriers must be overcome under pressure.

The Lack of Trust among Participants

Trust is the foundation for consensus building. The distressful situation concerning Hong Kong is the existence of a serious lack of trust among political actors, among elites, or between elites and the general public. Elites

Table 4.1
Trust in Governments

	Hong Kong		U.K.		PRC	
Trust	N	%	N	%	N	%
Very high	30	4.5	13	2.3	14	2.5
High	523	79.2	290	51.1	228	39.9
Low	99	15.0	237	41.8	267	46.8
Very Low	8	1.2	27	4.8	62	10.9
DK/NA	107	-	200	-	196	-
Total	767	100.0	767	100.0	767	100.0

are thus prevented from playing an effective role in the diffusion of ideas, while the system is deprived of legitimacy that otherwise could have been conferred by popular support.

The general public in Hong Kong is distrustful. The extent of distrust varies. According to a sample survey that we conducted in the summer of 1985, the Hong Kong people's trust of governments can be depicted as shown in Table 4.1.

It is evident from Table 4.1 that neither the British nor the Chinese government enjoyed sufficient trust among the people of Hong Kong. The lack of trust with regard to the Chinese government was more serious, especially because China is going to be the new master of Hong Kong. When asked whether they believed that "China would let Hong Kong people rule Hong Kong after 1997," 66.3 percent (N = 337) of those who gave answers (N = 508) responded in the negative. The large number of interviewees (259) who said that they "did not know" or refused to answer the question may also indicate distrust.

The high trust placed by the public on the Hong Kong government is unexpected in view of former Director of Home Affairs John Walden's remarks in 1979:

> For one thing there is a basic credibility gap that the Hong Kong Government has to overcome. There are seldom voiced but perfectly understandable doubts as to whether a government that is staffed at its upper levels mainly by expatriate civil servants, who are eventually going to retire and leave Hong Kong, can be expected to run things in the best interests of a predominantly Chinese society that is going to stay here for good. There are uncertainties as to whether Hong Kong is fully in control of its own affairs.[6]

In our survey, we also asked our respondents whether there were any social or political leaders they thought they could trust and, if yes, to name them. Only 24.5 percent of the respondents (N = 767) answered in the affirmative, compared with 47.8 percent in the negative. The response was even more discouraging when we turned their attention to leaders of pressure groups. A meager 12.5 percent of our subjects trusted those group leaders as against 58.5 percent who declared distrust.

From the other perspective, data on government's or leader's trust in the common people is hard to attain. In our 1982 study on the relationship between citizens, leaders, and officials in Hong Kong, it was found that leaders were generally elitist and authoritarian who denigrated the residents for being ignorant and apathetic.[7] A low level of trust held by government officials toward citizens has also been reported elsewhere.[8] Nevertheless, these findings must be interpreted with caution, for they address the problem of mutual trust at the local level only. They may be valid for our present purpose to the extent that the boundary between citywide and local politics is blurred, which is generally true, but we do not know how true it is.

The lack of trust among governments can only be conjectured. It is more than a courtesy for a government not to disclose its feelings toward its counterpart. However, one can hardly fail to observe a competition between the Hong Kong and the Chinese government over the initiative in shaping the governmental machinery for the future Hong Kong. Below the official level, there are more candid indications. Chinese authorities working in Hong Kong were reported to be suspicious about political reforms introduced by the Hong Kong government.[9] At the other end of the spectrum, high performers in the Hong Kong civil service were said to be unwilling to trust Chinese assurances.[10]

Dearth of Effective Leadership

Effective leadership is essential in a process of consensus building. J.M. Burns distinguished between two basic types of leadership: "the transactional and the transforming. A transactional leadership manifests itself in the exchange of material goods, such as jobs for votes. Transforming leadership is a relationship of mutual stimulation and elevation between leaders and followers. It is a kind of moral leadership that goes beyond mere preaching, uttering of pieties, or the insistence on social conformity." As Burns so aptly put it, "it emerges from and always returns to, the fundamental wants and needs, aspirations, and values of the followers."[11] Transforming leadership, which by its nature is more instrumental than the transactional leadership in shaping attitudes and beliefs, is conspicuously lacking in Hong Kong.

One can hardly expect the Chinese government to play any transforming leadership. With regard to social stability and economic prosperity, China's poor record of performance must have failed to provide a source of inspiration for the people of Hong Kong. It appears unbelievable for a socialist government to provide moral leadership for a capitalist society, which China has pledged to sustain. Since the Chinese government has publicly recognized the responsibility of Britain to govern Hong Kong until 1997, it is circumscribed in playing a transactional leadership. It can dispense with punishment and rewards only in an indirect and subtle way or with delayed realization.

As regards the Hong Kong government, transforming leadership can hardly be a proposition. In the first instance, all colonial governments are inherently handicapped to exude political morality in any convincing manner. The Hong Kong government has never been a reformist government. Its officials usually do not reach out to the people and publicly espouse any views on how government business should be conducted, at least not until recently. Instead of being a moral agent, the Hong Kong government can be expected to exercise transactional leadership. Its effectiveness is, however, undergoing severe tests because it is regarded as an outgoing government. Avoiding an impending authority crisis will depend not only on Hong Kong government's determination to rule but also on the self-restraint and cooperation on the part of the Chinese government.

It is apparent that Hong Kong badly needs locally rooted leadership if "Hong Kong people ruling Hong Kong" or a "representative government" is to be taken seriously. This leadership will have to provide a vision for the future, to tinker at the political escapism and refugee/immigrant reflexes in society, to cultivate political efficacy and self-identity among the attentive public, and to demonstrate ability to govern before the departure of the British administration. As the present situation stands, all of these things remain less than a reality.

True to its bureaucratic and secluded nature, the political system in Hong Kong has failed to nurture even a limited number of political leaders who can wield any moral authority. The prosperous economic sector has absorbed and will continue to draw away most of Hong Kong's talents. The dependent status of Hong Kong's future political system on an authoritarian central government will render the political career unattractive to some aspirants and even risky to others. The pragmatic public can be mobilized for short-term benefits but can hardly be enlightened on matters of long-term principles. In a nutshell, the political arena is too compressed for emergence of an effective transforming leadership.

At the transactional level, the dominant bureaucratic power that controls the authoritative allocation of values has condemned the would-be leaders to a dependent status. The new system of electoral representation can be of little help because it is introduced in such a small dosage that for some time, representation will remain divorced from power.

The Risk of Cumulative Frustration

Given the novelty of the situation, the lack of trust among participants, and faulty leadership mistakes, frustration is elevated. The cumulative frustration may reach a point where the people can never be commanded again. The invitation for further consensus often appears as a threat for a participant who has previously experienced frustration, for in him a siege mentality has developed that tends to reduce his readiness to compromise. Presented with no other choices, he may passively accept whatever is effectively imposed on him, but he will not likely commit himself to the imposed values and priorities.

The Hong Kong people are politically frustrated. According to findings from our 1985 survey, mentioned earlier, the majority of the Hong Kong people are voluntarists in the socioeconomic sense but fatalists in the political sense. With regard to the political future of Hong Kong, they were initially mesmerized by an optimism that the status quo under the British administration or at least with some form of British responsibility could be maintained after 1997.[12] This initial optimism was based on the arguments that as the Chinese government had, despite its rhetoric over territorial integrity or anti-imperialism, tolerated the British rule over Hong Kong for more than three decades for practical reasons, there should be no reason why it could not further tolerate the status quo for the sake of the country's Four Modernizations.[13]

When their dream was torn asunder, Hong Kong people became apprehensive of the possibility of being "sold out." This apprehension was prompted by the lack of any formal role for Hong Kong to play during the Sino-British negotiations, which were conducted under the veil of strict secrecy.[14] Finally, an assessment office was set up to test the acceptability of the agreement, but the people of Hong Kong were presented with the *fait accompli* of either accepting the Sino-British consensus or entering 1997 without any agreement.[15]

The deprivation of a formal role in the first phase calls for compensation in the current phase of consensus building concerning the postagreement reforms in Hong Kong's political system and the drafting of the Basic Law for Hong Kong after 1997. In the search for a lasting consensus on policy-making procedures, which should contribute to future stability and legitimacy, the attentive public demands to play an enhanced role beyond mere consultation. These demands include confirmation of status, vis-à-vis the government as well as among one's peers. It also involves a test of sincerity on the part of the government. Currently, the people of Hong Kong are observing the propriety of consultations to be conducted to prove beyond reasonable doubt that the formula of "Hong Kong people ruling Hong Kong" is not a deception.[16] Likewise, the process of consultation is also a confidence building process, in which misunderstandings can easily lead to cumulative frustrations, thereby reducing the chance for a commitment to a lasting constitutional framework for Hong Kong.

POSITION OF THE HONG KONG GOVERNMENT

In constitutional development, the Hong Kong government has always been cautious and hesitant. In the past, all constitutional reforms of some significance, such as the Young Plan of 1946 and the Dickinson Report on Local Government Reform of 1966, have proved to be abortive attempts. Recent reforms in political institutions are confined to the local and regional levels, limited in the scope of power devolution, and approached unprogrammatically. The issue of 1997 has indeed aroused a sense of urgency. To prepare for the departure of the British administration, power needs to be delivered eventually into the hands of reliable guardians, lest the Chinese government fill the vacuum. This is apparently the fundamental position of the Hong Kong government. To translate this position into concrete policies is a formidable task because new leadership cannot be developed overnight. At the same time, the Chinese government cannot be affronted, and most importantly, uninterrupted effective rule of the present government has to be ensured until 1997.

The initial intention of the Hong Kong government is well reflected in the *Green Paper* entitled *The Further Development of Representative Government in Hong Kong*. The *Green Paper* was published on July 18, 1984, after Sir Geoffrey Howe, the British foreign secretary, had informed the public in Hong Kong on April 20, 1984, that "it would not be realistic to think of an agreement that provides for British administration in Hong Kong after 1997." The aims of the proposals put forth in the *Green Paper* were "to develop progressively a system of government the authority for which is firmly rooted in Hong Kong, which is able to represent authoritatively the views of the people of Hong Kong, and which is more directly accountable to the people of Hong Kong."[17]

The initiative was clearly in line with Britain's past decolonialization experiences. It might even be regarded as a calculated move to win over public opinion in Britain, which favored democratization in Hong Kong as a bulwark against blatant Chinese intervention in the future. That explains why warnings were sounded from the Foreign Ministry of the PRC as well as from left-wing leaders in Hong Kong, such as He Saizhu, member of the Chinese People's Political Consultative Conference. Regardless of these warnings, the *White Paper* was published in November 1984.

According to the *White Paper*, an elective element was to be introduced into the Legislative Council of Hong Kong, which had so far been composed of official and appointed members only. Elections were held in September 1985, with 12 unofficial members elected by nine functional constituencies and another 12 by an electoral college comprising all members of the Urban Council, the newly constituted Regional Council for the New Territories, and the nineteen district boards.

The response of the voters to Hong Kong's first election to the Legislative Council was not enthusiastic. Voter registration of the functional constituencies was so low that a second registration had to be conducted. Electoral turnout for the said constituencies was 57.6 percent, on the low side in view of the high educational level of the eligible voters. Voter turnout in the contested electoral college constituencies was marked by intense intragroup rivalries with only three of the 409 eligible voters absent. At any rate, a new-face Legislative Council has thus been called into existence.

These reform measures are basically modest. No additional powers have been given to the Legislative Council; the elected members make up more than 42 percent of the total membership of the council. The Executive Council has not been affected; the position of the governor remains unchanged; direct election has been ruled out for the time being; the issue of introducing a ministerial system has been shelved; and most significant, the electoral arrangements are more corporatist than democratic (in terms of one person, one vote). On the one hand, the institution of functional constituencies might develop the strategic groups, such as industrial or professional, into a bulwark of the present capitalist system. The electoral college, on the other hand, is meant to placate public aspirations for political participation through the local and regional filters.

The general direction of the reform, however, looms alarming to left-wing observers who are worried about the direction of this constitutional development. They are mindful of those pitfalls such as "transfer of sovereignty to the people of Hong Kong before 1997" instead of "transfer of sovereignty to the Chinese government in 1997," and thus transferring a Hong Kong of people's sovereignty to China in 1997 rather than a Hong Kong without people's sovereignty as of the date of signing of the Sino-British Joint Declaration.

It is, however, erroneous to ascribe to the Hong Kong government a single-mindedness in developing representative government. First, the Hong Kong government is not monolithic. Second, it is not an ideological but a pragmatic government, preoccupied with the need to govern well. Although many tentative ideas abound, the basic policy as it stands is primarily to open up possibilities for a representative government without firm commitment to any ultimate form it should take and secondly to remain in control of the initiative in further development.

The *White Paper* is said to be solely concerned with 1985. What next then? Will the government yield to the pressures for more democratization? Will direct election to the Legislative Council be the next step in constitutional development? It is useful to stress again the pragmatic and cautious position of the Hong Kong government that no commitment to any measure will be made before the next review, which has been set for 1987. In the meantime, there are pressing issues such as land sales and passports that require not only the Hong Kong government's attention but also the goodwill of the Chinese government for the solutions. Moreover, the need for continued effective rule of the Hong Kong government is no less important than the development of a representative government. Recently, Peter Williams, the secretary for general duties, while speaking about the future of Hong Kong expressed the view that the priority is Britain's effective and manifest exercise of its responsibility for the administration of Hong Kong until June 1997. He further stressed that the authority of the Hong Kong government must be maintained and that it must not become a "lame-duck" government.[18] Throughout the speech, no emphasis whatsoever was given to constitutional development in Hong Kong. Instead, it was the first time a senior official of the Hong Kong government stated explicitly that constitutional development in Hong Kong and the drafting of the Basic Law will go forward together. The aim has now become to develop a kind of system that will be "suitable for incorporation in the Basic Law." Some other senior officials in the following weeks repeated the same theme.

The stress on the need for continued effective rule does not augur well for *democratization*, a term that government officials have often avoided. The question of governability will certainly take the edge away from those populist reforms that are perceived as frightening to investors and professionals. The same need for effective government also calls for governmental measures to strengthen its authority, for instance, through boosting the morale of the civil service and the police force. Can the government afford to expose the bureaucrats and policemen to erratic pressures for democratic scrutiny and control?

The recognition of the need for synchronization of the ongoing constitutional reforms and the forthcoming drafting of the Basic Law signals a possible replacement of the battle of initiative between the Hong Kong government and the Chinese government with concerted intergovernmental efforts to dampen the rising political expectations. Will consensus struck at the intergovernmental level be conducive to consensus between governments and people?

POSITION OF THE CHINESE GOVERNMENT

While the political responsibility still remains Britain's, the Chinese government is caught in a dilemma between the prudence of nonintervention in Hong Kong's affairs and the concern about the direction of political reforms that are taking place before 1997. So far the Chinese government has tried hard to adhere to the policy of nonintervention for good reasons. First, the political responsibility of administering Hong Kong still rests with Britain, which the Chinese government publicly recognizes. Moreover, the Chinese government has pledged itself to let Hong Kong people rule Hong Kong after the establishment of the Special Administrative Region. Any intervention would be interpreted in Hong Kong as a breach of the promise. To foster confidence, Chinese authorities in Beijing and in Hong Kong have taken great efforts to demonstrate to the world that the wishes of the people of Hong Kong are respected. It is in this spirit that we should interpret the Chinese government's position on the issue of democratization in Hong Kong. In spite of the superficial respect for public wishes, China has never officially committed itself to the democratization of Hong Kong. Some tend to interpret Premier Zhao Zhiyang's comment on this issue, expressed in a letter dated May 22, 1984, in response to the letter from the students of the University of Hong Kong, as an indicative of a firm Chinese commitment to democratization in Hong Kong. Premier Zhao stated in the letter: "It is self-evident that the future Hong Kong Special Administrative Region will practice a democratized political system that is what you call 'Hong Kong ruled democratically.'"[19] The statement is, however, open to interpretation since it was preceded by the statement that "it has been the fundamental principle of our State to protect the democratic rights of the people." Does it mean that democracy has to be understood the way the People's Republic of China has experienced? Moreover, there is also an important snag. The democratic principles listed in the students' letter to the premier had not been accepted but "would be considered" only by the authorities concerned. One may take the words of the Chinese government at their face value, but it would be dangerous to base one's expectations on a letter read out of context. Premier Zhao's gesture was fully appropriate when public opinion in Hong Kong must be won over for a proposition for a final settlement of the Hong Kong problem.

The same also applies to the interview with Li Zhuwen, deputy director of the Hong Kong branch of the New China News Agency on January 23, 1984. If there was any commitment, it was a promise to follow the consensus of the Hong Kong people. The relevant passage of the interview states that: "The demand for democracy on the part of Hong Kong's people is fully justified and should win the sympathy of all those with democratic aspirations—including the Chinese. If Hong Kong prefers direct elections to determine its officials, then it should strive for that, and it will have the support of the Chinese people.[20]

Since the conclusion of the Sino-British negotiation, the dual themes of nonintervention and deference to opinions in Hong Kong have been maintained in all official responses, which can most conveniently be documented by two interviews given by Wong Hanbin, secretary-general to the Standing Committee of the National People's Congress and deputy director of the Basic Law Drafting Committee. In response to questions about the political system in Hong Kong in general, the issue of direct election, the interface between the current development of representative government and the drafting of the Basic Law, and the desirability of political parties, Wang answered in the noncommittal formats of "no comment," "this is still under study," and "that requires consultation among the people in Hong Kong."[21]

Although the Chinese government is aware of the importance of respecting the public opinion in Hong Kong, it nevertheless believes that the issue of political reform is too important to be left alone to the people of Hong Kong. The way in which the future of Hong Kong will be molded involves stakes that far outweigh the issue of democratization, it is both the economic mission of Hong Kong in terms of China's Four Modernizations and the demonstration value of Hong Kong to the Republic of China in Taiwan that require the Chinese government to retain the ultimate control over the direction Hong Kong is taking in terms of "one country, two systems." From this perspective, the policy preference of the Chinese government involves two principles; one is "no change" in the transitional period, and the other is "control of initiative" by the Chinese government if changes are deemed necessary.

The Chinese preference for no change is understandable. The first reason is rhetoric. It has been said that the people of Hong Kong are afraid of change; hence any ill-conceived change may trigger false expectations detrimental to the stability and the prosperity of Hong Kong.

Second, the current governmental structure of Hong Kong is not unattractive to the Chinese government. Like any other colonial constitution, the political system in Hong Kong is (1) dependent on an external force for its legitimacy, (2) relatively immune from political pressures originated from the society, (3) executive centered rather than legislature dominant, and (4) operative in a top-down policy-making mode. It is in China's best interest to retain ultimate control over Hong Kong if these essential features are preserved while those "colonial" components, such as appointment of the governor by the queen, are removed. In essence, it involves nothing more than the replacement of the master.

Third, to the extent that China is more concerned with social stability and economic prosperity than political innovation, democratization in the form of mass volatility, group activism, and partisan and adversarial politics would render China's ultimate control much more difficult than a situation in which the bureaucratic government is stronger than the society. Otherwise, the Chinese government might be tempted into a visible and preemptive role in Hong Kong's political struggle, thereby threatening stability and prosperity.

In conclusion, the Chinese government does not share with the Hong Kong people the same sense of urgency for political reform. Accordingly, Ji Pengfei openly expressed the view that the proposition of "prosperity plus reform" is unacceptable and that "only those elements that run counter to the transfer of sovereignty, that exhibit colonial characteristics and that damage the honor of the Chinese people need to be changed while all others should remain unchanged."[22] Ji's strong concern with the pace and direction of *political* reform can never be misunderstood because no reform had ever been proposed concerning the social or economic systems. In his meetings with Hong Kong visitors in October 1985 Ji again delivered a message along the same line. In addition, he disclosed that Chinese government would prefer to wait until 1997 for resolutions of specific issues.[23]

Evidently, the Chinese government is uneasy with political changes made recently in Hong Kong. But it has little recourse because it is not the incumbent government and also because it has once propagated the concept of "Hong Kong people ruling Hong Kong." The implication thus seems to be that since change is considered inevitable, China must not lose control of the initiative. To achieve this end, the Basic Law Drafting Committee appointed by the National People's Congress in July 1985 will prove to be an important channel. The Hong Kong membership of this committee is composed largely of capitalists and conservatives who unmistakably testify to the Chinese government's preference for the status quo. The Basic Law Consultative Committee, which has been set up in parallel to the Drafting Committee, is bound to be a major public relations exercise. It is the Basic Law that will authoritatively determine the form of the government in Hong Kong after 1997 with the activities related to these two committees widely reported in the local press. Through a careful manipulation of the agenda, the Chinese government may greatly influence Hong Kong's public opinion.

There is another covert channel available to the Chinese government to exert initiative, the Sino-British Joint Liaison Group set up to facilitate the effective implementation of the Joint Declaration and to ensure a smooth transfer of government in 1997. The reason why this channel has not been used to discuss Chinese views on constitutional development in Hong Kong probably is due to the fear that the move would be interpreted as evidence of Chinese intervention in the internal affairs of Hong Kong when it is still under British rule. This fear could be removed once the public in Hong Kong concedes that it is not up to themselves but instead up to the Chinese and the British governments to synchronize the political reforms currently underway in Hong Kong and the design of the political system for 1997 and beyond.

In the final analysis, China has enough means to have the rising political expectations in Hong Kong at its disposal, and it will influence subtly the cultivated political attitudes and ideas to its best interest.

POSITIONS OF THE HONG KONG PEOPLE

The Sino-British competition for public support, the outcome of their negotiations, and the promises of "representative government" as well as "Hong Kong people ruling Hong Kong" have together brought about a politicization among the people of Hong Kong to an unprecedented degree. Activities include constitutional discussion, group formation, political alignment, and efforts to seek media exposure. Prominent among the many political overtures are calls for consensus building among the people. For instance, even Szeto Wah, president of the Association of Professional Teachers and a member of the Basic Law Drafting Committee, believes that both the Chinese and the Hong Kong governments would accept a proposal for political reform that carries a consensus of the people of Hong Kong. However, in view of the rift between the elites and the public, and among the elites themselves, a consensus among the people of Hong Kong will be difficult to secure.

Popular orientations toward political objects in Hong Kong have never been seriously studied until recently. In our survey research in the summer of 1985, political culture in Hong Kong was found to have taken on a very complex and sophisticated configuration. Here are some highlights of relevant findings.

It has been suggested that in the struggle for their future, the people of Hong Kong failed to avoid the pitfalls of Chinese nationalism.[24] This hypothesis is untenable simply because Hong Kong is not filled with compatriots who can be converted for the motherland's purposes. According to our findings, the majority of the respondents to the survey identify themselves as Hong Kongers rather than as Chinese. This identity lends additional support to Hugh D.R. Baker's thesis of "the emergence of Hong Kong man."[25] Apart from this, our findings add credibility to the results of a survey commissioned in 1982 by a political group renowned for its critical stand, vis-à-vis the Hong Kong government, according to which an absolute majority of 87 percent of the respondents (N = 3,299) opted for the status quo, whereas only 12 percent accepted that Hong Kong is to be returned back to China.[26]

Past studies of Hong Kong's political culture argued for the presence of a "don't-rock-the-boat" mentality in a refugee town, which was a kind of passive acceptance of the lesser evil.[27] Currently, the people of Hong Kong are much more sophisticated. They know the limits of their power, but they are ready to resort to pressure or violence. They have not been converted to the Sino-British consensus. It is still true that they prefer the political status quo but not because it is the lesser evil. They are positively attached to the status quo. It is this vital point that most democratic proponents in Hong Kong have failed to grasp. In contrast to them, the Hong Kong people do not view politics in structural terms. They are much more concerned with performance. The form of government is largely irrelevant to them, provided that they can maintain a minimal living. If forced to choose among some forms of government, they also would prefer a government by the philosopher king (but not of the Marxist brand), rather than what has been suggested in the name of democracy. This choice is related to the fact that government performance is evaluated highly and that bureaucrats are trusted more than politicians. It appears that after they have been sheltered from the trauma of Chinese politics for decades, they have become accustomed to trust professional knowledge and administrative skills more than the advocacy of political ideals and the politicians' ability to resolve conflicts. Most interestingly, the men on the street have hardened their appreciation of the current political system since the Sino-British negotiations. Asked whether the imperfect current system was still the best under the existing circumstances, 74 percent of the total sample (N = 767) in 1985 agreed, compared with only 54 percent (N = 953) in 1982.

With respect to the elites, the issue of 1997 is highly divisive. Elites can be categorized in many ways. A simple approach is to divide the elites of Hong Kong into the "ins" and the "outs." The "ins" have entrenched interests to defend. They stress the need for stability and continuity in political institutions. The "outs" are concerned about securing a high degree of autonomy for Hong Kong after 1997 and place their hope in a substantial extent of democratization. In terms of composition, the strategic elites, including those holding responsible positions in industry, commerce, banking, and the government, generally tend to be conservative. The democratic camp, on the other hand, commands support among a number of grassroots leaders, part of the intelligentsia, and many of the educated youth.

Regarding policy positions, both camps of elites have avowed support for stability and prosperity, and they are aware that a system rooted in Hong Kong has to be firmly established before or at the time of the departure of the British. They differ sharply on how this system should be constituted. The conservatives are afraid of too much democracy for the welfare implications and the unpredictability of the popular mood. The democrats, however, are afraid of too little democracy to give the future government sufficient popular legitimacy for its immunity from external intervention.

The conservative camp is by no means a vocal force. They have easy access to the power center, so they have no need to make outcries in public. So far only one well-drafted proposal on the Basic Law was made public by the conservatives. Its author is the industrialist Cha Chimin, a Hong Kong member of the Basic Law Drafting Committee.[28] The constitution he has recommended in the draft is largely a plutocratic oligarchy, the core of which is to be provided by a Council of Advisers. This council will be composed of socioeconomic notables, to be appointed by the governor for a life tenure. The major functions of the council are (1) to recommend candidate(s) for the governorship to the Central People's Government for appointment; (2) in consultation with the Legislative Council, to propose amendments to the Basic Law to the Central People's Government; (3) to elect among themselves one-third of the legislative councilors; and (4) to offer advice to the governor and the chief minister. According to Cha's proposal, besides those members elected by the Council of Advisers, one-third of the members of the Legislative Council will be elected indirectly by the functional constituencies and another one-third by the district boards (or by electoral districts). The powers of the Legislative Council shall remain unchanged, but it can be dissolved by the governor, who will then arrange for new elections. Such a system is believed to be conducive to Hong Kong's "continuity and stability."

On the other hand, the constitutional proposal submitted by the Hong

Kong Affairs Association (HKAA) represents the typical thinkings of the democratic forces.[29] The memorandum is drafted in the spirit of popular sovereignty, and the government structure proposed is to ensure the birth of a publicly elected government that is accountable to the people. The slogan is: "return the sovereignty to the people by 1997." The focus of this reform lies with the Legislative Council, which shall be fully elected by 1997 through direct and indirect elections. Official and appointed members of the Executive Council should also be gradually reduced to zero. The elected legislative councilors will head the various government departments. After 1988 the governor will no longer preside over the meetings of the Legislative Council and will cease his chairmanship of the Executive Council after 1994.

As revealed by the above two documents, the conservatives and the democrats are diametrically opposed to each other in ideological terms. There are certainly many levels of opinion that can be placed in between. Maria Tam, concurrent member of the Urban Council, District Board, Legislative Council, Executive Council, and the Basic Law Drafting Committee, is noted for her ambition to bridge the gap between the capitalists and the grassroots element.[30] However, the crucial issue of the constitutional development is whether stability and prosperity can be maintained better by leaving the capitalists and the bureaucrats in control of government for the sake of administrative efficiency or by giving power to the common people for the sake of political legitimacy. The possibility exists that agreements can still be reached over the procedural details of constitutional changes such as pace and proportion of different categories of councilors. The real anxiety and difference in opinions, however, is about the final state of affairs that is supposed to remain unchanged for many decades to come once it is established. It is extremely difficult to achieve consensus about this final state of affairs, more so when it is not conceptualized as a long-term goal but a target to be achieved within a decade or so. The difference in opinion about the final state of affairs is reinforced by the divergence in time perception: "time is on our side" versus "time is running out."

THE PROSPECT

We have delineated the barriers to consensus building with respect to political change in Hong Kong and have also laid a foundation regarding the value preferences and policy positions of the principal actors in the game. We now come to the hazardous task of contemplating the prospect. Will there be a consensus among all parties? If yes, what will then transpire? Will the consensus thereby achieved be sufficiently strong to sustain stability and legitimacy?

A rapidly changing society is unlikely to develop a single political consensus that is shared by all. However, to speak of a dominant consensus that sustains the political institutions and policies is useful. The present dominant consensus in Hong Kong favors a minimally integrated sociopolitical system. As Siu-kai Lau succinctly put it:

> The limited functions of the bureaucratic polity, the "self-sufficiency" and resourcefulness of the Chinese society, the tendency of both parties to avoid involvement in the affairs of each other, the absence of effective linkage mechanisms are forces inherent in the system which function to insure political stability by reducing political salience and by facilitating the process of "social accommodation of politics".[31]

In the past, there has already been a competing candidate for consensus in the form of an integrated system, in which electoral and party politics link. What is its chance of success? The promise of "representative government" and "high degree of autonomy" have apparently accelerated, but it has yet to beget a democratic movement in Hong Kong. It has to be reckoned with, however. But the outcome of a dominant consensus is likely to be something in between, a combined function of the barriers to consensus and the process of manipulative political persuasion.

Given the novelty of the situation, the lack of trust among participants, the paucity of effective leadership, the risk of cumulative frustration, and the time pressure under which agreement has to be reached, participants in the exercise of consensus building will eventually choose the one of familiarity, least resistance, and marginal gains. It is therefore likely that further reforms will not depart radically from the present system. In other words, existing institutions will be adapted to meet old and new demands. In the meantime, there will be some soul-searching activities and rhetorical games. But all this will end up in the realization that tradition is still the better mentor.

The recent debate over the concept of "democratic consultation" is typical. The term *democratic consultation* was mentioned several times in the Draft Regulations Governing the Basic Law Consultative Committee as a procedural rule of fundamental importance. Lui Yiuchu, a local lawyer and member of the Basic Law Drafting Committee, immediately and publicly voiced her dissent. As she rightly pointed out, this concept invited people to recall the Communist strategies for dealing with the other political groupings in the 1940s and early 1950s. Following a series of applause and rebuttal, the Basic Law Drafting Committee decided to retain in the regulations the concept of democratic consultation only in one place while the single term of consultation was used in the others. This interesting instance of linguistic war has not brought about the democratic procedural rules, but it forcefully reconfirmed the consultative mode of operations with all of the implications for initiative, status, and output. The happy ending is certainly better than the snarl of "democratic consultation." But it is a far cry from the ideal that democrats in Hong Kong would like to realize.

Consensus building is a process of communication and influence in which attitudes, beliefs, and orientations are acquired, changed, and hardened. Because we have established that existing political contenders for allegiance do not generally command moral authority, the path to consensus building will rely more on the capability to promise and deliver rather than on the ability to reason and persuade. Because of this capability, the democratic forces are at a disadvantage. There are indications that the Chinese government's and the British government's attitude are converging, and the strategic elites may also finally realize the dependence of their common interests on the persistence of the essential features of the existing system. Therefore, there seems to be an unholy alliance among the Communists, the capitalists, and the high-ranking bureaucrats who are likely to insist on an executive-centered and performance-oriented constitution. In the face of such a formidable contender, the democratic forces can assert themselves only if they have a mass base.[32] Devoid of an organizational base, the democratic forces acquire strength largely by playing up public opinion with the assistance of the competitive, free, and headline-hunting press. This strategy may be effective under certain circumstances when there exists a general dissatisfaction with government performance. The pressure of public opinion and the moral obligation to deliver in the wake of the promise of "high degree of autonomy" or "representative government" may move the government(s) to come to terms with the democratic forces through accommodating some of their demands.

Considering the various forces at work, we believe that if a dominant consensus could ever be achieved, it would be in the direction of a mixed constitution, the color of which is representative while the flavor is bureaucratic. There will not be a "government by the fat cats."[33] The introduction of electoral elements will surely contribute to the growth of government, of which the bureaucracy will be the immediate and chief beneficiary. Still wielding enormous power, the bureaucracy must ensure system performance and provide the backbone for continuity and stability. The Legislative Council will be chiefly responsible for the new game of adversarial politics advocating the aspirations and expectations of the aroused citizens. The chief executive has the unenviable job of balancing the interests of China and Hong Kong. Even if reality falls short of our predictions, Hong Kong will remain a fascinating laboratory to test many political theories.

NOTES

1. Text in *A Draft Agreement between the Government of the United Kingdom of Great Britain and Northern Ireland and the Government of the People's Republic of China on the Future of Hong Kong*, Hong Kong: Government Printer, September 26, 1984.

2. On the issue of sovereignty and related aspects, see Anthony Dicks, "Treaty,

Grant, Usage, or Sufferance? Some Legal Aspects of the Status of Hong Kong," *China Quarterly*, No. 95 (Sept. 1983), pp. 427–55.

3. George J. Graham, Jr., "Consensus," in *Social Science Concepts*, ed. Giovanni Sartori (Beverly Hills, Calif.: Sage, 1984), p. 111.

4. Jamie Walker, "Reform Up to HK—Renton," *South China Morning Post*, Nov. 1, 1985, p. 1.

5. Interview by Yuk-lin Lee with six legislative counselors who are concurrently members of the Basic Law Drafting Committee in *Pai Shing Semi-Monthly*, Oct. 16, 1985, p. 10.

6. John Walden, "Does Public Opinion Count in Hong Kong?" address to the Government and Public Administration Society, Chinese University of Hong Kong, Sept. 27, 1979, p. 1.

7. Siu-kai Lau, "Local Leaders and Local Politics in Hong Kong," in K. Aoi et al., eds., *Family and Community Changes in East Asia*, (Tokyo: Japan Sociological Society, 1985), pp. 374–96.

8. Hsin-chi Kuan and Siu-kai Lau, "Leadership, Participation, and Local Politics in Hong Kong," paper presented to the International Roundtable on Local Leadership and Government Performance, Nov. 15–20, 1985, in Bakersfield, California, p. 17.

9. Emily Lau, "One Small Step from Colonial Rule," *Far Eastern Economic Review*, Vol. 127, no. 11 (March 21, 1985), pp. 51–52.

10. Ian Scott, "The Sino-British Agreement and Political Power in Hong Kong," paper presented at the workshop The Future of Hong Kong on Apr. 19, 1985, at the University Joint Centre on Modern Eastern Asia, University of Toronto-York, Toronto, pp. 11–12.

11. J.M. Burns, *Leadership* (New York: Harper & Row, 1978), p. 4.

12. Joseph Y.S. Cheng, ed., *Hong Kong in Search of a Future* (Hong Kong: Oxford University Press, 1984), p. 79.

13. Byron S.J. Weng, "The Integration of Outlying Areas: The Case of Hong Kong," in *The End of an Isolation: China after Mao*, ed. Harish Kapur (Dordrecht: Martinus Nijhoff Publications, 1985), pp. 308–61, esp. 311–12, 337–38.

14. David Bonavia, *Hong Kong and 1997: The Final Settlement*, 2d ed. (Hong Kong: South China Morning Post, 1985).

15. *Assessments for Testing the Acceptability in Hong Kong of the Draft Agreement on the Future of the Territory: Report of the Assessment Office; Report of the Independent Monitoring Team and Submissions Made by Organizations to the Assessment Office* (Hong Kong: Government Printer, November 1984).

16. See, for example, Ho Li, "Chipenfa chüpu weichian (Jibenfa jubu weijian)" ["Out of Step Towards the Basic Law"], *The Nineties*, Vol. 88 (Sept. 1985), p. 20.

17. *Green Paper: The Further Development of Representative Government in Hong Kong* (Hong Kong: Hong Kong Government Printer, July 1984), p. 1.

18. Peter Williams, "Hong Kong: The Way Ahead," address to the Royal Institute of International Affairs, Sept. 30, 1984, in London.

19. Full text of the letter is printed in Kong Wai-man, *Hsiangkang chengchih yü kangjen chihkang (Xianggang zhengzhi yu gangren zhigang)* [*Political System of Hong Kong and Hong Kong People Ruling Hong Kong*] (Hong Kong: Wide Angle Press, 1984), p. 33.

20. Interview with Li Zhuwen by Melinda Liu, *Newsweek* (International edition), Vol. 103, no. 4 (Jan. 23, 1984), p. 48.

21. Interview with Wong Han-pin by the chief editor of *The Mirror*, Vol. 96 (July 1985), pp. 6–12; interview with Wong Han-pin by Lu Keng, *Pai Shing Semi-Monthly*, Vol. 106 (Oct. 16, 1985), pp. 15–17.

22. Interview with Louis L.Y. Cha, proprietor of the influential newspaper *Mingpao* and member of the Basic Law Drafting Committee. That interview was published as a series in *Mingpao* from July 23 to August 1, 1985. The relevant information referred to in the text can be found in the July 25, 1985, issue, p. 4.

23. Terry Cheng, "Ji Keeps on Sounding Beijing Alarm over HK Reforms," *South China Morning Post*, Oct. 31, 1985, p. 12.

24. Chalmers Johnson, "The Mousetrapping of Hong Kong: A Game in Which Nobody Wins," *Asian Survey*, Vol. 24, no. 9 (Sept. 1984), pp. 887–909.

25. Hugh D.R. Baker, "Life in the Cities: The Emergence of Hong Kong Man," *China Quarterly*, no. 95 (Sept. 1983) pp. 469–79.

26. *Hong Kong and Its Future*, prepared by Survey Research Hong Kong Ltd. for Hong Kong Observers, 1982, Table 20A.

27. Stephen Hoadley, "Hong Kong is the Lifeboat: Notes on Political Culture and Socialization," *Journal of Oriental Studies*, Vol. 8 (Jan. 1970), pp. 206–18. Ambrose King, "The Political Culture of Kwun Tong: A Chinese Community in Hong Kong," in *Social Life and Development in Hong Kong*, ed. Ambrose King and Rance P.L. Lee (Hong Kong: Chinese University Press, 1981), pp. 147–68.

28. Cha Chi-min, "Tui Hsiangkang Tepie Hsingcheng Ch'u Chengtse He Chipenfa Te Chianyi (Dui Zianggang Tebie Zingzhengqu He Jibenfa De Jianyi)" *Mingpao*, Aug. 7–12, 1985. An English version titled "Basic Policies and Constitution for the Hong Kong Special Administrative Region," June 20, 1985, was distributed in private circles.

29. Hong Kong Affairs Association, "Women Tui Chipenfa Te Yihsieh K'anfa (Women Duei Jibenfa De Isie Kanfa) [*Memorandum on the Development of Hong Kong's Political System*]," in *Kuotu Shich'i Te Hsiangkang Chengchi Yü Fachih (Guodu Shiqi De Xianggang Zhengzhi Yu Fazhi) [Hong Kong's Political and Legal System in the Transitional Period*], ed. Hong Kong Affairs Association, Hong Kong: Pai Shing Bimonthly, May 1985, pp. 76–95. A similar position can be discerned in the draft Basic Law prepared by Meeting Point, published in full in *Ta Kung Pao*, May 5, 1984, p. 2.

30. See, for example, the interview with Maria Tam by Hsu Sze-min on August 21, 1985, *The Mirror*, Vol. 98, pp. 28–31.

31. Siu-kai Lau, *Society and Politics in Hong Kong*, Hong Kong: Chinese University Press, 1982, p. 164.

32. In another paper we have gone to some length to explain why the democratic forces are still weak organizationally and prospects for organizational expansion are by no means encouraging. See Siu-kai Lau and Hsin-chi Kuan, "Hong Kong after the Sino-British Agreement," *Pacific Affairs*, vol. 59, no. 2 (Summer 1986), pp. 214–36.

33. William H. Overholt, "Hong Kong and China: A New Relationship," *Current History*, Vol. 84 (Sept. 1985), pp. 258–261, 273.

5

Hong Kong: The Human Rights Dimension

TA-LING LEE

Hong Kong has always had an anomalous and at times precarious existence. It does not neatly fit into any category. Although it has been ruled by the British as a crown colony since the Treaty of Nanking in 1842, the Chinese have always regarded the treaty as an unequal one with dubious validity. In fact, the government of the People's Republic of China (PRC), upon assuming a seat in the United Nations, formally informed the world body in 1972 that Hong Kong was not to be treated as a colony, a position that raised no objections at the time. In any event, with the leasehold on the New Territories expiring in 1997, the continued British rule over Hong Kong becomes academic. Hong Kong comprises only a small part of the whole area and depends on the hinterland for sheer survival. Moreover, the two parts have long since been fully integrated as a single entity, economically and in other respects.

Politically, the British ruled Hong Kong through appointed officials with enormous power and prestige, from governor on down to a host of civil servants in charge of the bureaucracy, with only advisory if not token participation by the local residents. Given the British tradition of the rule of law, however, the people of Hong Kong have long enjoyed a full range of freedoms and protections. Hong Kong, therefore, is a land where there is freedom but no democracy. The people have often sought to channel their views and energies through economic activities and a free press but not through a direct role in government via participatory democracy.

With the lease expiring in 1997 and the future uncertain, there had always been a sense that Hong Kong lived on borrowed time. With the future now sealed in the Joint Declaration, it is only natural that the residents believe the borrowed days are numbered. The tragedy of the whole situation is that the people of Hong Kong have had no voice in their own future. Like those in many other places caught in an untenable situation, they have unfortunately become pawns in an international game of power and pride. How do they feel about their own future? What was the attitude of the British government toward them during the negotiation? What do the people of Hong Kong themselves plan to do? What role can a third party play in the larger picture? In terms of legalities and politics, these questions really boil down to a fundamental question of human rights—the rights, or the lack thereof, of 5.5 million hard-working people to determine their own destiny.

The position of the United Nations on human rights is unequivocally clear. In the name of the peoples of the United Nations, the United Nations charter "reaffirm(s) faith in fundamental human rights, in the dignity and worth of the human person" in the Preamble. With the Soviet bloc abstaining, the General Assembly by a vote of 48 to 0 adopted the Universal Declaration of Human Rights in 1948 detailing the fundamental human rights including the right of life, liberty, and the security of persons (Article 3). Among other fundamental human rights of immediate relevance here are the freedom of movement, the right to choose one's nationality (Articles 13, 15), the right of freedom of thought and expression (Articles 18, 19) and the right to take part in government (Article 21). Although it should be readily admitted that these high ideals fall far short of realization elsewhere in the world, the prospect of severe curtailment of these rights for Hong Kong's 5.5 million people should still be a serious concern. Those who enjoy these rights owe it to themselves to raise this question and to keep the issue before the public. For the millions of residents there, the question of Hong Kong is more than its survival as a free-market economy; it is their own collective fate that is at stake. That is, can they continue to live with faith "in the dignity and worth in the human person" now that the 10-year "countdown to communism" has begun?

THE BRITISH GOVERNMENT

Prime Minister Margaret Thatcher was among the first to mention the interests of the people of Hong Kong during the initial stages of the negotiation. As early as September 1982, she made the now famous three-legged-stool analogy. For any Anglo-Chinese agreement to be acceptable she stated that it must be based on the consent of three parties: the PRC government, the British Parliament, and the "people of Hong Kong." If any one of the legs was not sturdy, the stool would collapse.[1] However, Thatcher and other British officials were soon to find out that they had neither the means nor the ability to see the third leg of the stool in place and have since vainly tried to argue their way out of the fix that they were in.

First, at present there are no formal institutions through which the people of Hong Kong can be consulted. Hong Kong has been, and still is, ruled by an appointed governor, other appointed civil servants, an appointed Legislative Council, and an appointed Executive Council; a setup "in all essentials exactly what it was when it was introduced on the colony's establishment in 1843," despite the recent addition of unofficial members to the two councils (UMELCO) and the election of local boards.[2] In short, the British have not been eager to bring the people of Hong Kong into the mainstream of Hong Kong's political life by opening up channels for participatory democracy, thereby taking full advantage of the often-assumed culturally based apolitical attitude of the local residents. Moreover, even if there were means to consult with the people of Hong Kong, such as a plebiscite, concerning their views, the standing veto from Beijing would make it utterly unrealistic. The British government did not initially demonstrate any strong desire to fight for the interests of the people of Hong Kong, having agreed to negotiate with Beijing on a bilateral basis from the beginning and thereby denying the participation of Hong Kong as a third party.

The repeated concessions the British made over the third leg of the stool during the negotiations are pathetic to recall. Every time the issue arose the British meekly retreated, sacrificing the interests of the people of Hong Kong. In addition, the attitude of calculated indifference and arrogance of the British government toward the people of Hong Kong has been evident. Consequently, the meekness toward Beijing and the strident attitude toward the people of Hong Kong would result in either an inability or an unwillingness to make the proclaimed British position any more than a mockery concerning the Hong Kong people's interest.

For example, when the Sino-British negotiation first got under way, London allowed it to focus on the unequal treaties of the nineteenth century rather than on the interests and free will of the 5.5 million population in Hong Kong, which certainly could have been forcefully raised and morally sustained at the forums of the international community. In the summer of 1983, Sir Edward Youde, the governor of Hong Kong, was added to the British negotiating team. At a press conference on July 7, in answer to a question as to whom he would be representing in the talks, Youde said: "I am the governor of Hong Kong.... Indeed I represent the people of Hong Kong. Who else would I represent?" This brought an immediate response from Beijing. The Chinese foreign ministry announced the next day: "Mr. Youde will take part in the talks as a member of the British government delegation. Therefore, he can only represent the British government in the talks."[3] Meanwhile, the PRC government began to take action. Chalmers Johnson summed up the subsequent developments:

> It denied a visa to Beijing for Peter Tsao, the Director of the Hong Kong Government Information Service, who was to accompany Youde. Tsao had already irritated the PRC by saying to a British newspaper, in May, that if Hong Kong's future involved coming under PRC sovereignty, he himself would emigrate. The British government made no protest over these developments: Youde joined the team as a British government official, Tsao stayed in Hong Kong and no representative of the people of Hong Kong has to date participated in the negotiation.[4]

Examples of British indifference and arrogance equally abound. When Sir S.Y. Chung, senior unofficial member of the Executive Council, went to London heading a UMELCO delegation to plead Hong Kong's case with Parliament in May 1984, he was cold-shouldered in humiliation.[5] When the Joint Declaration was presented to the people of Hong Kong for "approval," on a "take it or leave it" basis, Governor Youde's statements at a press conference on September 27, 1984, were a classic example of bureaucratic Catch–22. Youde announced the creation of an "Assessment Office" to allow the people of Hong Kong to "have an opportunity to state their view on the acceptability of the agreement as a whole," while the British government has already made it clear that there was to be no revision of any kind. A rejection would mean there was to be no agreement.[6] In other words, what Youde really wanted to say was that the people of Hong Kong had to say "yes" to the whole package.

The disregard of the will of the people of Hong Kong did not stop here. The pattern continued on the day Parliament was scheduled to take up the draft agreement. Only 50 out of 635 MPs bothered to show up to approve it, and the perfunctory debate over the future of 5.5 million people did not make the front page of a single newspaper in London.[7] In view of all this neglect, does the total exclusion of the people of Hong Kong from the decision affecting their destiny raise a moral question? Indeed, does the forced return of nearly 3 million refugees from mainland China to Communist rule against their will constitute a serious human rights violation?

From the very beginning it seems clear that the British government has avoided taking a strong stand concerning the rights of the people of Hong Kong to decide what constitutes their own best interest. By conceding that right to Beijing without even raising its voice on the moral issue, Britain has clumsily left itself only an amoral last line of defense: things could have been worse if there had been no agreement. That line of defense was invoked repeatedly by Prime Minister Thatcher in her December 22, 1984, news conference in Hong Kong, after her journey to Beijing, where she signed the Joint Declaration. When she faced a battery of Hong Kong reporters who bombarded her with tough questions, Thatcher rationalized the British position on the moral question. One exchange with a reporter went as follows:

Question 8: Prime Minister, on Wednesday, you signed an agreement with China promising to deliver over 5 million people into the hands of a Communist dictatorship. Is this morally defensible, or is it really true that in international politics the highest form of morality is one's own national interests?

Answer: Can I just say this to you. What do you think would have happened if we had not attempted to get an agreement? In 1997, 92 percent of the territory would automatically have returned to China without any assurance, without any of the advantages of the agreement that we have now. May I now put it to you that the situation now is vastly better for Hong Kong and [that it] accepts and honors and acknowledges the fact that China wishes the lifestyle of Hong Kong to continue under that agreement. I think you would have had great cause to complain had the government of Britain done nothing until 1997 and I believe that most of the people, indeed the overwhelming number of people in Hong Kong think the same. You may be a solitary exception.[8]

Repeatedly, she was to fall back on the fact that 92 percent of Hong Kong would go back to China in 1997 in any case, implying that whatever agreement she was able to exact from the Chinese government was really a gain for Hong Kong. However, when pressed, she refused to say specifically how her government was to defend the Joint Declaration in case of a violation:

Question 14: Why your government feels assured of China's commitment to the treaty does not need reiteration. But I think we need for the record to know what will your government do if the terms of this agreement are abused or broken? In short, are you prepared to defend this pact as you did in the Falklands, and by what means?

Answer: I believe that this agreement will be honored. I believe that firmly. If by any chance any question rose under the agreement, naturally a signatory to it would raise the matter with the Chinese government. If they had anything to raise with us, naturally they would have raised it with us. That is the normal procedure under an agreement. The signatories raise matters with one another.

Question 15: Are you prepared to go further to defend this?

Answer: I have indicated that if there is anything to raise under the agreement then of course we would raise it in the normal way but I believe it will be fully honored. Can I just say to you: In 1997, 92 percent of the territory would automatically return to China.[9]

After some digression, the moral question was brought up again and Thatcher was again evasive in her answer:

Question 19: Mrs. Thatcher, you have solved the historical problem of Hong Kong as a territory. Yet, you are left with a moral problem because since World War II this is the first time that 6 million people, by treaty, have transferred from what you yourself might call the free world to Communism. You have signed that treaty. How do you feel about it?

Answer: I think that we should have been negligent had we not, in fact, raised the post–1997 position as we did. We raised it. We have got an agreement which is acceptable overwhelmingly to the people of Hong Kong. That agreement will extend to 50 years beyond 1997. I feel we have done a good job for the people of Hong Kong. Just consider what sort of question you would be asking me now had there been no agreement and a totally unknown future.[10]

And the inescapable comparison with the Falklands eventually came up at the press conference:

Question 28: Prime Minister, how do you justify going to war over the Falkland Islands when the small population there didn't wish to be absorbed into Argentina and giving in to Communist China so easily, and handing over the 5.5 million people of Hong Kong to Communist China, when so many of those people voted with their feet to leave that country?

Answer: I do not quite understand how you can ignore the lease which terminates in 1997 and every question which has been put on the basis that you have put there has ignored that fundamental fact. I did not find it was being ignored in Hong Kong, that fundamental fact. I found that people wanted confidence and reassurance about post–1997, realizing that unless we entered into an agreement what would happen in 1997, therefore we negotiated with China—China and we were both anxious that the stability and prosperity of Hong Kong should continue—and the agreement is the result. I think you will find that had there not been agreement now, had we not entered into talks, Hong Kong people would have cause to be concerned because uncertainty is always very, very difficult. We have got an agreement and it has been overwhelmingly accepted by the people of Hong Kong.

Question 29: The international treaties were the ones that you cited two years ago when you went to Beijing when, at that point, the Chinese government had already stated that it wanted Hong Kong back. The treaties were the ones you stood by at that point. What, during the past two years, has caused the change?

Answer: We have, as I have indicated, now freely entered into a new agreement which we regard as legally binding, freely entered into. And our concern now is to implement that agreement and to honor it to the full—which both sides will.[11]

Instead of throwing in all the marbles at the outset, and thus finding herself having to defend a morally untenable position, London could have put forward the will of the 5.5 million people as paramount at the beginning of the negotiation. Or, to use the expression of the local newspapers in Hong Kong, London could have and should have played the "public opinion card." London should have raised the issue and stuck to it, thus bringing to world attention the fact that the Hong Kong issue was a moral/human rights issue rather than a simple territorial issue. With an appeal to global conscience, it would have been possible to put Beijing on the defensive if it chose not to hurt its image in the current modernization drive when China needs the assistance of the West. Unfortunately, this was not to be the case, for human rights considerations were easily outweighed by the prospects of trade and other benefits in the minds of policy-makers in London.

THE PEOPLE OF HONG KONG

Hong Kong's phenomenal rise to its present status, as one of the world's dynamic economies and financial centers, was a relatively recent development, primarily in the last three decades or so. For more than 100 years, it had existed largely as one of many British overseas possessions with no particular claim to economic importance other than being a medium-sized trading port with modest facilities. However, by the turn of the 1950s, the political change that had taken place in China was to bring about a revolutionary transformation of the British enclave on the South China coast. A major influx of mainland refugees took place as a result of the founding of the PRC in late 1949 and streams of Chinese fleeing the mainland have since continued to reach Hong Kong right up to the present. This continuous influx has helped to push the total population of Hong Kong to 5.5 million, 98 percent of them Chinese and more than 50 percent refugees from mainland China. It is largely through the hard work of these new arrivals that Hong Kong has grown steadily in importance, financially and economically, on a global scale during the past three decades. How do the people of Hong Kong view the 1997 issue? What do they plan to do about their own future?

The phenomenal growth of Hong Kong during this period is even grudgingly admitted by the Chinese Communists. When interviewed by a reporter of the Japanese *Yomiuri Shinbun* in his plush Hong Kong office, Wang Guangying, brother-in-law of the late Liu Shaoqi, the Chinese head of state who died of persecution during the Cultural Revolution, said that "Hong Kong began to prosper only when we were in our worst days," referring to the height of the Cultural Revolution in the late 1960s. Wang was a former capitalist who suffered grievously during the Cultural Revolution but has since been restored to good grace and sent to Hong Kong to oversee Chinese investment there in the post-Mao modernization drive because his entrepreneurial skills are again useful. He observed that:

> Hong Kong was not as good as Guangzhou [Canton] when I came here in 1956 and not as good as Shanghai when I came here in 1959. Even on the eve of the Cultural Revolution [1965–1966], Shanghai was still better than Hong Kong.... Now Hong Kong has turned out so well and this is to China's advantage. Many business transactions are done through Hong Kong. This is a place with great transportation and communications facilities. We can take advantage of these facilities and utilize them.[12]

Although Wang should be commended for his candor in admitting that "Hong Kong has turned out so well" in such a short time, what he probably knows well, but left out, was much more important, namely, the combination of factors that are behind the Hong Kong success story. One important factor is the fact that Hong Kong is a free society under the rule of law, which has made possible the release of human energy and creativity to perform wonders. The respect for fundamental human rights under the rule of law are particularly precious to those to whom these rights were once denied. To the millions of Hong Kong residents who have risked their lives and undergone untold hardships to escape to Hong Kong, the life in Hong Kong and the one they have forsaken on the Chinese mainland under a different system are a comparison about which there is no ambiguity in their minds. They have already voted with their feet. The choice to them is between two systems; neither is perfect. One offers freedom under the rule of law, hope, and human dignity. The other is a totalitarian rule of fear and human degradation.

Hong Kong is not a perfect society. It has the usual shortcomings associated with what is generally known as a capitalistic society, including crime, social inequities, indifference, and alienation. In addition, there is a conspicuous lack of local residents' political participation in the local government, a situation that is uniquely Hong Kong. Despite these shortcomings the people of Hong Kong persevered, pursued their jobs with diligence and creative energy, and made Hong Kong what it is today. From their experience, they have come to realize what they can accomplish under a system that allows the freedom to act and affords the protection against unchecked political power in the wrong hands.

Illustrative of how the people of Hong Kong feel about the free-wheeling life-style, there is a popular saying there that the local men fear their wives more than they do the government. In short, the people of Hong Kong have fondly grown accustomed to their way of life, despite all of its imperfections and shortcomings. Shielded from the external threat and protected from an abusive government, they have been able to concentrate on improving their own lots and have developed a strong awareness of control over their own destiny, despite the cloudy long-term prospect and uncertain legal status of Hong Kong itself. The far-sighted and learned observers may have deep worries, but the ordinary people in Hong Kong have successfully taken a day at a time and were unprepared for the "shock of 1997" as it first came into the open two years ago. The thriving newly industrialized country (NIC) suddenly was to sink into deep trouble and threatened to turn into a collapsing recently industrialized country (CRIC), with the stock market near collapse, capital flight, and the whole colony seemingly awaiting doomsday in despair.[13]

As the Sino-British negotiations got under way, the people of Hong Kong were to experience a shocking and cruel awakening that, in fact, they had no control over their own destiny. The prospect of having to live again under the system from which they have escaped is frightening; yet there is little they can do to avoid that fate. That sense of inability to control one's own future is at the heart of the pervasive mood of hopelessness, despair, and resignation. For the Hong Kong people as a whole, the crisis of confidence runs deep, even though, at times, it may be muted or hidden under a facade of euphoria. For almost two years, Hong Kong's fortune ebbed and flowed, in response to the progress of the negotiation. A snag would produce a downturn on the stock market and more capital flight. A reported breakthrough, however, in the highly sensitive but not always accurate local press would generate a short-lived euphoria. But all of the time the mood of despair and resignation lay just below the surface.

The people of Hong Kong clearly indicated their fear and anxiety over the future of their homeland several times even before the Sino-British Agreement was reached in September 1984. In a series of polls, they repeatedly and overwhelmingly favored the status quo. Chalmers Johnson provided a summary of these scientifically conducted polls:

> One of the earliest polls found that "maintenance of the status quo" was the preferred solution for 70 percent of the population. A later poll, dating from April 1983, found 95 percent in favor of no change. Only 42 percent thought that Hong Kong's becoming a "special administrative region" of Communist China was acceptable to them and when the question was phrased as "returning Hong Kong to China," support fell to 26 percent. Perhaps most revealing, no fewer than 22 percent of those people (in June 1982)—most of them in the 15–34 age group—would "try every means to leave" if Hong Kong reverted to China, a figure that would translate, the poll organizers say, into 710,000 people seeking to leave.[14]

Polls in 1984 showed little change in the perceived general mood. An unpublished survey found that 68 percent of the professional people polled in Hong Kong were considering leaving.[15] Another survey, taken by several local boards, showed that of more than 1,000 people interviewed, less than 30 percent expressed confidence in the Chinese Communist promise of no change of policy toward Hong Kong for 50 years, whereas 60 percent would consider emigration.[16] The suspense generated by the secrecy in which the negotiations were conducted and the open threat that Beijing would announce its own solution to the Hong Kong question, if none was produced through negotiation by September 1984, only added to the anxiety and created an almost suffocating atmosphere in Hong Kong that was only thinly camouflaged under the usual hustle and bustle to the unsuspecting eye.

When British Foreign Minister Sir Geoffrey Howe announced in late April 1984 that "it would not be realistic to think of an agreement for continued British administration in Hong Kong after 1997," dashing an earlier hope, he was greeted by dozens of demonstrators outside his Hong Kong hotel waving banners reading "No Communism to Hong Kong" and "Only Hong Kong People Understand Communism."[17] When the agreement was finally announced in September, it was greeted with a sigh of relief: it meant that the suspense was finally over and the worst did not happen. The hapless Hong Kong residents for a while were again in a state of euphoria. As expected, the Assessment Office duly reported Hong Kong's favorable opinion toward the agreement. Many community and business leaders showed public support, although privately they continued to harbor deep reservations.[18] Before the Assessment Office issued its report, one prominent UMELCO member commented: "I think the general impression that all of us have gained from public and private discussion . . . is that it will prove acceptable to the majority of the people of Hong Kong."[19] Other public and private opinion polls showed that the majority of the people of Hong Kong accepted the agreement, the PRC was quick to claim.[20] Even an American journalism professor, L. Erwin Atwood of Southern Illinois University, found in his survey that 70 percent of his correspondents considered the terms of the accord acceptable, although he took note of the fact that the respondents thought they were virtually powerless and that their opinion mattered little.[21] The stock market rebounded and achieved a four-year high. Before the agreement, "everything was doom and gloom," one Hong Kong broker said. "Now investors think this place is good for another 12 years—if not 62 years."[22]

This ostensible change of mood forcefully brings to mind the Anschluss of 1938, when Hitler gobbled up Austria after much suspense and tension. At that time one scholar observed:

> What made the whole conflict so intensely tragic was that the assassination of the Republic, greeted by the ringing of church bells, was acclaimed by the hand-clapping, cheering majority of its population, proclaiming their German nationality. The people were goaded into taking a position very much at variance with the one they had assumed a few days earlier by motives and convictions that can as yet be only dimly perceived.[23]

Analyzing the abrupt turnabout of the public mood, he offered the following observation, which was as true of Austria in March 1938 as it was of Hong Kong in September 1984, half a globe away and half a century later:

> The sudden relief of tensions, accompanied by an awareness of grossdeutch self-interest, prevailed over long-range sound judgment. . . . a mass psychological breakdown in March 1938 caused reversal of public opinion. . . . Many regarded the new situation as an ease of tension. Others welcome becoming citizens of a great power.[24]

With the change of a few words, the following passage could well have been written for Hong Kong:

> In the confused situation of the March (1938) days, the Austrian leaders were given no say in the plans that Hitler carried out for—or rather against—their own country. This was their last moment. Integrated almost immediately into the Nazi machinery, they had to pursue the total Anschluss solution in concert with the Fuhrer's will. For many of them, Austria soon became only a memory, perhaps a pathetic irrelevance, hopeless from the start.[25]

Speaking of the feeling of "helpless abandon and chilling fear which led to an affirmative vote of 99.7 percent of the electorate" in a plebiscite for Anschluss, another observer wrote the following with an equally familiar ring: "Even critical eye-witnesses of the events of those first few weeks find it as difficult to criticize the passivity of a stunned and bewildered population as to communicate to others the atmosphere of hysteria and fright."[26]

Behind the seeming euphoria in Hong Kong, the mood of resignation and gloom remains. Specific reactions and options vary a great deal with individuals and with one's background. The elite have many options, including emigration, taking a wait-and-see posture or "strategic readjustment." These options are by no means mutually exclusive. The high-level professionals and managers likewise have their options and can count on their skills and financial resources and contacts. Under the top layer of the elite and the professionals are the vast majority of Hong Kong residents whose options are severely limited. Among this silent majority are nearly 3 million refugees from mainland China who dread the prospect of returning to communism.

K.C. Chan, one of the two UMELCO members who refused to endorse the Joint Declaration, stated his reasons bluntly: "Over 2.7 million people had experience with political turmoil in China in the past and they will never believe China's promises.[27]

J.J. Swaine, the other abstaining member, called the agreement "the best of a bad deal," which Britain negotiated "with one arm tied behind her back." He warned that "infiltration of the system and suppression of dissent by pressure or fear is a great danger."[28]

Another member of the top elite, Lo Tak-shing, resigned his position as a senior member of the UMELCO in protest after the signing of the agreement. Lo, a prominent lawyer, went on to organize a company called the Hong Kong Freedom of Movement and Rights of Abode Ltd., to provide information and advice on immigration and investment opportunities abroad. He spoke of the need to provide a "fire exit, a safety net, and an option" for the Hong Kong people "who were suddenly confronted with the prospect of being thrust into the unknown."[29] Allen Lee, who also served on the UMELCO, said his business acquaintances were getting visas to other countries simply as an insurance. He said that he expected many of them to wait and see after 1997.[30]

Unfortunately, courageous leaders are difficult to find. Many have quietly moved their investments elsewhere while publicly speaking of Hong Kong's future in glowing terms. Others, including most of the sitting UMELCO members destined to play an active role in the years to come, are quick to become "political chameleons," in the words of one observer, eager to curry favor with Hong Kong's future masters despite their own well-known private misgivings and their intimate knowledge of people's fears and aspirations.[31]

Among the young professionals and Western-trained managers, the underlying concern about Hong Kong's future also runs deep. Numbering in the tens of thousands and just below the elite, they are the backbone of the vibrant Hong Kong economy. "They may not hold a foreign passport, but their talents and skills are much in demand by foreign companies. Employment with a foreign company is a ticket out if need be," a seasoned observer recently wrote.[32] "It is the hearts, minds and intentions of these people that will determine the future of Hong Kong," according to Jimmy D. McGregor, director of the Hong Kong Chamber of Commerce.[33] Two typical examples of this group can be cited. Christine Loh, a 28-year-old executive in the colony's financial district, said "it is all very well to say that we now have an agreement, but there is no guarantee that it will work out." She added: "I am still reserving the right to leave Hong Kong or to stay. I haven't made up my mind yet."[34] She was joined by Lawrence Chiu, a 36-year old director of a large investment firm: "To me, the fundamental uncertainty remains."[35] A British businessman in Hong Kong said: "I don't know of a single Chinese executive of tertiary education or successful business who has not worked out plans to leave.... The only people who say they won't leave are those who have no chance."[36]

Indeed, those who have no chance, particularly those who have fled the mainland, are in the majority. What is at stake is their very future, over which they have no control. For them, the fear and distrust of Beijing are deep and pervasive. A local financial daily, *Xin Bao*, summed up the mood best when it posed the question: "once Hong Kong becomes 'internal,' will Beijing [Peking] keep its promise?"[37]

Here is a typical case of one with tragic personal experiences, now hopelessly waiting to be returned to communism from which he escaped several years ago. Dismissing some "nationalistic" university students in Hong Kong as naive in their newly acquired sense of pride over Hong Kong's impending return to the "motherland," the intellectual emigrant said that what these students do not understand is that "first there must be regard for human dignity. Only then can one talk about *Chinese* dignity."[38] This emigrant was painfully educated as a nationalistic student who returned to the motherland from abroad in the 1950s imbued with a sense of pride and dignity. Expressing the kind of despair and resignation typical of the vast majority who cannot afford to leave, he said recently: "The doomsday fear is deepening here. We just don't know what to do." Speaking of his two teenage children who were spoiled by the material comforts in Hong Kong and are unconcerned about the perils awaiting them, he added: "If only they had been through the Cultural Revolution, they would not be like this!" He was joined by his wife, who managed, however, to transform her sense of despair to pity and hope for the next generation: "For us the 97 question is a constant worry. We just hope that our children will study hard so that when they finish high school, they can go to America for a college education. We fervently hope that the next generation can live in greater freedom and happiness than we have."[39]

This sentiment was shared by a group of individuals who commented on Hong Kong's future in similar terms: "We do not care what happens to Hong Kong for our own sake. We worry for our children."[40] Another intellectual, also an emigrant from the mainland, is convinced that Deng Xiaoping is ready to sacrifice Hong Kong's economic interest in favor of unfettered sovereignty. Citing an internal speech by Deng to high party cadres in 1984, he believes that Deng "wants to go down in history as the reunifier of China."[41]

Even a Communist cadre, on a recent business trip to Hong Kong, was shocked by the "97 phobia" among the people there. He admitted that he was completely unaware of this phobia while on the mainland. He said he never realized that people in Hong Kong "are more afraid of 97 than people on the mainland are afraid of class struggle!" He then commented that "if only we had waited another eight to ten years to raise the question of the return of Hong Kong's sovereignty, I am sure the 97 phobia would not be this serious here." In conclusion he said that, "Mandarin Deng is too impatient at this time!"[42] Desperately hoping that the British can somehow continue to provide some protection after 1997, one Hong Kong resident even suggested that the Sino-British liaison group should continue to function for 50 years after 1997 to "make sure there will be no change." "We want to be sure that Hong Kong's prosperity and stability continue, and that Hong Kong is truly run by the people of Hong Kong."[43]

In a public opinion survey conducted by the Assessment Office, specifically regarding Annex II of the Joint Declaration and the Sino-British Joint Liaison Group, the possibility for the Joint Liaison Group to operate beyond the year 2000 to 2047 was also raised in many responses.[44]

Popular sentiments are in many ways reflected in the Assessment Office report. Although a "preordained" document designed to give the agreement the expected ex post facto endorsement, the report does contain views expressed by what it characterizes as a "minority of individuals" and "a small number of organizations" that are significant.[45] Raw statistics can, however, be interpreted in ways to suit one's purposes. Qualitatively, therefore, it would seem absurd to equate a simple voice from the bandwagon with a heart-rending cry of fear and despair. It is in this sense that the views of the "minority of individuals" and "a small number of organizations" are worth careful noting.

The report states, with statistical precision, that out of a total of 430 professional and civic organizations, "an overwhelming majority of 334 have placed on record" the support of their members for the agreement, while relegating to a footnote certain important facts: that the Bar Association was unable to "pass a resolution recommending the ratification of the draft agreement"; that the Law Society "would not give its views on the draft agreement"; and that the Hong Kong Observers, formed by a group of concerned intellectuals, called the Assessment Office "a farce."[46]

Impersonal tabulations are cited to support the Assessment Office's conclusion that "most of the people of Hong Kong find the draft agreement acceptable," whereas the "proposition" that an agreement is preferable to "there being no agreement"—a thinly veiled threat—is "generally understood and accepted."[47] However, the details of individual responses, as always, reveal much more in terms of the depth of feelings and anxieties. The following two responses cited in the report are typical: "It is difficult to foresee the future. The draft agreement is a post-dated cheque. The result can only be known when it is proved." "The worry about Hong Kong being governed by people from Beijing or from the left-wing cannot be removed simply by the initializing of the draft agreement."[48]

The report states that in a number of cases "people expressed sadness at the severance of the link with Britain and the socio-economic system it has provided; disappointment at Britain's inability to maintain the status quo; resentment at the lack of involvement in the talks and frustration at the fact that the draft agreement could not be altered."[49] It cites the following representative response:

> [Because] I belong to the middle income group who do not have the means to emigrate to other countries and because I was born and educated in Hong Kong, I would wish to stay in Hong Kong. For the purpose of your statistics you can classify me as one of those who would accept the draft agreement, but I hope you will also take into account that I only accept it with much reluctance and with many reservations about the feasibility of its implementation. My heart is not truly at ease and I [do not have] full confidence in our future. The whole thing has not been a very fair play to us because we have not had any say and there is no other alternative other than not to have an agreement at all.[50]

In a vain effort, some even tried to challenge the validity of the agreement and the right of Britain and China to determine the future of Hong Kong, arguing either for the status quo or for self-determination. "They should render early support for the Hong Kong people to determine their own destiny by way of a referendum so as to avert the fate of future persecution by the Communists," declared the Cotton Bleaching and Dyeing Free Workers Union.[51]

The report cites "a minority of individuals" who rejected the draft agreement because they saw the basic incompatibility of the two systems. Recounting China's past history of political upheaval and their own past experiences, they appealed to the British government for compassion and moral responsibility as shown in the following two responses:

The British government ought to have compassion on those people who fled the cruelties of Communist China to Hong Kong so as to assist in resettling them elsewhere.

Britain cannot simply rescind a historic and moral responsibility of looking after her subjects. These people are legally British and cannot be made stateless.[52]

Left to their own devices and trying to do what they can under the circumstances, many people in Hong Kong have begun to organize. Denis Bray, a former secretary for home affairs, has warned: "If those who have built Hong Kong into the prosperous place it is today make no effort to preserve this prosperity, then there is real danger that this prosperity will be destroyed by those who do not understand the underlying realities of life in Hong Kong."[53] The recent local board elections saw more active participation than before and several political groups have formed as precursors of political parties. "If Hong Kong people don't want to run their affairs, China will send its own people," declared Yeung Sam, a leader of one such group. He added: "We want to fight for more chance to participate, and Britain should help us before it is too late."[54]

Already, prominent local leaders, including wealthy business people and active UMELCO members, are jockeying for power.[55] Whatever their motivations, the popular base of those leaders and groups remain to be proved. The public is still apathetic. As one observer put it, after living in an apolitical environment for decades, Hong Kong's people cannot be expected to "switch on to politics at a snap of a finger."[56] Above all, there is the prevailing mood of resignation on the part of the Hong Kong people over their inability to control the future of the territory. "In the end, Hong Kong's future lies in the hands of Beijing, so why should we bother?"[57]

Albert Hirschman, in his *Exit, Voice, and Loyalty*, wrote of exit and voice as two options in the decision-making process. Citing the exit from Europe in the seventeenth century and the "go-West" movement in nineteenth-century America, he eloquently said that "the United States owes its very existence and growth to the millions of decisions favoring exit over voice."[58] Unfortunately for most people in Hong Kong, such options do not exist.

THE PRC GOVERNMENT

To examine the PRC government's position on Hong Kong from the human rights point of view, one must logically start from the government's position on human rights in general. Two questions can be raised at the outset: How does Beijing define human rights? What is Beijing's human rights record? In the answers to these two questions will be seen Beijing's human rights position on Hong Kong.[59]

To Beijing, the "slogan" of human rights that includes freedom and equality is of Western origin, a product of Western history. According to this view, it was raised by the bourgeoisie to oppose feudalism, as in the American and French revolutions. Corrupted by the bourgeoisie, universal validity of human rights has been superceded by scientific Marxism. A sweeping explanation along these lines can be found in an authoritative article in the official press:

> History shows, on the one hand, the slogan of human rights has played an important role in breaking through the shackles of feudal ideology, encouraging people to rise to fight and propel the bourgeois revolution, and on the other hand, the slogan of human rights is after all a slogan of the bourgeoisie. Although it includes all nominal universal principles of man, in reality, it is nothing but the right of the bourgeoisie. In [the] capitalist society, the capitalists occupy the means of production and monopolize the ideology in society and propaganda machine.... It is not strange that the slogan of human rights was later turned into a tool for the imperialists and bourgeoisie to attack the proletariat and socialism....
>
> Unlike the slogan of human rights which reflects bourgeois ideas such as freedom and equality, Marxism puts forward the scientific viewpoint of freedom and equality. ...Establishment of the proletarian democratic dictatorship, abolition of private property, elimination of classes and eventual realization of Communism are the definitive Marxist statement on the equality and freedom of man.[60]

By rejecting the bourgeois "slogan" of human rights and by officially falling back on a rigid Marxist line, Beijing has sought to put the PRC in a category outside the Western concept of human rights and thus to avoid criticism from the West. Given this position, it is not surprising that Beijing's record on human rights is not enviable. As a totalitarian state under one-party rule, the PRC is a place where Western concepts of freedom, equality, and human dignity are only dimly understood and seldom practiced, especially by those who wield power at different levels. Coming out of one of the worst abuses of human rights in history during the Cultural Revolution, a major theme forcefully and painfully pursued by writers in their literary works has been the search and reaffirmation of human nature and the dignity of humankind.[61]

Although conditions have improved measurably since the end of the Maoist era, there has been no fundamental change either of the system or of the ideology, despite the current modernization drive. Indeed, Beijing has taken pains to tell the outside world that politically and ideologically, it has not abandoned socialism in favor of capitalism while rushing to borrow capitalist tools to rescue the nation's economy from near ruins caused by Maoist mismanagement. The "four insistings"—insisting on a socialist road, insisting on a proletarian dictatorship, insisting on Communist party leadership, and insisting on Marxism-Leninism and Mao Thought—have been repeatedly stressed in official pronouncements.

In the wake of the now famous *People's Daily* editorial on December 7,

1984, suggesting that Marxism-Leninism should not be relied upon to solve all of today's problems, a top Beijing Marxist theorist toured leading U.S. universities to explain that the PRC had not abandoned and would not abandon Marxism, but it would continue creatively to apply basic Marxist tenets to present-day China conditions. He particularly stressed the difference between what he called "structural" change and "systemic" change. What is taking place in China, he stressed, is structural change within the unchanged system.[62] The current economic reform, in other words, need not be accompanied by relaxation and freedoms in other areas such as freedom of speech and the tolerance of dissent. Indeed, the Amnesty International has found just the opposite in recent years with known cases of human rights violation on the increase.[63] Given this domestic record, it is a small wonder that the people of Hong Kong are deeply worried about the prospect of living under such a system.

There is no indication that Beijing understands or cares about the freedoms and the rule of the law that the people of Hong Kong now enjoy, and there is no indication that Beijing really wants to give the people of Hong Kong control over the future government of Hong Kong. Swept under the waves of nationalism in the name of sovereignty, the people of Hong Kong are justifiably worried about losing what they possess.

To the PRC, the issue concerning Hong Kong is one of sovereignty, not how the people there feel. The return of sovereignty to China is a matter of nationalism and therefore cannot be questioned. All that remains to be done is to give assurance to the people of Hong Kong that things would not change without bothering to find out what they are thinking. When three leading UMELCO members went to Beijing in late June 1984 to plead the Hong Kong people's case, Deng Xiaoping gave them a cool reception, telling them they could not speak for the people of Hong Kong because they were appointed to their posts by the British government and not elected. On their return to Hong Kong, the three told a news conference that they did not think Deng understood the concerns of the people of Hong Kong about falling under Chinese Communist rule. "We don't think we have convinced the Chinese leaders that there is a confidence problem in Hong Kong," said Sir S.Y. Chung, one of the three traveling UMELCO members whom Deng criticized for succumbing to a colonial mentality. Instead of listening, Deng lectured them: "Generally speaking, you have said that Hong Kong people do not have confidence. This is really your view, that you have no trust in the PRC. You said you have trust only in me. That's empty talk."[64]

Later, Deng made it clear to two other delegations from Hong Kong that the region would be run by local Chinese "patriots" after 1997. "We don't require them all to favor China's socialist system, but only ask them to love the motherland and Hong Kong," Deng said. Appealing to nationalism, he added: "[Hong Kong] must be administered by Hong Kong residents with patriotic Chinese as the main body."[65] Thousands of party cadres have already been sent in and recruitment of new party members will soon begin in Hong Kong. The local residents know full well there will be no shortage of "patriotic" Chinese in Hong Kong to run the region after 1997.

Deng's impatience and brusque way only added to the uneasiness. "Our policies toward Hong Kong will remain unchanged for 50 years and we mean what we say," he told the delegations from Hong Kong, suggesting that his personal assurance was all that was needed.[66] Earlier on television, he declared that troops would be stationed in Hong Kong after 1997, and he rudely scolded the former defense minister and the former foreign minister for suggesting the opposite, causing a near panic in the Hong Kong stock market.[67] Whether or not he realized it, Deng's emperorlike behavior was a strong factor contributing to the deepening of the crisis of confidence in Hong Kong. "Deng is an aging peasant revolutionary with very little knowledge of the outside world and no understanding of what makes Hong Kong tick," observed a Hong Kong-based Western diplomat. He also pointed out Deng's personal reason to be anxious about Hong Kong's return: "If he succeeds, he will be known in history for getting Hong Kong back."[68]

How long will Beijing tolerate Hong Kong with its freedoms? What impact will this have on the mainland? How does Beijing keep the ideological "Hong-Kongization" from spreading over the mainland? These are fundamental questions Deng has not answered; but they are the questions reflecting the Hong Kong people's fear that what they have possessed until now will by necessity be taken away, long before the 50-year guarantee period expires, when Hong Kong becomes an integral part of China, subject to "internal" rules and all of the uncertainties in the PRC.

THE THIRD PARTIES

What can the third party do to help the people of Hong Kong insofar as their human rights are concerned? Third-party countries have only provided havens for those people of Hong Kong who can afford to leave, but they have done little to help the others. Already, there is an influx of immigrants and capital from Hong Kong at several major North American cities with heavy Chinese concentrations. There is an adage in the New York Chinese circles that the Hong Kong Chinese already own Vancouver and half of San Francisco, are buying up Toronto, and will work on New York.[69] In the Flushing area of New York City, one half of the 50,000 ethnic Chinese in the thriving new "Chinatown" are recent immigrants from Hong Kong. "It's mostly Yuppies: engineers, doctors, attorneys as well as restaurant people," one community worker reported.[70] In the U.S. Congress, bills are introduced in both houses to raise the annual quota of immigrants from Hong Kong to 5,000 from the present 600.[71] In the Republic of China on

Taiwan, the government feels a special responsibility for the fellow Chinese in Hong Kong. Plans are made to welcome the Hong Kong people who are willing to immigrate by simplifying procedures, allowing them dual nationality and offering assistance for investment in the local economy.[72]

By providing immigration and investment opportunities, however, the third-party countries are helping only a small affluent minority in Hong Kong, leaving untouched the great majority of Hong Kong people who are unable to emigrate and therefore are most vulnerable. The general belief seems to be that a third party, for example, the United States, holds little leverage despite the fact that it may have heavy financial stakes in Hong Kong's present and future. Although holding 47 percent of all direct foreign investment in Hong Kong manufacturing, "Washington can only speak softly and hope the Chinese will keep Hong Kong as an open door between the regimented society and the outside world and an open door for technology, ideas and goods that are predominantly American in origin," as observed by a veteran observer.[73] He praised the Hong Kong people's hard work and untrammeled enterprise as particularly "inspiring" to Americans but spoke of Hong Kong's future in somber terms: "The greatest hope... lies in Hong Kong's increasing role in accelerating the present alteration of the PRC from a Marxist-Leninist dictatorship that turned its back on European and American ways to a less oppressively authoritarian regime that looks outward for inspiration."[74]

To attach Hong Kong's future to such uncertain hope, fashionable among many countries now scrambling for China trade, appears to be an abdication of moral responsibility to the people of Hong Kong who will soon be forced to trade their present freedoms and basic human rights for a Marxist-Leninist dictatorship. Is it true that Washington and the West in general—the major suppliers of technology to the PRC—have no leverage on the PRC concerning the future welfare of the Hong Kong people? Is it conceivable, for example, to insist on a linkage between technology transfer and respect for human rights? This linkage has been the time-honored U.S. policy toward the Soviet Union.

In addition, there is no reason why Western nations and Japan should not boldly speak out on the human rights of the people of Hong Kong before world forums, including the United Nations, to keep the issue alive in the public conscience. Indeed, the people of Hong Kong themselves have suggested that their rights and freedoms should be protected by filing complaints, if necessary, with the Human Rights Committee of the United Nations.[75] Unfortunately, such prospects do not look good, for "the reality is that the very nations who should be most concerned about securing Hong Kong against the vagaries of Chinese Communism are themselves blindly scrambling to attach financial fortunes and geopolitical schemes to the swirling uncertainties of China's future."[76]

NOTES

1. Chalmers Johnson, "The Mousetrapping of Hong Kong: A Game in Which Nobody Wins," *Asian Survey*, Vol. 24, no. 9 (Sept. 1984), p. 900.

2. Evan Luard, *Britain and China* (London: Chatto & Windus, 1962), p. 179.

3. Johnson, "The Mousetrapping of Hong Kong," p. 901.

4. Ibid.

5. Emily Lau, "Scramble for Power," *Far Eastern Economic Review*, Vol. 130, no. 16 (Apr. 18, 1985), p. 46. Hereafter cited as *FEER*.

6. See the following excerpts from the press conference:

(Beacroft) Nick Beacroft, Radio Hong Kong. Referring to the white paper, Sir Edward, Her Majesty's government says there is no possibility of an amended agreement, and the alternative to acceptance of the present agreement is to have no agreement at all. Therefore, why bother to have an assessment office? Is it like some labor MPs have said, who have visited the territory, just window dressing?

(Youde) The reason for having an assessment office is very simple. It is that it has always been stated that the objective was to find an agreement which could be acceptable to the people of Hong Kong. It is therefore in my mind, essential to be sure that the people of Hong Kong do have an opportunity to state their view on the acceptability of the agreement as a whole, and the assessment office is a very good way of giving them the opportunity to do that. I cannot think why anybody would wish to deny them that opportunity.

(Beacroft) But if they say no, what will happen?

(Youde) I recommend the agreement to the people of Hong Kong because I believe that it is a good agreement and it is an agreement which I believe they will find acceptable, so the question is hypothetical.

(Biddulph) Jim Biddulph, BBC. What if people say it's not agreeable? You say it's hypothetical, but surely you have given them the opportunity to say yes or no. What if they say no?

(Youde) Well, the answer is set out in the white paper where the UK government made quite clear that there is to be a transition in 1997. It can be a transition on the basis of what I believe to be a good and acceptable agreement, or a transition without that agreement. I have little doubt as to which is the best course.

"Governor Sir Edward Youde's Press Conference on PRC-UK Declaration on Hong Kong," *Foreign Broadcast Information Service, China*, Sept. 28, 1984, p. W1. Hereafter cited as *FBIS*.

7. James Bartholomew, "The Short Goodbye," *FEER*, Vol. 129, no. 51 (Dec. 20, 1984), p. 16.

8. "Iron Lady Defends Pact," *Hong Kong Standard*, Dec. 22, 1984, p. 2.

9. Ibid.

10. Ibid.

11. Ibid.

12. Azumao Kocho, "Wang Guangying yu Huzhang Dongfu de jingcai duihua [An Interesting Conversation between Wang Guangying and Azumao Kocho]," *Jing Bao* [*The Mirror*], no. 1 (Jan. 1985), p. 20.

13. Johnson, "The Mousetrapping of Hong Kong," p. 886.

14. Ibid., pp. 900–901.

15. Christopher S. Wren, "Hong Kong Stew: And Now a Dash of Democracy," *New York Times*, July 17, 1984, p. A2.

16. "Survey Asks British Protection, Shows No Confidence in Chinese Guarantee," *Zhong Bao* [*Centre Daily News*], May 10, 1984, p. 9.

17. "Britain to Relinquish Hong Kong," *New Haven Register*, Apr. 21, 1984, p. 8.

18. Emily Lau, "Time to Face the Challenge of 1997," *FEER*, Vol. 129, no. 47 (Nov. 22, 1984), p. 32.

19. Ibid., p. 33.

20. Zhongguo Xinwenshe Correspondent, "1984 in Hong Kong in Retrospect," Dec. 31, 1984, in *FBIS*, *China*, Jan. 2, 1985, p. E3.

21. Helen Goebel, "Poll Shows Hong Kong People Helpless over 1997 Problem," *Free China Journal* (Taiwan), Feb. 3, 1985, p. 1.

22. "Stocks Surge in Hong Kong," *New York Times*, May 6, 1985, p. D12.

23. Radomir Luza, *Austro-German Relations in the Anschluss Era* (Princeton, N.J.: Princeton University Press, 1975), p. 52.

24. Ibid.

25. Ibid., p. 48.

26. Karl R. Stadler, *Austria* (New York: Praeger, 1971), pp. 152, 183.

27. *Arrangement for Testing the Acceptability in Hong Kong of the Draft Agreement on the Future of the Territory, Report of the Assessment Office and Report of the Independent Monitoring Team* (Hong Kong: Hong Kong Government Printer, Nov. 1984), p. 41. Hereafter cited as *Report*.

28. Ibid.

29. Emily Lau and Mary Lee, "Hong Kong: More Problems Ahead," *FEER*, Vol. 130, no. 2 (Jan. 10, 1985), p. 21.

30. Wren, "Hong Kong Stew," p. A2.

31. Lau, "Time to Face the Challenge of 1997," pp. 32–33.

32. Steve Lohr, "Hong Kong, Despite Accord, Is Still on Edge," *New York Times*, Aug. 5, 1984, p. A6.

33. Ibid.

34. Ibid.

35. Ibid.

36. Wren, "Hong Kong Stew," p. A2.

37. Miriam London and Ta-ling Lee, "Hong Kong: Before the Anschluss," *The American Spectator*, Vol. 17, no. 11 (Nov. 1984), p. 30.

38. Ibid.

39. Personal Correspondence, July 30, 1984.

40. *Report*, p. 31.

41. London and Lee, "Hong Kong: Before the Anschluss," p. 31.

42. Li Min, "Dengdaren chaozhi guojile [Mandarin Deng Is too Impatient]," *Cheng Ming* (Hong Kong), no. 82 (Aug. 1984), p. 18.

43. Chau Men, "Yingjiandu liushisan nian [Supervision Should Last Sixty-three Years]," *Cheng Ming* (Hong Kong), no. 82 (Aug. 1984), p. 16.

44. *Report*, p. 28.

45. Ibid., pp. 19, 20.

46. Ibid., p. 17. (The footnote, by the way, avoided harsher criticisms altogether. For example, in her *FEER* column, "Time to Face the Challenge of 1997," p. 33,

Emily Lau reported that the Assessment Office has been thoroughly discredited, being labeled as a "charade to mask a diplomatic defeat," "a farce," and "a sick joke.")

47. Ibid., p. 15.

48. Ibid., p. 19.

49. Ibid.

50. Ibid.

51. Ibid., p. 20.

52. Ibid.

53. Lau and Lee, "Hong Kong: More Problems Ahead," p. 21.

54. Wren, "Hong Kong Stew," p. A2.

55. Lau, "Scramble for Power," p. 43.

56. Lau and Lee, "Hong Kong: More Problems Ahead," p. 21.

57. Emily Lau, "A New Political Era," *FEER*, Vol. 130, no. 8 (Feb. 21, 1985), p. 26.

58. Albert Hirschman, *Exit, Voice, and Loyalty* (Cambridge, Mass.: Harvard University Press, 1970), p. 106.

59. A recent book on human rights in the People's Republic of China is John F. Copper, Franz Michael, and Yuan-li Wu, *Human Rights in Post-Mao China* (Boulder, Colo.: Westview Press, 1985).

60. "Commentary," *Heilongjiang Ribao* (Harbin), May 20, 1981, p. 3, in *FBIS, China*, June 17, 1981, p. k17.

61. This theme is most pronounced in the so-called wounded literature that came out during the early years of the post-Mao era, when writers poured out their hearts about the Cultural Revolution in their writings. Most representative of these works is Dai Houying, *Ren Ah Ren!* [*People, Oh People!*] (Guangdong: Huacheng chubanshe, 1980).

62. Su Shaozhi, director of the Institute of Marxism, Leninism and Mao Zedong Thought, Chinese Academy of Social Sciences, toured the United States in April 1985 and delivered lectures at Harvard, Columbia, and Yale universities among other places. See "Beijing bingwei fangqi Makesi lilun [Beijing Has Not Abandoned Marxism]," *Zhong Bao* [*Centre Daily News*], Apr. 1, 1985, p. 2, for his Columbia lecture. I attended his lecture at Yale on April 12, 1985.

63. *China: Violations of Human Rights* (London: Amnesty International Publications, 1984), pp. 5–51, 83.

64. Christopher S. Wren, "Some in Hong Kong Question Peking's Intentions," *New York Times*, July 1, 1984, p. A10.

65. "China Plans 'Patriotic' Hong Kong," *New Haven Register*, July 1, 1984, p. A16.

66. Ibid.

67. "Deng Xiaoping Announces Troops in Hong Kong after '97," *Zhong Bao* [*Centre Daily News*], May 26, 1984, p. 1.

68. Christopher S. Wren, "Hong Kong as Territorial Imperative," *New York Times*, July 22, 1984, p. E4.

69. Marvine Howe, "Hong Kong's Plight Alters Look of Flushing," *New York Times*, Apr. 14, 1984, p. A1.

70. Ibid.

71. "Senate Bill Proposes Sharp Increase in Hong Kong Immigrants," *Zhong Bao* [*Centre Daily News*], Apr. 3, 1985, p. 4.

72. "Nationalist Government Welcomes Hong Kong People to Settle in Taiwan," *Zhong Bao* [*Centre Daily News*], March 16, 1984, p. 1.

73. Robert Elegant, "Our Hong Kong Connection," *Parade*, July 15, 1984, pp. 8–9.

74. Ibid.

75. *Report*, p. 27.

76. London and Lee, "Hong Kong: Before the Anschluss," p. 31.

6

In the Shadow of 1997: Interaction between Hong Kong and Its Economic Partners and Neighbors

YUAN-LI WU

THE NATURE OF THE GAME

The Chinese authorities are well aware of the economic importance of Hong Kong to the People's Republic of China (PRC), and this is the basic reason why the Sino-British Agreement of 1984 proposed to maintain the prosperity of Hong Kong under a basic law that would try to preserve the same conditions under which Hong Kong has been able to operate until now for another 50 years after 1997. One might assume, therefore, that given rational behavior on the part of the Chinese, there would be no further question about the future of Hong Kong. One can find further support for an optimistic prognostication by pointing to the relative calm Hong Kong has enjoyed since the signing of the agreement.[1]

However, other factors must also be considered. First, fires that rage out of control may be started in various ways: by persons who underestimate the pains they can cause their perpetrators, by children who play with matches and accidentally start them, and by those who fail to gauge how quickly a small conflagration can spread. The assumption of rational behavior on the part of PRC leaders after 1997 also overlooks the fact that the transfer of sovereignty from British to Chinese hands is tantamount to a radical change in one of the principal parameters of Chinese calculations of benefits and costs. There is a distinct possibility that rational behavior after 1997 will not be identical to rational behavior before that time. At least twice in recent history the Chinese Communists had the possibility of overrunning Hong Kong; both times they stopped short of doing so. This happened in 1950 when the victorious People's Liberation Army took South China and could have driven right across the border into the New Territories. A second time came when Maoist radicals were in control of Beijing during the Cultural Revolution and stirred up a disturbance in Hong Kong that could have spelled much deeper trouble for the colony's administration than it actually did. In the first case, a Chinese takeover would have led to far wider diplomatic consequences than a mere confrontation with Great Britain. British recognition was more important than whatever military power and resistance Britain might have mustered at that time. On the second occasion, the radicals in Beijing and the Red Guards running rampant at Mao's urging were primarily battling their domestic enemies; they were not preoccupied with foreign affairs. Thus in both instances cooler heads prevailed. Had Hong Kong been under Chinese sovereignty but British administered, it is difficult to assert with assurance that a Communist takeover would not have occurred in the early 1950s had there been no Korean War.[2] Under similar conditions, a revolutionary committee could very well have been organized in Hong Kong in 1967–1968, which might then have gotten out of control. The point is whether the removal of an important external constraint to drastic Chinese Communist action might not in the future alter Chinese behavior and reduce caution.

Still another factor to be considered is the impact of China's, as well as Hong Kong's, actions on other nations, partners as well as competitors, in the two parties' respective economic and political relations and the resultant interaction among them. How would the British, the Japanese, the Americans, and the Republic of China on Taiwan react before and after 1997, in response to their particular perceptions of Chinese Communist policy and its impact on Hong Kong as well as Hong Kong's impact on China? Will the Chinese action produce responses on the part of other nations that are stabilizing in their effect on Hong Kong or will they have the opposite effect? Timing will make a difference. Anticipation of certain developments after 1997 may result in actions both before and after that date. The effects of these actions may or may not be immediately visible. In short, one has to think in terms of dynamic relationships, with anticipation, uncertainty, and divergent strategies being employed by "players" who do not necessarily share the same interest in a complex "game" in which it is sometimes hard to distinguish the pawns from the players. Since alternative courses of development after 1997 are theoretically possible, one should look for the plausible and probable developments and be prepared for such developments. How will other countries' approach affect Hong Kong? These are issues that need to be explored.

LAW, ORDER AND FAIR COMPETITION

At the risk of some overlapping with previous discussion, it is, nevertheless, useful to enumerate sequentially the principal conditions under British rule that have made Hong Kong a prosperous and developing economy expanding from a port for transit trade to a world trade, manufacturing, and international banking center in the post–World War II period. The first among these conditions has been the maintenance of law and order under a system where arbitrary rule by the courts can be discounted and where minimal governmental intervention in business operations within the private sector can be counted upon. The Chinese Communists have promised continuation of the same kind of "legal" system but suffer from three disadvantages. First, the Basic Law for Hong Kong has not been drafted. One must, therefore, wait to see what will become of it in the drafting. Second, the Chinese Communist concept of law, like that of the Soviet Union, is the codification of rules to be followed by the individuals, but those rules are subservient to the policy of the Chinese Communist party and will change with it. Law is not, as in the West, meant to protect the rights of the individuals. Third, by any objective standard, Communist rule in China since 1949 has not been able to inspire confidence in those in power either in their benevolence or in their truthfulness.[3]

If the future Hong Kong government is to adopt the work style of Beijing, not only that of Mao, especially in his final decade, but even that of the present Dengist reformist government, it would probably be more than a little inclined toward intervention in the court's operations. The Chinese Communist legal system and work style have never favored an independent judiciary. Arbitrary intervention in the performance of contracts and in free-market operations would seem to be entirely natural and consistent with Chinese practice to date. In that case business contracts may no longer be entirely determined by the market. With the expectation of a greater role to be played by mainland-related enterprises after the Chinese takeover of Hong Kong, economic favoritism may be practiced as it has been practiced in Beijing. This work style of corruption and favoritism based on special relationships to be dispensed by those in power is probably endemic in the PRC, independent of which Communist faction is in power. The situation might even become worse under the conservative Communists who are more prone to intervene than under the radicals who do not know the difference between intervention and everyday governance. For many years, especially since the conclusion of the 1984 agreement, there have been noticeable PRC attempts to infiltrate Hong Kong institutions and to seize real control of the economy and of key organizations in Hong Kong. These efforts to increase the number of Communist-trained activists in Hong Kong's electorate and political scene only enhance the likelihood of a more flexible and pliant court system amendable to PRC suggestions.

TAXATION AND LABOR COST

A second reason Hong Kong has prospered is its relatively low tax burden.[4] This low tax is partially a result of the nature of the British colonial government, which has not been as concerned about economic and social welfare as a popularly elected government that must be more responsive to the vast majority of the population. However, until now the Hong Kong government seems to have met the minimum requirements of the population, perhaps because many who had come from China have been able to look forward to an improved economic well being and, for a small number, the possibility of eventually emigrating with their savings garnered through hard work. After the PRC's takeover, however, since China wants to derive a large and hopefully increasing flow of foreign-exchange income from Hong Kong, one may reasonably expect that China might take the measures of transferring it unilaterally to China in some form, including taxation. The key issue is how much the increase will be. This increase tends to become higher if the PRC's budget requirements demand it. This is not only a matter of the central government's budget but also one of the provincial Guangdong (Kwangtung) government's budget. The provincial budget is relevant because Hong Kong borders this southernmost Chinese province from which it draws both water and food and is no less dependent upon the province than upon China as a whole. This dependence can and probably will become very costly if fiscal conditions on the Chinese side are deteriorating either due to failure in the current economic reform or in the case of successful economic expansion, an increasing demand for investment financing. Both provincial politics on the other side of the border and factional strife in the Central People's Government can be indirectly important factors affecting the tax burden in Hong Kong. In this connection, the Chinese Communists will have replaced the British government as a recipient of such remittances. At the same time, sale of public land for industrial development will no longer be a reliable source of government revenue as it was before the collapse of the local land boom. The private sector may also be required to bear unexpected burdens of government crisis intervention. Extra government spending during a financial crisis, even of non-Hong Kong origin, would probably have to be borne by the private sector, and such crises can be expected to occur from time to time. Furthermore, unilateral transfers may not be confined to taxes. Donations of some kind, such as "patriotic contributions," and higher price for supplying water, electricity, and other consumer goods may play an equally important role. Finally, the future Hong Kong government may increase its social expenditures more than the British administration, thus raising the demand for revenue.

A third condition concerning Hong Kong's success is that Hong Kong has benefited economically from low labor cost and a relatively nondisruptive labor market with little strife. An important reason for the low labor cost has been the continuing inflow of refugees from China at a regulated pace. Will a PRC-dominated Hong Kong government be able to keep the entry of PRC citizens into Hong Kong under control as before, based solely on Hong Kong's requirements? Can PRC authorities, for internal political reasons, justify a policy of regulated exit to Hong Kong against potential domestic party critics? Won't the PRC workers for their part be seeking entry into Hong Kong at a faster pace? That, however, depends upon the living and employment conditions in China. During the Great Proletarian Cultural Revolution and in 1962, at the time of the largest economic crisis China had experienced until then, the PRC authorities were either unable or unwilling to control the refugees' flight into Hong Kong. For highly placed PRC cadres, Hong Kong may serve both as a vacation resort and a potential place of personal and even family refuge. This immigration pressure from the PRC will increase if economic conditions in China are poor or if factional strife is rampant.

As long as Hong Kong can retain a degree of independence, it may be possible to keep wages low by maintaining immigration from China at the desired rate, but whether the labor cost will or will not rise is a different matter. After the Chinese takeover, disorderliness on the labor market may increase while the efficiency of labor may decline, and the social cost of maintaining labor peace may rise. These adverse effects may not be of the highest order in affecting the advantages Hong Kong has hitherto enjoyed in worldwide competition; the advantages are bound to decline after 1997. With an increasing demand for investment in social welfare and infrastructure, the tax burden is bound to rise as previous discussions suggested.

The next consideration is the supply of those skilled workers who have given Hong Kong a considerable advantage in its industrial and financial development. The supply of well-trained, white-collar workers and middle-level managers will probably fall. Some in this group may actually be drawn to China to work on business related to the foreign sector, either in foreign firms or in Chinese enterprises dealing with foreign customers, such as hotel workers, supervisors, and management. Other such white-collar workers may speed up their departure from Hong Kong as emigrants, that is, if emigrants from Hong Kong continue to be permitted by foreign governments elsewhere and if exit from the city remains free. If Hong Kong should suffer a decline in its international financial business, service workers in this sector will be less in demand, and they, too, may try to move to other occupations or areas.

PITFALLS A FREE FOREIGN-EXCHANGE MARKET PRESENTS

At the heart of Hong Kong's free economy is the free-exchange market, in which the Hong Kong dollar as an independent currency has enjoyed complete convertibility. The PRC has promised to maintain the Hong Kong dollar as a separate currency and to keep the free-exchange market. However, will a free-exchange market in Hong Kong and an independent Hong Kong dollar encourage the flight of capital from China if the underlying conditions of capital flight exist, and will this in turn undermine the maintenance of a strict balance-of-payments regime in the PRC's planning that is geared to the modernization and development of China itself rather than Hong Kong? The PRC's promise to allow the free-exchange market toop-erate in Hong Kong may come under pressure if Hong Kong becomes a gateway of capital flight from China to Hong Kong and from China and Hong Kong to other parts of the world. This condition that seems to be emerging may become worse as access to Hong Kong by Communist cadres and "capitalist roaders" becomes easier and such persons become more numerous.[5]

A related development would be the growth of commodity and currency smuggling between the PRC and Hong Kong. Import smuggling (aided and financed initially by overvaluation of legitimate imports and conversion of the excess foreign exchange received into private foreign bank deposits in Hong Kong) would require the maintenance of foreign-exchange accounts in Hong Kong banks by private or semiprivate residents in China. Additionally, export smuggling through undervaluation of legitimate exports and banking the excess payment received in Hong Kong for use later will have the same impact. Conversion of PRC currency into Hong Kong dollars could occur through the outward smuggling of PRC money and, therefore, result in the emergence of a black market of Chinese currency in Hong Kong. Alternatively, residents in China who cannot leave the country themselves may wish to put their money into a more reliable medium such as gold. This would encourage the inward smuggling of gold and foreign currencies. These are practices in which residents on both sides of the Hong Kong border are well versed.

If the Hong Kong exchange market is one of managed float or if it is virtually pegged as it has been since November 1983, the monetary authorities may find it necessary to intervene after 1997. If this transpires, one must ask whose reserves will be used for such a stabilization operation. Will the Bank of China be intervening on behalf of the Hong Kong government? Can one perceive the PRC's Bank of China intervening at the bidding of a still independent Hong Kong government? Will the independence of the Hong Kong government have to be compromised, or will the Bank of China push the responsibility onto the local monetary authorities and their exchange reserves? Would the alternative in such an eventuality be the abandonment of free convertibility of the Hong Kong dollar? Or will the local monetary authorities then be forced to resort to devaluation at frequent intervals? If and when Hong Kong dollars flood the exchange market in outward flight, the authorities undertaking the stabilization operation will have to absorb the Hong Kong dollars. Will this reduction in money supply be offset by the monetary authorities? The above issue of foreign-exchange reserves is tied to that of the identity of the final arbiter of money supply. Currently, Hong Kong does not have a central bank. Presumably, neither the British government nor the two major banks will continue to serve in both capacities after 1997. Who will be ultimately responsible for the Hong

Kong dollar both externally and internally? Tendencies toward intervening in the foreign exchange market are bound to encourage corruption in both China and Hong Kong. Such a development would reverberate on the maintenance of a fair and incorruptible government and court system and the strict enforcement of laws.

FREE TRADE AND FREE ACCESS TO THE WORLD

Parallel to the free-exchange market, Hong Kong's prosperity is built upon free trade, a prerequisite of which is free access to the world's markets and sources of supply. After 1997, however, trade control may become a potential option to Chinese economic planners given their innate inclination toward controls. If there is a large decline of Hong Kong exports to markets other than China, or if there is a serious drop of income from financial services, tourism, and so on, or if there is a large capital repatriation from Hong Kong, the Hong Kong balance-of-payments deficit could be very serious.

At the same time, Hong Kong's exports to the world outside China could decline as a result of action by Hong Kong's trade partners. Conceivably even the MFN (most favored nation) status and Hong Kong's present GSP (generalized system of preference) standing could be lost due to the transfer of sovereignty. How individual trade partners will treat the PRC and how Hong Kong will be treated under PRC sovereignty are both questions not yet resolved because the transfer is yet to come. Even if the question were resolved for the time being, the settlement would not necessarily remain unchanged over time if other circumstances change. A reduction of Hong Kong's textile and other quotas by counting some of these exports from Hong Kong under the PRC quota without increasing the latter should not be excluded as among such possibilities in the future. As a transit trade center, Hong Kong is not just an entrepôt redirecting a part of its imports, with or without repackaging, to other foreign destinations, nor is the China market the primary destination of its reexports. Goods imported from the PRC, largely from the Shenzhen Special Economic Zone (SEZ), for minor assembly and processing for reexportation to the United States as Hong Kong products are officially reported by the PRC as goods exported to Hong Kong (not to the United States). This practice has been a most important reason why U.S. statistics of imports from China have consistently exceeded Chinese statistics of exports to the United States. By not counting its exports to Hong Kong, especially of textiles and garments, which are subsequently reexported to the American market as exports to the United States, China has often reported a trade deficit vis-à-vis the United States and has used this phenomenon as an argument in bilateral negotiations to demand larger access to the American market. By counting China's exports originally manufactured there (including the Shenzhen SEZ), which have been reexported from Hong Kong after minor "transformation" (such as sewing together in Hong Kong the sleeves on knitwear made in China), the United States has reported much larger imports from China. This statistical discrepancy has blown up as a major political issue in the textile dispute between the United States and China that centers on the latter's use of Hong Kong's share in the textile import quotas of the United States. Clamping down on this practice, through, for instance, more stringent enforcement of a stricter certificate or origin system, could reduce Hong Kong's nominal exports, China's indirect exports, to the United States.

Still another consideration that has been at the root of Hong Kong's international economic prowess is the freedom to travel for business and personal reasons. What might happen to persons holding a local Hong Kong passport after 1997 is not yet clear. Will that person be freely admitted if admission to the United Kingdom is not automatic? Will that person be free to enter the PRC and leave at will? Will that person be required first to secure an exit permit from Hong Kong before going anywhere? Will the PRC directly or indirectly restrict exit from Hong Kong? For PRC citizens in Hong Kong, new entrants from the PRC into Hong Kong, and Hong Kong's present residents born anywhere, will there be differential treatment? Will foreign countries change their quotas for Hong Kong immigrants and visa regulations for travelers from Hong Kong? How does one differentiate if differentiation in visa regulations of different countries emerges? These are questions far beyond the already complex issue of Hong Kong residents holding a special type of British passport not being able to enter the United Kingdom. The latter issue may appear to be a complex legal question for Westminster and the British conscience, but the problems for Hong Kong citizens and residents and others who must be free to travel to and from Hong Kong after 1997 if they are to conduct business extend far beyond that one problem. (Ordinary business people, and perhaps tourists, undoubtedly will be caught up in a maze of international bureaucracy.)

Finally, might Hong Kong residents be picked up for internal exile in China on some pretext? This possibility is the reverse side of the freedom to travel, which might be regarded as a freedom not to travel. Will political kidnappings then follow? If the freedom to travel is restricted, Hong Kong's ability to maintain its position as a trading center would be seriously jeopardized.

FOREIGN INVESTORS' PROPERTY RIGHTS AND FINANCIAL PRIVACY

Since Hong Kong is not only a trade center but also a manufacturing and financial center, its investment climate is all important to its economic well being. Whether Hong Kong is good for foreign investment is a derivative issue based on all of the points already discussed, including the vital issue of capital repatriation. Conceivably, at some point in the future Hong Kong's otherwise free foreign-exchange market might be circumscribed by restrictions of outward capital movement. Will proceeds from the sale of an existing investment in Hong Kong, assuming that there still is a buyer, be repatriable in convertible currencies in ordinary times and during a crisis? In the case of U.S. investments in Hong Kong, this is a matter that eventually must be faced in the coverage of the investment treaty that has been under negotiation between Washington and Beijing. If such a treaty is signed and covers the risk of expropriation and the right of repatriation, both the negotiators and the two governments must publicly answer the question whether investments in Hong Kong would be covered by the same treaty after the transfer of sovereignty. If a new treaty, or a new protocol, has to be negotiated to cover Hong Kong, this would add to the uncertainty of investments in Hong Kong up to the conclusion of the new agreement, which may never materialize. If such a U.S.-PRC treaty will cover all American investments in Hong Kong, there might then be a rush to convert all investments in Hong Kong that are not owned by residents, or even if they are beneficially owned by residents, nominally into legal investments by Americans. One could easily accomplish this purpose through the registration of non-American firms as American firms or through sale or reincorporation in the United States. But if this process occurs, would such transfers not amount to the conversion of all investments, including possibly local investments and certainly all non-Chinese foreign investments in Hong Kong, into the foreign liabilities of an economically independent Hong Kong under Chinese sovereignty in the future?

The same issue, however, can be directly raised by non-American investors whose government does not have an investment treaty with the PRC and is not negotiating one. One can imagine British, Japanese, and all Western European investors following suit. Any attempt by China or Hong Kong to define foreign investments, to segregate them by date, or in any manner to make them identifiable for unequal treatment later would sow distrust and general market instability right away. Unfortunately, this dilemma has already become a reality.

Hong Kong's status as an international financial center is predicated upon the existence of a free-exchange market. Obviously, depositors are willing to keep their monies in Hong Kong only as long as they are able to repatriate their funds freely. But a free-exchange market is not the sole condition for a financial haven. Any policy on the part of the PRC to monitor illegally the private, unauthorized bank deposits of residents of China and their other financial dealings, including smuggling of currencies, commodities, and gold across the Hong Kong-PRC border, would require reporting by Hong Kong's financial institutions, including banks, deposit-taking companies, insurance firms, and others to some agency controlled by the local government and somehow under the PRC's surveillance. The Hong Kong government or PRC-controlled banks could perform this function after 1997. Since accounting and law firms can act for their clients, reporting by them may also be required. Thus banking secrecy in the widest sense and privacy in legal and accounting agent-client relationships will be compromised. The PRC's ongoing practice in placing some of the legal immigrants from China in employment with various banking, legal, and accounting firms in Hong Kong under the pretext of learning local business practice in order to serve the Hong Kong community better after 1997 has ominous implications.[6] Foreign depositors in Hong Kong's financial institutions, whether they are Chinese or locally owned, or branches of foreign firms, must therefore think twice before leaving their monies in Hong Kong. Anyone who desires a high degree of confidentially would wish to leave Hong Kong or be ready to do so at short notice.

INTERNAL VERSUS EXTERNAL CONSTRAINTS OF PRC POLICY TOWARD HONG KONG

Having surveyed the manner and likelihood of PRC intervention in ways that would undermine the conditions for Hong Kong's prosperity and economic viability as a free trade, financial, exchange, and manufacturing center, the factors involved can be grouped into two categories. One category consists of Chinese actions alone, but these actions are not dependent solely upon developments in China itself or just the success or failure of present Chinese economic reform measures. Success in economic reform may result in a lesser tendency for government intervention partially because the real success in this respect is dependent upon the increased practice and scope of the free market in China itself. However, success in economic growth in China, with whatever degree of "marketization," does not necessarily mean less intervention in Hong Kong's affairs. A part of the success of economic development in China may be dependent upon the greater exploitation of Hong Kong in the form of taxes and transfers.

In a second category are those conditions contributing to Hong Kong's prosperity that could be undermined by protectionism and other trade restrictive measures adopted by countries outside Hong Kong. Because the international financial market is really a single global market, it is also conceivable for the financial stability of Hong Kong to be threatened by developments outside Hong Kong. For instance, in connection with the 1985 Pan-Electric crisis in Singapore there have been reports of investors in Hong Kong trying to liquidate their local assets to increase their liquidity in Singapore. The possibility that Hong Kong may become involved indirectly in the world's economic affairs raises the question of how the burden of adjustment and response to such crises might be borne and whether the Chinese authorities would direct monetary and other public authorities in Hong Kong after 1997 to insulate themselves from the world's economic cross-currents. The reversion of sovereignty over Hong Kong from British to Chinese hands removes a major constraint to Chinese intervention through the PRC government, the Chinese Community party, and their central and local agencies and personalities. The tendency of coordinated as well as ad hoc intervention will be most dominant. Having had the British constraints removed, one must ask whether a substitute constraint might not be desirable. As an analogy, an alcoholic desirous of quitting alcohol can seek support from others to increase his own determination not to fall back into the habit. The same may be said of a nation having a tendency to intervene in the free market. It may be necessary and even desirable for the PRC's sake to establish some other constraint to make it unmistakably clear to all of the internal factions in Beijing and the provinces on what must *not* be done to maintain Hong Kong's economic and political autonomy.

I suggest that the adverse factors that could undermine Hong Kong's prosperity as a result of foreign intervention could actually serve as the basis to construct a new external constraint. More explicitly, this means that foreign governments, such as the government of the United States, could individually make the preservation of Hong Kong's independent economic status free from Beijing's state, party, or provincial intervention as a precondition for granting or continuing such external treatments as independent quotas for imports from Hong Kong, the MFN status, the General Agreement on Tariffs and Trade membership benefits, participation in various bilateral and multilateral trade agreements such as the Multifiber Arrangement, and even special visa privileges and immigration quotas. Since all of this is based on each country's own perception of Hong Kong's status after 1997 and in the years before that date, internal legislation can be enacted individually. An international common understanding may be desirable but again is certainly not indispensable. The agreement of China would certainly be desirable but again not *prima facie* necessary. As more self-government devolves upon Hong Kong before 1997, an agreement with Hong Kong based on the assumption that it will be economically autonomous should present no special objection in principle.

The Chinese Communists may consider this seemingly provocative proposal as imperialistic, but the criticism itself would serve a dual purpose. It could be used as a political argument by those Chinese leaders who really wish to carry out reform and who would like to preserve the usefulness of Hong Kong to China as a free market because they can then blame all of the things they must not do on imperialist foreigners. On the other hand, given such a real constraint, the PRC government will have greater incentive to act more prudently, in China no less than it should in regard to Hong Kong, than it had done previously during the Cultural Revolution and in the early 1950s.

What incentives will foreign nations have to help construct a new barrier to restrain the PRC's behavior after 1997? To answer this question one should examine the nature of self-interest of the major foreign economic partners of Hong Kong. What leverage do they have on China and what special measures might they be willing to undertake to protect their own interests?

First, in regard to trade, the major trade partners of Hong Kong are the United States, Japan, Singapore, and Taiwan. After 1997, considering the trade of Hong Kong and of China as a single unit with these trading partners, there is no particular reason why the total should increase faster than it might otherwise do without any transfer of sovereignty, all things being equal. On the other hand, one should also consider the possibility of a decline of this trade. In this connection, one can divide the total trade of Hong Kong into three components: (1) trade in transit to countries other than China, pure and simple; (2) indirect trade with China through Hong Kong; and (3) direct trade with the Hong Kong market itself. From the point of view of Hong Kong's trading partners, with the possible exception of Taiwan, there is no reason why all of these components should not continue as before. The transfer of sovereignty will have no effect on their willingness to trade with China and Hong Kong or through Hong Kong with any other country. They do not wish to see this trade decline or become less profitable, which might happen if Hong Kong's economic role suffers as a result of PRC intervention in its market economy. However, direct trade with Hong Kong, which is the principal component that would suffer most, is relatively small in the worldwide trade of these countries, Taiwan excepted. Domestic manufacturers that compete with imports from Hong Kong may actually wish to observe Hong Kong's exports, for instance, of textiles and garments, decrease as a result of the PRC's intervention so that they would not suffer directly if Hong Kong lost its competitiveness. Exporters in the same countries would like to see Hong Kong remain as a prosperous market, with the exception of Taiwan. The third component of their trade with Hong Kong is relatively small in their respective total trade so that these export interests are unlikely to possess a strong political voice. Furthermore, any decline of trade with Hong Kong could be more than compensated through an expansion of direct trade with China so that self-interest based on the perception, right or wrong, of a rapidly expanding China market might silence criticism when confronted with PRC intervention in Hong Kong.

The United States and Japan both have a strong leverage in their dealings with China in the form of technology transfer. But the volume of their trade with Hong Kong itself being so small, even fear of total loss of this trade may not provide enough motivation for them to take action on behalf of Hong Kong's economy. Weightier arguments would have to be found.

Taiwan's trade with Hong Kong is potentially far more susceptible to the impact of the transfer of sovereignty over Hong Kong. On the PRC side, Beijing will be tempted to use the China and Hong Kong market to attract

Taiwan's exporters in support of its political designs against Taiwan. This effort is likely to be eventually accompanied by demands of a political nature that, if accepted, could undermine Taiwan's standing as an international entity. At the same time, the PRC's ability to import from the world, including Taiwan, is limited, and it will not lightly increase the importation of consumer manufactures. Besides, such imports would be in competition with China's domestic products. Hence any expansion of Taiwan's exports to the China-plus-Hong Kong market would be limited to the Taiwan-Hong Kong part (i.e., the third component of Hong Kong's trade with Taiwan). In that respect, the post–1997 effect would not differ very much from the corresponding trade between Hong Kong and its other major trade partners and would be subject to the same influences.

On Taiwan's side, however, the very possibility of Beijing's combining political demands with the continuation of trading relations between Hong Kong and Taiwan is viewed as a strong probability. Hence protective measures are bound to be taken, leading to a potential reduction in all three components of overt trade after 1997, if not before. Taiwan would, therefore, have an incentive to see the development of a new external constraint to PRC intervention in Hong Kong.

However, Taiwan's interest is more complex because it is not entirely predicated on trade. Offering a refuge to those in Hong Kong who wish to leave before the PRC takeover is a matter of strong moral appeal. A heavy outflow of skilled middle-management from Hong Kong would act as another constraint to the PRC. Such an outflow, however, is not likely to occur much before 1997 and may prove too late to influence the drafting of Hong Kong's Basic Law. Some Taiwan leaders may also wish to attract capital from Hong Kong, but other alternative destinations like the New York financial markets and California real estate take precedence in the investors' minds. Yet when 1997 comes even nearer and Taiwan's offshore financial services become more developed, this factor may grow in importance. Taiwan's minimal interest is to have the farcical nature of the 1984 Sino-British Agreement demonstrated to the world. This wish will most likely be fulfilled, but its realization will bring little consolation to Hong Kong residents.

PROTECTING FOREIGN INVESTMENTS IN HONG KONG

This analysis suggests that the chief economic concern of the United States, Japan, and others, excluding Taiwan, about the impact of the sovereignty transfer has little to do with current trade, but rather with investments and the environment of investment, as a result of intervention and the risk of expropriation. For countries with large investments in Hong Kong the protective measures that might be taken depend upon the estimate of risk and therefore the perception by these countries and their investors of the future economic policy of China and its intervention in Hong Kong. One could assume nevertheless that for all of these investors, prudence dictates that minimal protection be undertaken. This is true especially for investors who cannot liquidate real investments tied to immovable assets. In this situation the best minimal protection would be to transfer registry of ownership outside Hong Kong. Consequently, large British firms like the Jardine interests have moved their head office out of Hong Kong. Others like the Hong Kong and Shanghai Banking Corporation reputedly already have the greater part of their assets outside Hong Kong. How many resident Chinese and other firms of foreign origin, including Taiwanese firms, may have actually transferred their registry and nominal ownership to outside interests in the United States or elsewhere is not known. There is no information based on official reporting systems currently available. Furthermore, a very natural tendency on the part of operators in this area is to conceal information and to spread disinformation. Persons wishing to sell their immovable assets with the intent of transferring proceeds outside Hong Kong are motivated to promote the opinion that nothing will ever happen to Hong Kong. Unless they do so, they would have greater difficulty in liquidating their own holdings. Not only is such information unavailable, but available information may be very misleading. However, a priori, those investors in Hong Kong who are unable to liquidate before the signing of the 1984 agreement for lack of suitable alternatives or a desirable market condition may now be gradually moving out of Hong Kong to avoid a stampede later when a crisis arises due to intervention by China or for any other reason. This is meant to avoid crowding at the gate when exit becomes obviously necessary to everyone. On the basis of this reasoning, the more gradually one plans one's exit, the better it can be carried out. This process, however, must precede 1997 by a margin. Thus the outward calm that Hong Kong has exhibited in the short period after the signing of the agreement does not necessarily reflect *real* conditions or concerns on the part of investors now still in Hong Kong, even if potential investors elsewhere are contemplating the broader China market.

Finally, a distinction has to be made between private foreign investors in Hong Kong who must consider whether or not to plan an orderly exit and foreign governments that are primarily concerned with strategic and political considerations. Many Americans, for instance, have been preoccupied or even obsessed with the U.S.-Soviet-China triangular relations. These relations have been an issue in the United States ever since the early 1970s. More recently, some Westerners have indulged in wishful thinking assuming that a prosperous China, bent on modernizing and reforming its economy with the purpose of increasing efficiency, would necessarily benefit the West's strategic interest. The basic assumptions are twofold. First, it is assumed that an economically stronger China would be a better counterweight and potential member of a U.S.-China coalition against the Soviet

Union. This assumes that the PRC will be siding with American interests vis-à-vis the Soviet Union when China is more capable to do so. There is no persuasive evidence that this will be Beijing's real intention, whatever may be China's capability in the future, Chinese protestations of their abiding interest in the United States and the West notwithstanding.

The second assumption is that a Chinese economy with a greater role reserved for the free market will also be a China devoted to greater domestic democratic interests at home. This convenient identification of the market system, vis-à-vis centralized planning, with democracy is something that may be true in the long run but is not necessarily true in the short run, especially in a political system that rests on the Communist political ideology and Communist party rule. In making this assumption one conveniently overlooks the fact that a more modern totalitarian party and government bureaucracy can be an even more efficient system that oppresses its population. (For instance, a better computerized filing system could provide tighter control over the billion plus Chinese than the antiquated but nevertheless efficient system of individual dossiers that have hitherto been used to control the Chinese population for more than three decades.) There is, therefore, a potential conflict between the foreign governments' perception of national interests and foreign investors in Hong Kong who are out to protect their own economic interests. Some of these governments may even contribute to information that would mislead their own investors by exaggerating the stability and calm of the Hong Kong economy. As more private investors in Hong Kong are misled by such estimates and the less they do now to protect their interests before any eventual crisis, the greater is the chance of an ultimate exit stampede. "Crowding at the gate" could eventually lead to a crisis.

Equally unfortunate is the fact that although the development of an external constraint to substitute for the previous one represented by the British administration of Hong Kong is really beneficial to the PRC, this will not be recognized as such by the Chinese Communists as long as their thought process and work style preclude such an interpretation of reality. Given this Chinese Communist attitude, foreign governments that cater to it for their own reasons have avoided upsetting the Chinese by not pointing to the potential possibilities discussed in this chapter. This "let's-not-rock-the-boat" approach on the part of foreign chancelleries only serves to confirm the Chinese in their own approach.

Is the final tragedy unavoidable? Much depends upon (1) whether able local leadership will emerge as more responsibilities of government devolve upon the local population, (2) whether local Hong Kong leadership can lobby foreign governments in the interest of erecting new constraints to Chinese behavior, and (3) whether the same foreign interests can restrain China from advancing the takeover before 1997.

NOTES

1. Among such indices the Hong Kong stock market price index rose from 684.9 during the last week of September 1984 to 1159.1 in the last week of December 1985. The Hong Kong dollar, thanks to the local government's stabilization scheme, remained at HK$7.80 to US$1.00 in the entire period. *Wall Street Journal*, Sept. 28, 1984, p. 52; Dec. 30, 1985, p. 31.

2. The economic value of Hong Kong to the PRC rose sharply at the end of 1950, when China sent its troops across the Yalu River to join those of North Korea. This action triggered a full-scale United Nations export embargo against Beijing and made Hong Kong doubly useful as an open shopping center of China.

3. See the discussion on the alienation of Chinese from the Communist party in John Copper, Franz Michael, and Yuan-li Wu, *Human Rights in Post-Mao China* (Boulder, Colo: Westview Press, 1985), p. 80.

4. For a discussion on taxes in Hong Kong, see Alvin Rabushka, *Value for Money: The Hong Kong Budgetary Process* (Stanford, Calif.: Hoover Institution Press, 1976).

5. A sharp increase in the unexplained "statistical discrepancy" item in the PRC balance of payments in 1984 suggests the presence of large unreported trade and remittance items during that year. *Renmin Ribao* [*People's Daily*] Sept. 2, 1985, p. 2.

6. Those with long memories will recall what happened to bankers and industrialists in Shanghai in 1950–1956 when they had to accommodate similar "apprentices." The possibility that sponsors of these "apprentices" of PRC origin may also have personal reasons does not exclude the motive noted in the text. Both personal and PRC public objectives can coexist.

7

Can the Hong Kong Settlement Serve as a Model for Taiwan?

AN-CHIA WU

Beijing's news media have been vigorously trumpeting the concept of "one country, two systems" since the Sino-British Agreement was initialed on September 26, 1984. The propaganda has focused on the following three major points Deng Xiaoping had emphasized:

1. The concept of "one country, two systems" is a strategy for the settlement of issues involving Taiwan and Hong Kong. After China is reunified, the 1 billion people on the Chinese mainland will follow the socialist system while people in Hong Kong and Taiwan will continue their capitalist ways of life.
2. This concept, which was announced by Zhao Ziyang in his "Report on the Work of the Government" at the Second Session of the Sixth National People's Congress on May 15, 1984, is not a measure of expediency or a fraudulent scheme.
3. This concept provides a model for the peaceful settlement of international disputes.[1]

In reality, Deng Xiaoping first introduced this concept of the "one country, two systems" in September 1982 at a reception in honor of British Prime Minister Margaret Thatcher, when the two exchanged views on how to settle the Hong Kong problem. Earlier, the principle put forth by Ye Jianying, then chairman of the Standing Committee of Beijing's National People's Congress, in September 1981 with regard to Taiwan also falls within the framework of "one country, two systems," although the term as such was not used. At that time, Ye said that after the unification of China, Taiwan could become a Special Administrative Region with a high degree of autonomy. It may retain its own armed forces, continue its existing social and economic systems and life-style, and maintain its existing economic and cultural relations with foreign countries.[2]

In his reception of Yang Liyu (Winston Yang), a professor at Seton Hall University, on June 26, 1983, Deng Xiaoping dealt at length with the question concerning unification. According to Deng:

After reunification of the motherland, the Taiwan Special Administrative Region will have its own independent character and can practice a system different from that on the mainland. It will have its independent jurisdiction and judicial organs and the court of final appeal should be based in Taiwan rather than in Beijing. Taiwan can maintain its own army, but this should not constitute a threat to the mainland. The mainland will neither station troops nor civilian officials in Taiwan. Taiwan can maintain its party, government and army. In addition, Taiwanese people will be selected to assume posts in the Central Government.[3]

As a matter of fact, the concept of "one country, two systems" was originally aimed at solving the Taiwan issue but was later applied to Hong Kong first when negotiations between Beijing and London on the future of Hong Kong began to make progress.

The concept of "one country, two systems" as now being propagandized by the Chinese Communists is based on the following four premises:

1. A situation of "peaceful coexistence" and "peaceful competition" is possible between the socialist system and the capitalist system for the time being. However, the slogans of "peaceful coexistence" and "peaceful competition" are primarily designed to make the capitalist world less vigilant toward the Communist threat.
2. The concept of "one country, two systems" is advantageous to the Chinese Communists in their modernization program.
3. The mainland under Chinese Communist rule will continue to practice socialism. The capitalist system practiced in Hong Kong is only a supplement to the socialist economy in mainland China, and it will not turn mainland China into a capitalist society.
4. "One country, two systems" is a "transitional model" for the settlement of the Hong Kong issue.

These four premises are closely connected with the Communists' ideological edifice. It is the purpose of this chapter to examine the feasibility of the Hong Kong model from the ideological perspective. The focus of the analysis is on mainland China's strategic goals and the ideological confusion that is bound to appear, and already has appeared, as a result of its attempts to achieve these goals.

THE STRATEGIC GOALS

The Chinese Communists have long considered the strategy of a "united front" as one of the "three magic weapons" for defeating their enemies. The two others are armed struggle and party building.[4] This was the gist of a speech by Xi Zhongxun, a member of the Chinese Communist party (CCP) Central Politburo, at the National Conference on the Theory of United Front Work held in February 1985. He maintained that without the full use of that magic weapon it would be impossible for the Chinese Communists to accomplish all of the important tasks. According to him, under the new circumstances, Beijing's "united front" should be made to serve the purposes of achieving economic structural reform, socialist modernization, and the three great tasks of reunifying the mother-land, opposing hegemonism, and defending world peace.[5] In his closing speech at the conference, Yang Jingren, director for the United Front Work Department of the CCP Central Committee and president of the China United Front Theory Research Association, pointed out that the new subjects to be studied include: (1) the "united front and our efforts to build socialism with Chinese characteristics," (2) "the status and role of the democratic parties during the new historical period," (3) the relationship between reform and the united front," (4) "united front work in the course of opening our country to the outside world," (5) "the concept of 'one country, two systems' and the patriotic united front," and (6) "the third cooperation between the Kuomintang and the Communist Party."[6] From what Xi and Yang have said, it is clear that the unification of China is one of the major tasks to be undertaken by the Chinese Communists and that the study of the concept of "one country, two systems" is the focal point of Beijing's current study on the theory of "united front."

To be precise, the term *united front* in Chinese Communist parlance means forming an alliance with all of the forces that can be "united," organizing them into a camp of "uniformity," and then employing all possible means of struggle against the enemy. When there are many enemies who cannot be struck down all at once, the target area must be narrowed and a coalition formed with the "secondary enemies" in order to get rid of the "principal enemy." Only when that is done will one proceed to annihilate the others, one by one, with the same method. When the enemy is too strong to be defeated by frontal attacks, measures of infiltration are to be used to induce divisiveness within the enemy's camp before exterminating the enemy. Furthermore, the precise ways to carry out the "united front" can be changed to suit the specific circumstances and situations. Nevertheless, the most important and unvarying principle is, as Chalmers Johnson pointed out, "the creation of panoply of vague but plausible-sounding slogans and the use of them to avoid spelling out the PRC's true policies."[7] "One country, two systems" is just one of such plausible-sounding slogans, and the Chinese Communists have called it a "scientific concept" and "strategic policy" of the "patriotic united front during the new historical period." The "one country, two systems" slogan is presumably aimed at achieving the following strategic goals.

First, the slogan may lead some people in capitalist countries to believe that the Chinese Communists are willing to settle for "peaceful coexistence" with them. Once this impression is established in the capitalist world, it will be easier for Beijing to obtain the capital, technology, and management expertise needed for its Four Modernizations. On the other hand, the same slogan is being used to deceive people in Taiwan, Hong Kong, Macao, and other overseas Chinese communities by replacing "nationalism" with "patriotism."[8] It is also used to prod people in the above-mentioned areas to form a "patriotic alliance" for the unification of China.[9]

Second, the slogan may have the effect of making Taiwan and Hong Kong into local governments that can carry on their existing political, economic, and social systems, although only for a certain time and without any authority in foreign and defense affairs. Thus the governments of these two areas will receive their legitimacy to govern from Beijing. This kind of political structure is described by the Chinese Communists as a "unitary state which has some of the characteristics of the composite state."[10]

Third, the slogan will make the post–1997 Hong Kong government, nominally administered by the people of Hong Kong, as a "united front regime" and a transitional model for the settlement of the Taiwan issue as well.[11] On the concept of a transitional model, one Chinese Communist scholar, Cheng Linsheng, has said:

> Lenin once pointed out: "Before we have achieved real communism, no form should be considered as final. We are not so much conceited about ourselves as to say that we know the right road. Nevertheless, one thing we are sure is that we will unswervingly march toward communism." For the same reason, on the question concerning the unification of our motherland, the method of "one country, two systems" which conforms with the situation in our country is used in the transitional period before socialism is realized throughout our country to take the place of capitalism. Since this new "model" is in line with the Marxist theory on the staged development of socialism, we should not have any doubt about it... As to the question of when and how Taiwan will change from its existing system to the socialist system, it will be decided by history.[12]

Fourth, the slogan will induce the government of the Republic of China to the negotiation table. While propagating the concept of "one country, two systems," the Chinese Communists, on the one hand, have emphasized that the goal of unification, which is the common aspiration of the Chinese people, should be achieved even if it will take 100 years or 1,000 years.[13] On the other hand, the Chinese Communists pointed out that Taiwan could be offered more generous terms because the situation in Taiwan is different from that in Hong Kong. For example, Beijing declared that Taiwan will be allowed to retain its armed forces after the unification, only if it is put under the unified leadership of the People's Liberation Army (PLA).[14]

Whether these strategic goals can be achieved will depend on whether the Chinese Communists can solve the long-standing contradictions between the socialist and capitalist systems, whether the "Basic Law for the Hong Kong Special Administrative Region," which is to be drafted by Beijing, will serve the interests of the people of Hong Kong, and whether the Republic of China is willing to change its long-standing anti-Communist stand.

IDEOLOGY

The concept of "one country, two systems" has given rise to two ideological problems for the Chinese Communists. One problem is: how can they solve the long-standing contradictions between socialism and capitalism. The other is: how can they dispel people's fear of capitalism and their disbelief regarding the supposed superiority of socialism?

The Chinese Communists used to criticize capitalism as a "decadent" and "moribund" social system, maintaining that revolutionary and violent measures should be adopted to get rid of this kind of system and to replace it with a socialist one. Today, however, as the Chinese Communists have launched the concept of "one country, two systems," they have also begun to say that it is necessary to make use of the merits of the capitalist system to reform the socialist system so as to enhance the nation's socialist material civilization. By making these statements, they have downgraded the supposed superiority of the socialist system. They have also asserted that it will be possible for socialism and capitalism to "coexist, to help each other, to reinforce each other, and to engage in peaceful competition."[15] The change in their attitude toward capitalism is for no other purpose than to promote the "one country, two systems" concept.

From Marxist writings, the Chinese Communists have been trying to find a rationale for their affirmation of the merits of capitalism. For example, Xu Jiatun, director of the Hong Kong branch of the New China News Agency, tried to justify the "one country, two systems" formula and Beijing's open-door policy by citing Marx's writings. In the "Manifesto of the Communist Party," according to Xu, Marx was of the opinion that the bourgeois class has played a "revolutionary role" in history and that the productivity created under its rule in less than 100 years was greater than that created in any other era. Marx also had said that with the development of capitalism, the self-sufficient and exclusive way of production has been replaced by exchange between different nations. Besides quoting Marx's theory to justify the merits of capitalism, Xu also stated that since the socialist system had been in practice for less than 70 years whereas the capitalist system had been in practice for more than 300 to 400 years, some of the superiorities of socialism remain to be discovered. Therefore, mainland China has to take up a part of capitalism as a supplement to socialism.[16]

In defense of the view that it will be possible for socialism and capitalism to coexist, Chen Linsheng referred to Marx's theory by stating that since socialism emerges from the capitalist society, it is thus in every respect—economically, morally, and intellectually—still stamped with the birthmarks of the old society from whose womb it has emerged. He maintained that the application of the "one country, two systems" formula to Hong Kong and Taiwan, which would allow these two areas to continue their capitalist system for a certain period, conforms with the Marxist viewpoint.[17]

Huan Xiang, an adviser to the Hong Kong and Macao Affairs Office in the State Council and simultaneously adviser to the Chinese Academy of Social Sciences, also said that some capitalist economic elements could exist in mainland China's economy. According to him, the socialist society will exist for a long period, and during that historical period, there will be a process for the capitalist system and the socialist system to coexist. He maintained that mainland China's economy would take a variety of forms, including the state-run, collective, and individual economies. Besides, foreign business people should be allowed to invest in mainland China either jointly or individually. In conclusion, he stated that the three forms of economic systems currently existing in mainland China are the socialist economy now undergoing reforms, the special-zone economy, and the capitalist economy.[18]

In their propaganda overseas, the Chinese Communists have played down the role of ideology, with the intention of giving the capitalist countries and societies a favorable impression. For example, Qian Jiaju, a renowned Chinese Communist economist, expressed in an article that it was wrong for people in the 1950s to argue that the capitalist system and the socialist system were irreconcilable. According to Qian, relations between different countries are decided by their history, politics, and geographic conditions but not by their ideological edifice. Likewise, he said, whether a country can become unified will depend on the composition of nationalities in that country, and the cultural background, languages, customs, and habits of these different nationalities. He also said that capitalist and socialist countries could enjoy long-term "peaceful coexistence," and that the two systems could also be applied in the same country and reinforce each other.[19]

In stating that the socialist and capitalist systems can enjoy "peaceful coexistence," the Chinese Communists are clearly trying to provide a rationale for the formula of "one country, two systems."[20] For many years, the Chinese Communists had assumed a hostile attitude toward capitalism. Only a few years ago, on March 30, 1979, Deng Xiaoping castigated capitalism by insisting that there is no way by which capitalism can ever eliminate the extraction of superprofits by its millionaires or ever get rid of exploitation, plundering, and economic crises. Nor can capitalism ever generate common ideals and moral standards or free itself from appalling crimes, moral degradation, and despair. In conclusion, from Deng's viewpoint, mainland China will never learn from or import the capitalist system.[21] In 1983 Hu Yaobang, general secretary of the CCP Central Committee, also said that the capitalist world and the Communist world will continue to stand apart. In dealing with the capitalist world, he proposed to adopt dual tactics: on the one hand, resolutely to implement an open-door policy in order to take in foreign capital and technology; on the other hand, to resist with vigor decadent capitalist things, including the bourgeois ideology and way of life.[22]

In 1983 Qian Junrui, a theoretician and an adviser to the Chinese Academy of Social Sciences, wrote a series of articles criticizing the capitalist system. To him, the socialist system and the capitalist system are interdependent but must struggle against each other. He said:

> Interdependence is a form of struggle. The ultimate goal of the struggle by a capitalist country is a vain attempt to eliminate socialism and perpetuate capitalism. On the socialist side, the ultimate goal is to drive out capitalism and enable socialism and communism to achieve an all-out victory throughout the world. The fundamental economic law in the new historical period is that the socialist countries will be interdependent with the capitalist countries and meanwhile struggle against them with the ultimate goal of replacing capitalism with socialism throughout the world.[23]

From the foregoing statements by Chinese Communist leaders and economists, it is clear that the current propaganda on the "peaceful coexistence" of capitalism and socialism is only a case of the united-front tactic in practice. The objective of the new propaganda is to reduce the capitalist world's fear and hostility toward the Communist world, so that mainland China will be in a better position to obtain the capital, technology, and management expertise from the capitalist countries.

Evaluating the tactic of "one country, two systems," two mainland Chinese scholars, Zhou Yizhi and Shi Handong, contended that the theoretical basis for that tactic was a creative development and the application of Lenin's strategic theory of promoting socialism with capitalism.[24] In recent years, the Chinese Communists have been trying to copy Lenin's New Economic Policy for the purpose of achieving economic development. For example, peasants on the Chinese mainland are now allowed to sell their surplus food, individuals are allowed to run small-scale industrial and commercial enterprises, and foreign business persons are allowed to invest in the Chinese mainland either individually or in joint ventures with Chinese business people. According to Donald S. Zagoria, the analogy is striking between the Chinese mainland since 1978 and the Soviet Union of the 1920s, when the latter adopted its New Economic Policy.[25] It is interesting to note that Lenin's New Economic Policy was only a strategic retreat.[26] Lenin said that the retreat is for an eventual attack.[27] In other words, some flanking methods are used to seize some positions first and then make an all-out attack on the capitalist world when the Communists are better prepared.[28] Since this policy of retreat helped the Soviet Union to emerge out of its economic depression, Chinese Communist scholars have all highly recommended it.[29]

Chinese Communists first advanced the theory of "peaceful coexistence" on April 29, 1954, when China and India signed an agreement on trade and communication between Tibet and India. At that time, the Chinese Communists put forth "Five Principles of Peaceful Coexistence."[30] Expounding on the importance of the five principles, Beijing's late Premier Zhou Enlai maintained that the principle of "peaceful coexistence" for the socialist world and the capitalist world does not mean that the two different systems will coexist forever. It also does not mean that the struggle between these two systems has come to an end. In the process of "peaceful coexistence," struggle is not displayed in the form of war but in the form of "peaceful competition." He emphatically pointed out that the capitalist system would eventually "go to the grave."[31] Nevertheless, Zhou Enlai's slogan of "peaceful coexistence" did not last long. In the 1960s when the Chinese and Soviet Communists were engaged in polemics, the Chinese Communists criticized Khrushchev's theory of "peaceful coexistence, peaceful transition, and peaceful competition" with the capitalist world for being "revisionist" and violating "proletarian internationalism."[32] The Chinese Communists did not mention "peaceful coexistence" again until 1979, when Ye Jianying touched upon it at a mass rally in celebration of the 30th anniversary of the founding of the Beijing regime. Later, on July 18, 1984, at a symposium in commemoration of the 30th anniversary of the Five Principles of Peaceful Coexistence, Zhao Ziyang affirmed that the principle of "peaceful coexistence" was the basic principle in handling international relations.[33]

The principle of "peaceful coexistence" is similar in many ways to the convergence theory advanced by some Western scholars in the 1960s. At that time, four presumptions for that theory were advanced:

1. Industrialization and urbanization give rise to a common culture in all modern societies. Eventually, this culture will produce similar political institutions.
2. Industrialization produces increasing diversity and complexity in society. More and more technical specialties and interest groups will emerge, and the function of the Communist party will play a mediating, brokerage role, comparable to that of governments and political parties in Western democracies.
3. Industrialization creates affluence. Affluence undermines political disciplines and ideological orthodoxy. The age of ideology has already come to an end in Western Europe, the United States, and Japan. It will soon come to an end in the Soviet Union. If Khrushchev did succeed in raising the Soviet standard of living above that of the United States, he would not achieve communism; he would bury it.
4. Industrialization will give rise to the stage of high mass consumption. In such a society, a high-powered political dictatorship cannot survive. Communism is but a "disease of the transition." At that stage, the Soviet Union and the United States will enter into a phase of "mutual discovery," in which they will learn from each other. Through the importation of machines, techniques, or even a form of social organization, the Soviet Union, which has been more of a closed society than Western countries, will inevitably experience the greatest immediate change resulting from this increased contact.[34]

The theory of "peaceful coexistence" and the "convergence theory" have a major characteristic in common. Both maintain that ideology is no longer a cause for the antagonism between the socialist society and the capitalist society. Nevertheless, history has shown that despite their high degrees of industrialization, the United States and the Soviet Union today still feel mutual antagonism for each other. President Ronald Reagan castigated the Soviet Union as the "focus of evil in the modern world," urging people to "leave Marxism-Leninism on the ashheap of history." Secretary of State George P. Shultz also said: "So long as the Soviet system is driven by ideology and national ambition to seek to aggrandize its power and undermine the interests of the democracies, true friendship and cooperation will remain out of reach."[35]

Notwithstanding the fact that the "one country, two systems" concept may help Beijing achieve its united-front objectives abroad, the Chinese Communist leaders are still afraid that people on the mainland may be exposed to the erosion of the capitalist ideology while they are being asked to emulate the capitalist countries in developing technology and management expertise. Some CCP members are afraid that there will be no room left for socialism in the Chinese mainland after the policy of "one country, two systems" comes into effect. As a precautionary measure against ideological confusion, the Chinese Communists have time and again called to the people's attention the view that mainland China will never deviate from the socialist road. In his reception for a delegation composed of people from Hong Kong's industrial and commercial circles in June 1984, Deng Xiaoping emphasized that socialism remains dominant in mainland China, and that the opening of some cities to the outside world and the adoption of some capitalist policies are only a supplement to the development of the socialist economy.[36] In his article mentioned earlier, Qian Jiaju also pointed out that the "one country, two systems" model is to be used specifically in Hong Kong and Taiwan but not throughout the Chinese mainland. Furthermore, in carrying out its economic structural reform, the CCP does not intend to give way to capitalism because there is a clear line of demarcation between socialism and capitalism in regard to the ownership of means of production. In mainland China, the heavy and light industries, transportation and communication services, banking and finance, commerce, and public services are all owned by the state; no individual capitalists are allowed to own means of production, and the labor force is not allowed to be traded as commodities.[37] Through its news media, Beijing has tried to instill into people the idea that the implementation of capitalism in Hong Kong will produce only a limited adverse effect on the Chinese mainland because Hong Kong is separated from the mainland geographically and therefore will provide little chance for a direct conflict between the two.[38]

Concerning the main reason for practicing "one country, two systems" in Hong Kong and Taiwan, Deng said that "without capitalism, we will be unable to maintain prosperity and stability there."[39] This is tantamount to a denial of the Communist propaganda that "only socialism can save China."[40]

In short, the formulation of the "one country, two systems" concept does not mean that the Chinese Communists have abandoned their long-cherished conviction that the socialist system will eventually replace the capitalist system.

DRAFTING THE BASIC LAW

After the Sino-British Joint Declaration on Hong Kong was initialed, the people of Hong Kong expressed a deep concern over the validity of the "one country, two systems" concept. According to Xu Jiatun, their anxiety is mainly about the following four things:

1. Antagonism and conflict between the socialist and capitalist systems will be inevitable since they are two diametrically different systems.
2. Since socialism is the dominant form in the Chinese mainland and the capitalist system exists in a small area, it is possible that under certain circumstances, the areas that are currently practicing capitalism will be forced to follow socialism.
3. Since Beijing's Constitution is of a socialist nature, it probably will not be able to provide an adequate legal basis for the existence of capitalism.
4. After Hong Kong's future position is decided, Beijing may send a large number of people to Hong Kong, thus creating a heavy social burden on Hong Kong.[41]

Since the future of Hong Kong is in the hands of the Chinese Communists, the helpless people of Hong Kong can only hope that the "Basic Law for the Special Administrative Region of Hong Kong," which Beijing is expected to formulate before 1990, can provide them with some favorable terms.

The Basic Law, also referred to as the "miniconstitution," will become the major law to be followed by the post–1997 Hong Kong government, which is to be composed of the local people in Hong Kong. However, Beijing insists that: (1) it has the legislative and interpretative powers of this law; and (2) under this law, Hong Kong should not be allowed to become an independent political entity. On April 10, 1985, Beijing's Sixth National People's Congress adopted at its Third Session a "Decision on the Basic Law Drafting Committee of the Hong Kong Special Administrative Region." Based on that decision, the drafting committee is to be responsible to the National People's Congress (NPC). When the NPC is in adjournment, that committee will be responsible to the Standing Committee of the NPC. The list of members of that committee will be decided jointly by the Commission of Legislative Affairs of the NPC, the Office for Hong Kong and Macao Affairs of the State Council, the Hong Kong branch of the New China News Agency, and some other departments concerned before it is submitted to the NPC Standing Committee for approval in June 1985.[42] Members of that committee will probably include some NPC delegates, members of the Chinese People's Political Consultative Conference, and a few foreigners in Hong Kong. Officials of the British government in Hong Kong will be excluded from the committee because they may create a problem of dual loyalties.[43] Maintaining that Hong Kong should not be made an independent political entity, Beijing has repeatedly emphasized that the special policy and system for Hong Kong should be formulated in the Basic Law in accordance with Article 31 of Beijing's Constitution. In the Basic Law, Hong Kong will become a local administrative region under the unified leadership of the central government but not as a member state. The power of the Hong Kong Special Administrative Region is to be governed by the law formulated by the NPC relating to special administrative regions.[44]

In the process of formulating the Basic Law for Hong Kong, the Chinese Communists are expected to meet some problems resulting from the different conceptions held by people in the Chinese mainland and in Hong Kong, the contradictions between the Basic Law and Beijing's Constitution, and the power to interpret the Basic Law.

With regard to the question concerning the different conceptions of law, it can be said that the "rule of law" is followed in Hong Kong while the "rule by law" is followed in the Chinese mainland. The concept of the rule of law places the law above the government and respect for people's rights, whereas the concept of the rule by law places the government above the law and tends to transgress the law whenever it fails to serve the political purpose of the government. In other words, the Chinese Communists regard law simply as the manifestation of class will." A. James Gregor argued that this notion of law creates the preconditions for ideocracy and the legal foundations for totalitarianism. *Ideocracy* is a political system that bases its legitimacy on the purported truth of its ideology, such as "Marxist-Leninist thought," or the "thought of Mao Zedong." This kind of political system is different from systems in democratic countries. Democratic systems, for instance, are rooted in ideas such as the rule of law, respect for human dignity, and limited government. But ideocratic systems are built on a narrow and rigid set of ideas or propositions, and their legitimacy rests on the absolute acceptance of these ideas, at least by the ruling elite. Under democratic systems, by contrast, legitimacy rests on the free suffrage of the citizens.[45] Although Hong Kong is a British colony, it is ruled by a code that is patterned after the British law. Under the rule of that law, the people of Hong Kong are respected for their dignity and social values and can enjoy a wide range of freedoms. It is questionable how long they can continue to enjoy these freedoms once Hong Kong falls under the rule of the Chinese Communists.

How to solve the contradictions between the Basic Law and Beijing's Constitution is a matter closely connected with the public's confidence in

Beijing's concept of "one country, two systems." For example, although it may be stipulated in the Basic Law that the existing social and economic systems and life-style in Hong Kong will remain unchanged, people will continue to doubt how long this will last. This doubt is because Article 1 of the Chinese Constitution has the following stipulation:

> The People's Republic of China is a socialist state under the people's democratic dictatorship led by the working class and based on the alliance of workers and peasants. The socialist system is the basic system of the People's Republic of China. Sabotage of the socialist system by any organization or individual is prohibited.[46]

In addition, Article 5 of the Constitution states: "The state upholds the uniformity and dignity of the socialist legal system. No law or administrative or local rules and regulations shall contravene the Constitution."[47]

Any possible stipulation in the Basic Law for the continuation of Hong Kong's capitalist economic and social system will, in fact, be contradictory to the position stated in the Constitution. According to the preamble of the Constitution,

> The exploiting classes as such have been eliminated in our country. However, class struggle will continue to exist within certain limits for a long time to come. The Chinese people must fight against those forces and elements, both at home and abroad, that are hostile to China's socialist system and try to undermine it.[48]

This emphasis on class struggle is further expounded by the *People's Daily* on November 6, 1982:

> The exploiting class has only been eliminated in the scope of rule by the PRC. There is a part of PRC territory [Hong Kong and Macao] that we have not yet recovered, and there is also a part [Taiwan] that has not yet been reunified with us. There are, of course, still bourgeoisie in Hong Kong and Taiwan. Do the bourgeoisie in those places have no effect on us at all? We will certainly recover these places and fulfill the great cause of reunifying the motherland. After we have recovered these places and achieved reunification, we will not, in accordance with Party principles, change the social system there, that is to say, the bourgeoisie in those places, of whom the great majority are patriotic, hope for the early reunification of the motherland and desire to contribute to the motherland's Four Modernizations; however, there are also some people who apply non-economic and political methods and also obscene methods, to influence and corrupt certain unsteady and unpatriotic elements. Taiwan radio stations are continually producing reactionary propaganda, and Taiwan's special agents engage in all kinds of activities to sabotage our system and our cause of socialist construction. They are enemies of the Chinese people. Therefore, it is evident that the class struggle in this respect still exists.[49]

In addition to the above anticapitalist and antimarket economy phraseology, what has also made the public in Taiwan and Hong Kong question the Beijing proposition of "one country, two systems" is the so-called high degree of autonomy for Hong Kong. It does not, however, provide any credible guarantee that Beijing will not interfere in the legislative and administrative operation of Hong Kong. For example, Article 31 of Beijing's Constitution contains certain restrictions on the power of a Special Administrative Region. "The state," according to this article, "may establish special administrative regions when necessary. The systems to be instituted in special administrative regions shall be prescribed by law enacted by the National People's Congress in the light of the specific conditions."[50] This stipulation has two implications. First, it means that the Special Administrative Region is not a permanent part of the state organ but is established only when necessary, and it may be dissolved when Beijing no longer regards it as necessary. Second, the NPC decides the establishment of the Special Administrative Region and the institution of the systems, and the NPC may change the law governing the systems for such a region or may dissolve the region altogether. When compared with the autonomous nationality areas, Hong Kong is granted even less autonomy because the power of autonomy and the administrative organizations of the nationality autonomous areas and the relationship between the central government and these areas all have been prescribed by the Constitution in its Articles 112 to 115 and Articles 117 to 122. In other words, the Standing Committee of the National People's Congress does not have the right to change these stipulations. Therefore, a high degree of autonomy for Hong Kong can be better guaranteed only when the power of autonomy and the duration of the Special Administrative Region are written into the Constitution.

Of serious concern to the people in Hong Kong is the interpretation of the Basic Law. In accordance with Article 67(3) and (4) of the Constitution, the NPC Standing Committee has the power to revise and interpret the Basic Law. Because the National People's Congress meets in session only once a year and each session lasts for a short time, there will be problems in settling questions of revision or interpretation of the Basic Law when the NPC is in recess. On this matter, Chang Hsin, a research fellow in the Institute of Contemporary Asian Studies of the University of Hong Kong, has suggested that the legislative, judicial, and administrative organs in the Special Administrative Region of Hong Kong should be granted certain interpretative powers of the Basic Law.[51]

For the formulation of the Basic Law, Beijing has established the "Basic Law Consultative Committee" to solicit opinions from the people of Hong Kong with regard to that law. Yet no one is sure to what extent that committee can meet the expectations of the people of Hong Kong, because there is no legal connection between the "Basic Law Drafting Committee" in Beijing and the "Basic Law Consultative Committee" in Hong Kong. The Drafting Committee will accept or reject opinions given by the Consultative Committee of its own will and without having to give any reason. Moreover, whether the opinions advanced by the "Consultative Committee" really represent the general will of the people of Hong Kong is an open question, and wether their criticism or comments of the views expressed by the leftist organizations in Hong Kong will be made known to the "Drafting Committee" remain to be seen.[52]

The formulation of the Basic Law is only one of the tasks Beijing has undertaken with regard to the Hong Kong issue. There are two concrete measures that have been adopted. One measure is to expand the organic structure of the Office for Hong Kong and Macao Affairs. This office of the State Council was established in 1978 under the open-door policy. The number of its staff members has been increased from a little more than 40 to more than 100. It has three major tasks:

1. To report to the State Council the political and economic situation and public opinion in Hong Kong and Macao.
2. To assist in the formulation of principles and policies concerning Hong Kong and Macao affairs.
3. To handle Hong Kong and Macao affairs in coordination with departments concerned with the established principles and policies. The Office for Hong Kong and Macao Affairs in the Foreign Ministry is in charge of diplomatic affairs between Beijing and Britain and Portugal in matters involving Hong Kong and Macao.[53]

Another measure is to intensify connections between the Chinese mainland and Hong Kong. According to a New China News Agency report of April 11, 1985, Hong Kong products exported to the Chinese mainland in 1984 totaled HK$11.3 billion, an increase of 81.3 percent over 1983. Today, the Chinese mainland has become the second largest market for Hong Kong (it was ranked 37th in 1978). Products exported from mainland China to Hong Kong in 1984 totaled HK$55.8 billion, an increase of 130.4 percent over 1983. In the past four years, Chinese Communists have invested about US$4.0 billion in Hong Kong. In addition, an automatic telephone system has been built between Hong Kong and 11 Chinese cities, and an aviation network has been built between Hong Kong and 13 Chinese cities. The number of travelers from Hong Kong to the Chinese mainland rose to 8,036,452 in 1984, an increase of 8.7 times over 1974. In the period from December 23, 1982, to the end of 1984, a total of 77,543 persons visited Hong Kong from mainland China. Beginning from 1979, a total of 16 provinces, municipalities, and autonomous regions have conducted exhibitions of exportable goods in Hong Kong.[54] These connections between Hong Kong and the Chinese mainland are expected to increase as time goes on.

REPUBLIC OF CHINA'S RESPONSE

Based on its long experience in dealing with the Chinese Communists and its understanding of the nature of communism, the government of the Republic of China has maintained the following position. It is convinced that Beijing's overture for negotiations, the call for "three links and four exchanges,"[55] and the slogan of "one country, two systems" are all aimed at confusing the Free World by creating an illusion of "peaceful coexistence."[56]

There are several major reasons for the Republic of China refusing to negotiate with the Chinese Communists. The first reason is that Taipei and Beijing do not possess any common basis for negotiation because of their different ideological edifices. The Republic of China is dedicated to the fulfillment of Dr. Sun Yat-sen's Three Principles of the People, which embraces the essence of Chinese culture with the final objective of implanting in China what Abraham Lincoln called in his Gettysburg Address a "government of the people, by the people and for the people." With regard to the distribution of wealth, the system of private ownership is followed in the Republic of China, and peaceful measures have been adopted for an equitable distribution of wealth. On the Chinese mainland, however, Marxism-Leninism is regarded as the guiding principle, the system of public ownership is practiced in all spheres, and violent measures have been used for the distribution of wealth. In a speech in early 1985, Deng Xiaoping said that it would be impractical to unify China with the Three Principles of the People. He maintained that China should rely on socialism and communism.[57] What Deng said is unacceptable to the Republic of China on Taiwan. It is an undisputable fact that under the Three Principles of the People, Taiwan has developed into a free and prosperous region. This prosperity is in sharp contrast to the situation in the Chinese mainland where the baneful influence of constant "class struggles" based on Communist theories exists, and the people have suffered from serious economic dislocations under an ideological bondage. As a result, the vast majority of the people on the mainland have lost confidence in communism.

Second, being a lawful government in effective control of Taiwan, established in accordance with a constitution, the Republic of China is naturally unwilling to accept an arrangement that will turn it into a local government under the People's Republic of China. Since their seizure of the Chinese mainland in 1949, the Chinese Communists have used a variety of united-front slogans toward Taiwan, including "liberate Taiwan with arms," "peaceful liberation of Taiwan," "democratic transformation of Taiwan," "three links and four exchanges," "a third cooperation between the Kuomintang and the Communist Party," "negotiation between the Kuomintang and the Communist Party on a reciprocal basis," and the "Hong Kong model" or the "one country, two systems" formula. The constant changes in their slogans toward Taiwan are an indication that Beijing intends to annex Taiwan by making it a province or a Special Administrative Region either through violence or by peaceful means. The "one country, two systems" model, which has been suggested by Deng, is completely different from the model of "one country, two systems" practiced in Germany and Korea. In Deng's model, the two different systems to be followed respectively by the mainland and Taiwan are in the nature of a central government and a specific local government, whereas in East and West Germany and in North and South Korea, the two different systems are practiced by two separate political entities, each of which has sovereignty over the areas under its jurisdiction and enjoys an independent international legal status.[58] If Taipei should accept Deng's concept of "one country, two systems" and negotiate with Beijing, the Republic of China would eventually become a local government. This is contrary to the wishes of the people in the Republic of China on Taiwan. Therefore, the Republic of China has no reason to accept Beijing's overture for negotiations.

The third reason for the Republic of China's refusal to enter into negotiation with the Chinese Communists is that it would immediately trigger four crises if it agreed to start negotiations. The first crisis is about its legitimacy. Since 1947 the government of the Republic of China has unswervingly assumed an anti-Communist stand. If the government begins to negotiate with the Chinese Communists, the people's will to resist communism may erode, just as the Chinese Communists are worried that the influx of capitalist ideology would detach the mainland people from Communist doctrines. The second crisis is the possibility of causing instability in Taiwan. Having led a peaceful and prosperous life over the past long years, the 19 million people in Taiwan certainly do not want to come under the Chinese Communist sovereignty, and they would resort to all possible means to show their discontent with the government if the latter should accept the Communist overture for negotiations. The third crisis is a possible military adventure by the Chinese Communists. Negotiations between Taipei and Beijing would give the impression that tension in the Taiwan Straits has been reduced and that it is no longer necessary for the United States to sell defensive arms to Taiwan as provided under the Taiwan Relations Act of 1979. Consequently, if Taiwan's defensive strength should become weakened, the Chinese Communists might be induced to launch a military attack against Taiwan. The fourth crisis is economic. If the Republic of China government should begin negotiations with the Chinese Communists on the Hong Kong model, the situation in Taiwan would be the same or even worse than that in Hong Kong when the United Kingdom began to negotiate with the Chinese Communists on the colony's future. A large amount of capital invested in Taiwan would be moved to other countries, and foreign business people would hesitate to invest in Taiwan. This would cause serious damage to Taiwan's economic development.

The fourth reason for the Republic of China's refusal to negotiate with the Chinese Communists is that the people in Taiwan would not be willing to undertake such socialist transformation as the Chinese Communists would dictate. Although the Chinese Communists said that within the framework of "one country, two systems" Taiwan may continue to follow the capitalist system, what they have said should be viewed only as a matter of expediency at a time when Taiwan is still beyond their control. As I mentioned earlier, the "one country, two systems" formula is only a "transitional model" used by the Chinese Communists for the settlement of the Taiwan and the Hong Kong issues. To transform Taiwan into a socialist society has been the consistent policy of the Chinese Communists. In his speech at the telephone conference for important cadres in Fukien on April 8, 1975, Pi Dingjun, the late commander of the Fuzhou Military Region, said that Taiwan will have to experience three stages of transformation after it is liberated. In the first stage, Taiwan will be made a province or a Special Administrative Region, and it will be allowed to retain the capitalist system for a period as long as it accepts the leadership of the central government. In the second stage, socialist transformation will be gradually undertaken in Taiwan. In the third stage, a thorough transformation will be made, to make Taiwan exactly the same as other provinces and autonomous regions.[59]

On December 28, 1979, at a meeting attended by cadres responsible for overseas Chinese affairs, Liao Chengzhi, the late director of the Administrative Office for the Overseas Chinese Affairs, said:

> After the peaceful reunification of China, Taiwan will have to take the socialist road eventually. It is unreasonable to believe that under the leadership of a proletarian Party, China would implement a socialist system on one side [of the Taiwan Straits] and a capitalist system on the other side. However, our most important task at the present time is to realize peaceful reunification and to end the split that has lasted for 30 years... Now, when the authorities and compatriots on Taiwan as well as the majority of overseas Chinese still refuse to accept our socialist system, our emphasis on socialism will only deepen misunderstandings and produce various unfavorable factors for reunification. Therefore, tactically, we must avoid empty talks about socialism. We should first point out the necessity of reunification from the viewpoints of national interests, the future of our country, the hope of the world, and the aspirations of all Chinese at home and abroad. Then we should further clarify the issue with examples from geopolitics, blood lineage, cultural background and the history of the development of Taiwan. This is a better method than indulging in empty talks about socialism, for it will easily inspire among the people an affection for their motherland and make them identify themselves with it psychologically.[60]

Subsequently, an editorial entitled "A Comment on the Controversy in Taipei over Multi-System Countries," which was published in Hong Kong's *Wen Wei Po* on March 17, 1984, stated:

The present reality raises the following possibility: the first step is to realize reunification of the motherland through negotiations between the Chinese Communist Party and the Kuomintang; and the next step is gradually to carry out the transition to the unification of social systems over a fairly long period. To unify the motherland in two steps is in the best interests of the whole country and the people.[61]

From these speeches by Communist leaders, it becomes evident that the "one country, two systems" formula is a tactical measure modeled after Mao Zedong's theory of the "development of revolution by stages."

The fifth reason is that the people in Taiwan have grave doubts about whether the Chinese Communists will keep their promise. It is noted that on September 22, 1937, the CCP Central Committee published a "Declaration" showing its willingness to cooperate with the Kuomintang. In that declaration, the CCP pledged that it would work for the complete realization of Dr. Sun Yat-sen's Three Principles of the People and would abandon its policy of armed uprisings against the central government.[62] Nevertheless, when the War of Resistance against Japan broke out shortly thereafter, the Chinese Communists availed themselves of that opportunity to increase their own strength. Consequently, by the time the eight-year war ended in 1945, Communist troops had increased from the original 25,000 to 1,400,000.[63]

The case in Tibet also made the people on Taiwan reluctant to believe the Chinese Communists. According to Article 4 of the 17-article agreement signed between Beijing and the Tibetan government on May 22, 1951, on the "peaceful liberation" of Tibet, the Chinese Communist authorities would not alter the existing political system in Tibet and would not alter the established status, functions, and powers of the Dalai Lama.[64] However, when Tibet was made an autonomous region, the Chinese Communists began to exert pressure on that region and force Tibetans to undertake socialist transformation. The Tibetan people's discontent with the Chinese Communists culminated in the 1959 anti-Communist rebellion, which was ruthlessly suppressed. The Dalai Lama was then forced to flee to India in exile.

A more recent instance that undermined the confidence of the Chinese people in Taiwan in the Chinese Communists was when Deng Xiaoping, in his reception for Yue-kong Pao, chairman of the Worldwide Shipping Corporation in Hong Kong, disclosed that he had asked British Prime Minister Margaret Thatcher to persuade President Ronald Reagan to accept the concept of "one country, two systems" and ask the U.S. government to help in solving the Taiwan issue.[65] This is certainly not in accord with Beijing's previous attitude that the Taiwan issue is China's internal affair and that no other countries should interfere.

In Hu Yaobang's talks with Lu Keng, publisher of a Hong Kong based magazine *Pai Shing*, on May 10, 1985, he further undermined the confidence of Chinese people in Taiwan in Beijing when he said:

We have not yet the military power to attack Taiwan. This temporary period may last four, five, or seven, eight years. We have to wait until our economy is on the right track. Military power is based on economic power. Say, for instance, in seven to ten years' time, we may attain a strong economy equipped with modernized defense. By then if most Taiwan people wish to return (to the mother country) and only a few saying no, we will have to use some force on them.[66]

The final reason for the Republic of China's refusal to negotiate with the Chinese Communists is that the Hong Kong model is inapplicable to Taiwan because there are many differences between Hong Kong and Taiwan. Unlike Taiwan, Hong Kong does not have a government that conducts its own foreign affairs, nor does it have a defense capability to the same extent that Taiwan has. As a colony, the fate of Hong Kong is in the hands of others. The Republic of China on Taiwan is a sovereign country, and it can decide its own fate. With the Taiwan Straits as the natural barrier, Taiwan is not under immediate Chinese Communist military threat as Hong Kong is.

If Beijing insists on its current terms for unification, the future of peaceful unification will be bleak. Why should the Chinese people in Taiwan, who enjoy ten times more per capita income than those on the mainland, place their fate in the hands of the Chinese Communists?

In fact, Beijing's current policy still includes the threat of the use of force, international isolation, and other possible pressures in an attempt to force the Republic of China and its 19 million people to accept its terms. Under such circumstances, the possibility of peaceful unification between Taiwan and the mainland remains remote.[67]

The best way to solve this unification question was suggested by former Premier Sun Yun-sun: "If the political, economic, social and cultural gaps between the Chinese mainland and free China continue to narrow . . . the conditions for peaceful reunification can gradually mature . . . the obstacles to unification will be reduced naturally with the passage of time."[68]

NOTES

1. Deng Xiaoping, *Jianshe you zhongguo tese di shehui zhuyi* [*Building Socialism with Chinese Characteristics*] (Guangdong: People's Publishing House, Dec. 1984), pp. 22, 29, 32, 40, 55.

2. Ye Jianying, "The Principles for Taiwan's Return to the Motherland so as to Realize Peaceful Unification," *Sanzhong quanhui yilai zhongyao wenxian xuanbian* [*Collections of Important Documents Since the Third Plenum*], Vol. 2 (Jilin: People's Publishing House, 1982), p. 966.

3. Deng Xiaoping, *Building Socialism with Chinese Characteristics*, pp. 17–18; Yang Li-yu, "Deng Xiaoping's Latest Concept on Peaceful Reunification," *Foreign Broadcast Information Service, Daily Report*, Vol. 1, no. 151 (June 10, 1982), p. W1.

4. Mao Zedong, "Introducing *The Communist*," *Selected Works of Mao Zedong*, Vol. 2, (Peking: Foreign Languages Press, 1965), p. 288.

5. *People's Daily*, Feb. 7, 1985, p. 4.

6. *Wen Wei Po* (Hong Kong), Feb. 13, 1985, p. 3.

7. Chalmers Johnson, "The Mousetrapping of Hong Kong: A Game in Which Nobody Wins," *Asian Survey*, Vol. 24, no. 9 (Sept. 1984), p. 897.

8. There are probably three reasons for the Chinese Communists to use the slogan of "patriotism" to take the place of "nationalism": (1) for fear that the use of "nationalism" may give rise to national independence among the 50-odd minority nationalities in China; (2) "patriotism" can be used to cover a wider range of targets, including people on the Chinese mainland, and compatriots in Hong Kong, Taiwan, and other Chinese communities; (3) since people have lost their confidence in communism, to use the slogan of "patriotism" at present would bring about great effect.

9. Deng Chao, " 'One Country, Two systems' and the Patriotic United Front," *Guangming Daily* March 5, 1985, p. 3.

10. Yan Jiaqi, "The Scientific Meaning and the Characteristics of 'One Country, Two Systems,' " *Honggi* (Red Flag), no. 6 (March 16, 1985), pp. 18–19.

11. See note 8.

12. Cheng Linsheng, "A Brand New Undertaking of the Socialist Practice in Our Country—A Preliminary Discussion on 'One Country, Two Systems,' " *Shehui Kexue* [*Social Science*] (Shanghai), no. 11 (Nov. 15, 1984), p. 37.

13. Deng Xiaoping, *Building Socialism with Chinese Characteristics*, p. 31.

14. "Deng Yingchao's Talks in Her Reception for Reporters from Hong Kong and Macao," *Wen Wei Po* (Hong Kong), March 30, 1985, p. 2.

15. At the symposium held in Hangzhou on July 15, 1984, on the "strategy for economic and social development and on the theory for the comprehensive reform of the economic structure," Qian Junrui, an adviser to the Chinese Academy of Social Sciences, conveyed the CCP leadership's call for "peaceful coexistence" of the socialist system and the capitalist system. He also asked mainland people to accept the concept of "one country, two systems," *Wen Wei Po* (Hong Kong), July 18, 1984, p. 2.

16. Lu Keng, "An Interview with Xu Jiatun," *Pai Shing* (Hong Kong), no. 89 (Feb. 1, 1985), p. 5; Karl Marx, "Manifesto of the Communist Party," *Selected Works of Karl Marx and Frederick Engels*, Vol. 1 (Moscow: Foreign Languages Publishing House, 1962), p. 36.

17. See note 11; Karl Marx, "Critique on the Gotha Program," *Selected Works of Karl Marx and Frederick Engels*, Vol. 2 (Moscow: Foreign Languages Publishing House, 1962), p. 23.

18. Huan Xiang, "The Background for the Principle of One Country, Two Systems," *Wen Wei Po* (Hong Kong), Sept. 29, 1984, p. 15.

19. *Wen Wei Po* (Hong Kong), Sept. 30, 1984, p. 7; Qian Jiaju, "Will China Change Its Nature—on Question Concerning 'One Country, Two Systems,' " *The Mirror* (Hong Kong), no. 90 (Jan. 1985), p. 55.

20. Chen Ziyun, "A General Discussion on Theoretical Questions Concerning the United Front in the New Period," *Guangming Daily*, March 18, 1985, p. 3.

21. Deng Xiaoping, "Uphold the Four Cardinal Principles" (March 30, 1979), *Selected Works* (Peking: Foreign Languages Press, 1984), 175–176.

22. Hu Yaobang, "On Questions of Ideological and Political Work," *People's Daily*, Jan. 2, 1983, p. 1.

23. Qian Junrui, "Prospects for the World Economic Situation in the 1980s and

Some Questions about the World Economy," *Shijie Jingji* [*World Economy*] (Peking), no. 8, Aug. 10, 1983, p. 5.

24. Zhou Yizhi and Shi Hanrong, "The One Country, Two Systems as Viewed from the Hong Kong Issue," *Guangming Daily*, Oct. 15, 1984, p. 3.

25. Donald S. Zagoria, "China's Quiet Revolution," *Foreign Affairs*, Vol. 64, no. 4 (Spring 1984), p. 880.

26. Lenin, "The New Economic Policy and the Tasks of the Political Education Department" (Report to the Second All-Russia Congress of Political Education Department, October 17, 1921), *Collected Works*, Vol. 33 (Moscow: Progress Publishers, 1966), p. 63.

27. Lenin, "Seventh Moscow Gubernia Conference of the Russian Communist Party" (Oct. 29–31, 1921), *Collected Works*, Vol. 33, ibid., p. 96.

28. Lenin, "The Role and Functions of the Trade Unions under the New Economic Policy" [Decision of the Central Committee of the Russian Communist Party (B.), Jan. 12, 1922], *Selected Works*, Vol. 33, ibid., p. 184.

29. Chen Huijun, "On the Retreat Made by the Soviet Union at the Early Stage When the New Economic Policy Was Enforced," *Shijie Lishi* [*World History*] (Peking), no. 1 (Feb. 7, 1982), p. 9.

30. *People's Daily*, Apr. 30, 1954, p. 4.

31. Shi Lü, *Can Peaceful Coexistence Be Realized?* (Peking: Popular Literature Publishing House, July 1957), p. 18.

32. "The Two Diametrically Opposed Policies on Peaceful Coexistence" in *Polemics on the General Line for the International Communist Movement*, Vol. 1 (Peking: People's Publishing House, 1965), p. 299.

33. *People's Daily*, July 19, 1984, p. 1.

34. Zbigniew Brzezinski and Samuel P. Huntington, *Political Power: USA/USSR* (New York: Viking Press, 1964), pp. 10–13.

35. "Reagan and Communism," *Christian Science Monitor*, March 10, 1983, p. 17; *The Times* (London), June 9, 1982, p. 4: George P. Shultz, "New Realities and New Ways of Thinking," *Foreign Affairs*, Vol. 63, no. 4 (Spring 1985), p. 706.

36. Deng Xiaoping, "One Country, Two Systems" (June 22 and 23, 1984), in *Building Socialism with Chinese Characteristics*, p. 30.

37. Huan Xiang, "The Background for the Principle of One Country, Two Systems," p. 15.

38. Ling Yun, "The Origin of 'One Country, Two Systems,'" *Guangjiao Jing* (*Wide Angle*, Hong Kong), no. 143 (Aug. 16, 1984), p. 14.

39. Deng Xiaoping, *Building Socialism with Chinese Characteristics*, p. 40.

40. The Propaganda Department of the CCP Central Committee and the Research Office of the Secretariat of the CCP Central Committee, "Some Opinions on the Education for the Propaganda of Patriotism" (July 2, 1983), *Xinhua Yuebao* (Peking), no. 7 (Aug. 30, 1983), p. 31.

41. Xu Jiatun, "One Country, Two Systems: The Cornerstone for the Settlement of the Hong Kong Issue," *Wei Wei Po* (Hong Kong), Apr. 5, 1985, p. 15.

42. *Ta Kung Pao* (Hong Kong), Apr. 11, 1985, p. 1.

43. Ibid., Apr. 6, 1985, p. 1.

44. Wang Shuwen, "It is Our Country's Important Policy Decision to Establish Special Administrative Region," *People's Daily*, Sept. 28, 1984, p. 5.

45. A. James Gregor, *The Republic of China and U.S. Policy* (Washington, D.C.: Ethics and Public Policy Center, 1983), pp. 4–6.

46. "Constitution of the People's Republic of China," *Beijing Review*, Vol. 25, no. 52 (Dec. 27, 1982), p. 12.

47. Ibid.

48. Ibid., p. 11.

49. Editorial, "Correctly Evaluate and Handle the Class Struggle at the Present Stage," *People's Daily*, Nov. 6, 1982, p. 1.

50. See *Wen Wei Po* (Hong Kong), Feb. 13, 1985, pp. 10 and 13.

51. Chang Hsin, "The Interpretative Power of the Basic Law for Hong Kong as Viewed from the Way of the Interpretation of Chinese Law," *Ming Pao* (Hong Kong), Feb. 28, 1985, p. 17.

52. Chiang Chih, "The New Situation for the Consultation of the Basic Law," *Ming Pao*, March 5, 1985, p. 2.

53. *Wen Wei Po* (Hong Kong), Apr. 4, 1985, p. 3; Apr. 6, 1985, p. 2.

54. *A Summary of Broadcasts of Mainland Radio* (Taipei), no. 8016 (Apr. 12, 1985), Economic Section, pp. 7–8.

55. Hua Guofeng, "Report on the Work of the Government Presented at the Second Session of the Fifth National People's Congress," *Honggi* (Peking), no. 7 (July 3, 1979), p. 27. He said that China should establish links with Taiwan in trade, transport, and postal services and start economic, scientific, cultural, and sports exchanges with it.

56. Chiang Ching-kuo, "Reunification of China under the Three Principles of the People Will Finally Be Achieved—A Special Message to His Countrymen on the Eve of the 1984 ROC National Day," *In Support of Freedom* (Taipei: Kwang Hwa Publishing Company, Nov. 1984), p. 11.

57. Deng Xiaoping, "Talk at the Third Plenary Session of the CCP Central Advisory Commission," *People's Daily*, Jan. 1, 1985, p. 1.

58. "A Free Discussion of China's Future by the Leftists, Middle of the Roaders, Rightists, and Taiwan Independents—A Record of the Symposium on 'China's Future,' " *Pai Shing* (Hong Kong), no. 85 (Dec. 1, 1984), p. 5.

59. The CCP's classified document obtained by the Intelligence Bureau, Ministry of National Defense of the Republic of China, unpublished.

60. Document 87 issued by the "Office for Overseas Chinese Affairs of the State Council." This document is also obtained by the Intelligence Bureau, Ministry of National Defense, of the Republic of China.

61. *Wen Wei Po* (Hong Kong), Mar. 17, 1984, p. 2.

62. *Kangri Minzu Tongyi Zhanxian Zhinan* [*The Guide to the Anti-Japanese National United Front*], Vol. 2 (Yenan: Liberation Press, Apr. 1938), p. 18. In its declaration of willingness to cooperate with the Kuomintang, the Chinese Communist party made the following four pledges: (1) Dr. Sun Yat-sen's Three Principles of the People are indispensable to China today, and the CCP is willing to work for their complete realization, (2) the CCP is to abandon its policy of armed uprising against the National government and its communization movement and to cease its policy of forced confiscation of the landlord's land, (3) the present Soviet government is to be abolished and democratic rule is to be enforced so as to achieve unification of government throughout the country, (4) the Red Army is to drop its title and

identity and reorganize itself into National Revolutionary Forces placed under the command of the National Military Council of the National government.

63. Zhou Enlai, "The Negotiation in the Past Year and Its Prospect," *Zhou Enlai Xuanji* [*Selected Writings of Zhou Enlai*], Vol. 1 (Peking: People's Publishing House, Dec. 1980), p. 251.

64. *Tibet, 1950–1967*, (Hong Kong: Union Research Institute, 1968), p. 21.

65. *Ta Kung Pao* (Hong Kong), Dec. 21, 1984, p. 1.

66. Lu Keng, "An Interview with Hu Yaobang," *Pai Shing* (Hong Kong), no. 97 (June 1, 1985), p. 6.

67. Hungdah Chiu, "Prospects for the Unification of China: An Analysis of the Views of the Republic of China on Taiwan," *Asian Survey*, Vol. 23, no. 10 (Oct. 1983), p. 1092.

68. *Foreign Broadcast Information Service, Daily Report*, Vol. 1, no. 112 (June 10, 1982), p. vi.

SELECTED DOCUMENTS

A

The Sino-British Joint Declaration on the Future of Hong Kong

On 19 December 1984, the Prime Minister of the United Kingdom of Great Britain and Northern Ireland, Mrs Margaret Thatcher, and the Prime Minister of the People's Republic of China, Mr Zhao Ziyang, acting on behalf of their respective Governments, signed the following Agreement on the future of Hong Kong:

JOINT DECLARATION
OF THE GOVERNMENT OF THE UNITED KINGDOM OF GREAT BRITAIN AND NORTHERN IRELAND
AND
THE GOVERNMENT OF THE PEOPLE'S REPUBLIC OF CHINA ON THE QUESTION OF HONG KONG

The Government of the United Kingdom of Great Britain and Northern Ireland and the Government of the People's Republic of China have reviewed with satisfaction the friendly relations existing between the two Governments and peoples in recent years and agreed that a proper negotiated settlement of the question of Hong Kong, which is left over from the past, is conducive to the maintenance of the prosperity and stability of Hong Kong and to the further strengthening and development of the relations between the two countries on a new basis. To this end, they have, after talks between the delegations of the two Governments, agreed to declare as follows:

1. The Government of the People's Republic of China declares that to recover the Hong Kong area (including Hong Kong Island, Kowloon and the New Territories, hereinafter referred to as Hong Kong) is the common aspiration of the entire Chinese people, and that it has decided to resume the exercise of sovereignty over Hong Kong with effect from 1 July 1997.

2. The Government of the United Kingdom declares that it will restore Hong Kong to the People's Republic of China with effect from 1 July 1997.

3. The Government of the People's Republic of China declares that the basic policies of the People's Republic of China regarding Hong Kong are as follows:

(1) Upholding national unity and territorial integrity and taking account of the history of Hong Kong and its realities, the People's Republic of China has decided to establish, in accordance with the provisions of Article 31 of the Constitution of the People's Republic of China, a Hong Kong Special Administrative Region upon resuming the exercise of sovereignty over Hong Kong.

Source: Bill Knight, ed. *Hong Kong: 1985*, Hong Kong: Government Publications Center, n.d., pp. 1–16.

(2) The Hong Kong Special Administrative Region will be directly under the authority of the Central People's Government of the People's Republic of China. The Hong Kong Special Administrative Region will enjoy a high degree of autonomy, except in foreign and defence affairs which are the responsibilities of the Central People's Government.

(3) The Hong Kong Special Administrative Region will be vested with executive, legislative and independent judicial power, including that of final adjudication. The laws currently in force in Hong Kong will remain basically unchanged.

(4) The Government of the Hong Kong Special Administrative Region will be composed of local inhabitants. The chief executive will be appointed by the Central People's Government on the basis of the results of elections or consultations to be held locally. Principal officials will be nominated by the chief executive of the Hong Kong Special Administrative Region for appointment by the Central People's Government. Chinese and foreign nationals previously working in the public and police services in the government departments of Hong Kong may remain in employment. British and other foreign nationals may also be employed to serve as advisers or hold certain public posts in government departments of the Hong Kong Special Administrative Region.

(5) The current social and economic systems in Hong Kong will remain unchanged, and so will the life-style. Rights and freedoms, including those of the person, of speech, of the press, of assembly, of association, of travel, of movement, of correspondence, of strike, of choice of occupation, of academic research and of religious belief will be ensured by law in the Hong Kong Special Administrative Region. Private property, ownership of enterprises, legitimate right of inheritance and foreign investment will be protected by law.

(6) The Hong Kong Special Administrative Region will retain the status of a free port and a separate customs territory.

(7) The Hong Kong Special Administrative Region will retain the status of an international financial centre, and its markets for foreign exchange, gold, securities and futures will continue. There will be free flow of capital. The Hong Kong dollar will continue to circulate and remain freely convertible.

(8) The Hong Kong Special Administrative Region will have independent finances. The Central People's Government will not levy taxes on the Hong Kong Special Administrative Region.

(9) The Hong Kong Special Administrative Region may establish mutually beneficial economic relations with the United Kingdom and other countries, whose economic interests in Hong Kong will be given due regard.

(10) Using the name of "Hong Kong, China", the Hong Kong Special Administrative Region may on its own maintain and develop economic and cultural relations and conclude relevant agreements with states, regions and relevant international organisations.

The Government of the Hong Kong Special Administrative Region may on its own issue travel documents for entry into and exit from Hong Kong.

(11) The maintenance of public order in the Hong Kong Special Administrative Region will be the responsibility of the Government of the Hong Kong Special Administrative Region.

(12) The above-stated basic policies of the People's Republic of China regarding Hong Kong and the elaboration of them in Annex I to this Joint Declaration will be

stipulated, in a Basic Law of the Hong Kong Special Administrative Region of the People's Republic of China, by the National People's Congress of the People's Republic of China, and they will remain unchanged for 50 years.

4. The Government of the United Kingdom and the Government of the People's Republic of China declare that, during the transitional period between the date of the entry into force of this Joint Declaration and 30 June 1997, the Government of the United Kingdom will be responsible for the administration of Hong Kong with the object of maintaining and preserving its economic prosperity and social stability; and that the Government of the People's Republic of China will give its cooperation in this connection.

5. The Government of the United Kingdom and the Government of the People's Republic of China declare that, in order to ensure a smooth transfer of government in 1997, and with a view to the effective implementation of this Joint Declaration, a Sino-British Joint Liaison Group will be set up when this Joint Declaration enters into force; and that it will be established and will function in accordance with the provisions of Annex II to this Joint Declaration.

6. The Government of the United Kingdom and the Government of the People's Republic of China declare that land leases in Hong Kong and other related matters will be dealt with in accordance with the provisions of Annex III to this Joint Declaration.

7. The Government of the United Kingdom and the Government of the People's Republic of China agree to implement the preceding declarations and the Annexes to this Joint Declaration.

8. This Joint Declaration is subject to ratification and shall enter into force on the date of the exchange of instruments of ratification, which shall take place in Beijing before 30 June 1985. This Joint Declaration and its Annexes shall be equally binding.

Done in duplicate at Beijing on 19 December 1984 in the English and Chinese languages, both texts being equally authentic.

For the
Government of the United Kingdom
of Great Britain and Northern Ireland

Margaret Thatcher

For the
Government of the
People's Republic of China

Zhao Ziyang

ANNEX I

ELABORATION BY THE GOVERNMENT OF THE PEOPLE'S REPUBLIC OF CHINA OF ITS BASIC POLICIES REGARDING HONG KONG

The Government of the People's Republic of China elaborates the basic policies of the People's Republic of China regarding Hong Kong as set out in paragraph 3 of the Joint Declaration of the Government of the United Kingdom of Great Britain and Northern Ireland and the Government of the People's Republic of China on the Question of Hong Kong as follows:

I

The Constitution of the People's Republic of China stipulates in Article 31 that "the state may establish special administrative regions when necessary. The systems to be instituted in special administrative regions shall be prescribed by laws enacted by the National People's Congress in the light of the specific conditions." In accordance with this Article, the People's Republic of China shall, upon the resumption of the exercise of sovereignty over Hong Kong on 1 July 1997, establish the Hong Kong Special Administrative Region of the People's Republic of China. The National People's Congress of the People's Republic of China shall enact and promulgate a Basic Law of the Hong Kong Special Administrative Region of the People's Republic of China (hereinafter referred to as the Basic Law) in accordance with the Constitution of the People's Republic of China, stipulating that after the establishment of the Hong Kong Special Administrative Region the socialist system and socialist policies shall not be practised in the Hong Kong Special Administrative Region and that Hong Kong's previous capitalist system and life-style shall remain unchanged for 50 years.

The Hong Kong Special Administrative Region shall be directly under the authority of the Central People's Government of the People's Republic of China and shall enjoy a high degree of autonomy. Except for foreign and defence affairs which are the responsibilities of the Central People's Government, the Hong Kong Special Administrative Region shall be vested with executive, legislative and independent judicial power, including that of final adjudication. The Central People's Government shall authorise the Hong Kong Special Administrative Region to conduct on its own those external affairs specified in Section XI of this Annex.

The government and legislature of the Hong Kong Special Administrative Region shall be composed of local inhabitants. The chief executive of the Hong Kong Special Administrative Region shall be selected by election or through consultations held locally and be appointed by the Central People's Government. Principal officials (equivalent to Secretaries) shall be nominated by the chief executive of the Hong Kong Special Administrative Region and appointed by the Central People's Government. The legislature of the Hong Kong Special Administrative Region shall be constituted by elections. The executive authorities shall abide by the law and shall be accountable to the legislature.

In addition to Chinese, English may also be used in organs of government and in the courts in the Hong Kong Special Administrative Region.

Apart from displaying the national flag and national emblem of the People's Republic of China, the Hong Kong Special Administrative Region may use a regional flag and emblem of its own.

II

After the establishment of the Hong Kong Special Administrative Region, the laws previously in force in Hong Kong (i.e. the common law, rules of equity, ordinances, subordinate legislation and customary law) shall be maintained, save for any that contravene the Basic Law and subject to any amendment by the Hong Kong Special Administrative Region legislature.

The legislative power of the Hong Kong Special Administrative Region shall be vested in the legislature of the Hong Kong Special Administrative Region. The legislature may on its own authority enact laws in accordance with the provisions of the Basic Law and legal procedures, and report them to the Standing Committee of the National People's Congress for the record. Laws enacted by the legislature which are in accordance with the Basic Law and legal procedures shall be regarded as valid.

The laws of the Hong Kong Special Administrative Region shall be the Basic Law, and the laws previously in force in Hong Kong and laws enacted by the Hong Kong Special Administrative Region legislature as above.

III

After the establishment of the Hong Kong Special Administrative Region, the judicial system previously practised in Hong Kong shall be maintained except for those changes consequent upon the vesting in the courts of the Hong Kong Special Administrative Region of the power of final adjudication.

Judicial power in the Hong Kong Special Administrative Region shall be vested in the courts of the Hong Kong Special Administrative Region. The courts shall exercise judicial power independently and free from any interference. Members of the judiciary shall be immune from legal action in respect of their judicial functions. The courts shall decide cases in accordance with the laws of the Hong Kong Special Administrative Region and may refer to precedents in other common law jurisdictions.

Judges of the Hong Kong Special Administrative Region courts shall be appointed by the chief executive of the Hong Kong Special Administrative Region acting in accordance with the recommendation of an independent commission composed of local judges, persons from the legal profession and other eminent persons. Judges shall be chosen by reference to their judicial qualities and may be recruited from other common law jurisdictions. A judge may only be removed for inability to discharge the functions of his office, or for misbehaviour, by the chief executive of the Hong Kong Special Administrative Region acting in accordance with the recommendation of a tribunal appointed by the chief judge of the court of final appeal, consisting of not fewer than three local judges. Additionally, the appointment or removal of principal judges (i.e. those of the highest rank) shall be made by the chief executive with the endorsement of the Hong Kong Special Administrative Region legislature and reported to the Standing Committee of the National People's Congress for the record. The system of appointment and removal of judicial officers other than judges shall be maintained.

The power of final judgment of the Hong Kong Special Administrative Region shall be vested in the court of final appeal in the Hong Kong Special Administrative Region, which may as required invite judges from other common law jurisdictions to sit on the court of final appeal.

A prosecuting authority of the Hong Kong Special Administrative Region shall control criminal prosecutions free from any interference.

On the basis of the system previously operating in Hong Kong, the Hong Kong Special Administrative Region Government shall on its own make provision for local lawyers and lawyers from outside the Hong Kong Special Administrative Region to work and practise in the Hong Kong Special Administrative Region.

The Central People's Government shall assist or authorise the Hong Kong Special Administrative Region Government to make appropriate arrangements for reciprocal juridical assistance with foreign states.

IV

After the establishment of the Hong Kong Special Administrative Region, public servants previously serving in Hong Kong in all government departments, including the police department, and members of the judiciary may all remain in employment and continue their service with pay, allowances, benefits and conditions of service no less favourable than before. The Hong Kong Special Administrative Region Government shall pay to such persons who retire or complete their contracts, as well as to those who have retired before 1 July 1997, or to their dependants, all pensions, gratuities, allowances and benefits due to them on terms no less favourable than before, and irrespective of their nationality or place of residence.

The Hong Kong Special Administrative Region Government may employ British and other foreign nationals previously serving in the public service in Hong Kong, and may recruit British and other foreign nationals holding permanent identity cards of the Hong Kong Special Administrative Region to serve as public servants at all levels, except as heads of major government departments (corresponding to branches or departments at Secretary level) including the police department, and as deputy heads of some of those departments. The Hong Kong Special Administrative Region Government may also employ British and other foreign nationals as advisers to government departments and, when there is a need, may recruit qualified candidates from outside the Hong Kong Special Administrative Region to professional and technical posts in government departments. The above shall be employed only in their individual capacities and, like other public servants, shall be responsible to the Hong Kong Special Administrative Region Government.

The appointment and promotion of public servants shall be on the basis of qualifications, experience and ability. Hong Kong's previous system of recruitment, employment, assessment, discipline, training and management for the public service (including special bodies for appointment, pay and conditions of service) shall, save for any provisions providing privileged treatment for foreign nationals, be maintained.

V

The Hong Kong Special Administrative Region shall deal on its own with financial matters, including disposing of its financial resources and drawing up its budgets and its final accounts. The Hong Kong Special Administrative Region shall report its budgets and final accounts to the Central People's Government for the record.

The Central People's Government shall not levy taxes on the Hong Kong Special Administrative Region. The Hong Kong Special Administrative Region shall use its financial revenues exclusively for its own purposes and they shall not be handed over to the Central People's Government. The systems by which taxation and public expenditure must be approved by the legislature, and by which there is accountability to the legislature for all public expenditure, and the system for auditing public accounts shall be maintained.

VI

The Hong Kong Special Administrative Region shall maintain the capitalist economic and trade systems previously practised in Hong Kong. The Hong Kong Special Administrative Region Government shall decide its economic and trade policies on its own. Rights concerning the ownership of property, including those relating to acquisition, use, disposal, inheritance and compensation for lawful deprivation (corresponding to the real value of the property concerned, freely convertible and paid without undue delay) shall continue to be protected by law.

The Hong Kong Special Administrative Region shall retain the status of a free port and continue a free trade policy, including the free movement of goods and capital. The Hong Kong Special Administrative Region may on its own maintain and develop economic and trade relations with all states and regions.

The Hong Kong Special Administrative Region shall be a separate customs territory. It may participate in relevant international organisations and international trade agreements (including preferential trade arrangements), such as the General Agreement on Tariffs and Trade and arrangements regarding international trade in textiles. Export quotas, tariff preferences and other similar arrangements obtained by the Hong Kong Special Administrative Region shall be enjoyed exclusively by the Hong Kong Special Administrative Region. The Hong Kong Special Administrative Region shall have authority to issue its own certificates of origin for products manufactured locally, in accordance with prevailing rules of origin.

The Hong Kong Special Administrative Region may, as necessary, establish official and semi-official economic and trade missions in foreign countries, reporting the establishment of such missions to the Central People's Government for the record.

VII

The Hong Kong Special Administrative Region shall retain the status of an international financial centre. The monetary and financial systems previously practised in Hong Kong, including the systems of regulation and supervision of deposit taking institutions and financial markets, shall be maintained.

The Hong Kong Special Administrative Region Government may decide its monetary and financial policies on its own. It shall safeguard the free operation of financial business and the free flow of capital within, into and out of the Hong Kong Special Administrative Region. No exchange control policy shall be applied in the Hong Kong Special Administrative Region. Markets for foreign exchange, gold, securities and futures shall continue.

The Hong Kong dollar, as the local legal tender, shall continue to circulate and remain freely convertible. The authority to issue Hong Kong currency shall be vested in the Hong Kong Special Administrative Region Government. The Hong Kong Special Administrative Region Government may authorise designated banks to issue or continue to issue Hong Kong currency under statutory authority, after satisfying itself that any issue of currency will be soundly based and that the arrangements for such issue are consistent with the object of maintaining the stability of the currency. Hong Kong currency bearing references inappropriate to the status of Hong Kong as a Special Administrative Region of the People's Republic of China shall be progressively replaced and withdrawn from circulation.

The Exchange Fund shall be managed and controlled by the Hong Kong Special Administrative Region Government, primarily for regulating the exchange value of the Hong Kong dollar.

VIII

The Hong Kong Special Administrative Region shall maintain Hong Kong's previous systems of shipping management and shipping regulation, including the system for regulating conditions of seamen. The specific functions and responsibilities of the Hong Kong Special Administrative Region Government in the field of shipping shall be defined by the Hong Kong Special Administrative Region Government on its own. Private shipping businesses and shipping-related businesses and private container terminals in Hong Kong may continue to operate freely.

The Hong Kong Special Administrative Region shall be authorised by the Central People's Government to continue to maintain a shipping register and issue related certificates under its own legislation in the name of "Hong Kong, China".

With the exception of foreign warships, access for which requires the permission of the Central People's Government, ships shall enjoy access to the ports of the Hong Kong Special Administrative Region in accordance with the laws of the Hong Kong Special Administrative Region.

IX

The Hong Kong Special Administrative Region shall maintain the status of Hong Kong as a centre of international and regional aviation. Airlines incorporated and having their principal place of business in Hong Kong and civil aviation related businesses may continue to operate. The Hong Kong Special Administrative Region shall continue the previous system of civil aviation management in Hong Kong, and keep its own aircraft register in accordance with provisions laid down by the Central People's Government concerning nationality marks and registration marks of aircraft. The Hong Kong Special Administrative Region shall be responsible on its own for matters of routine business and technical management of civil aviation, including the management of airports, the provision of air traffic services within the flight information region of the Hong Kong Special Administrative Region, and the discharge of other responsibilities allocated under the regional air navigation procedures of the International Civil Aviation Organisation.

The Central People's Government shall, in consultation with the Hong Kong Special Administrative Region Government, make arrangements providing for air services between the Hong Kong Special Administrative Region and other parts of the People's Republic of China for airlines incorporated and having their principal place of business in the Hong Kong Special Administrative Region and other airlines of the People's Republic of China. All Air Service Agreements providing for air services between other parts of the People's Republic of China and other states and regions with stops at the Hong Kong Special Administrative Region and air services between the Hong Kong Special Administrative Region and other states and regions with stops at other parts of the People's Republic of China shall be concluded by the Central People's Government. For this purpose, the Central People's Government shall take account of the special conditions and economic interests of the Hong Kong Special Administrative Region and consult the Hong Kong Special Administrative Region Government. Representatives of the Hong Kong Special Administrative Region Government may participate as members of delegations of the Government of the People's Republic of China in air service consultations with foreign governments concerning arrangements for such services.

Acting under specific authorisations from the Central People's Government, the Hong Kong Special Administrative Region Government may:

- renew or amend Air Service Agreements and arrangements previously in force; in principle, all such Agreements and arrangements may be renewed or amended with the rights contained in such previous Agreements and arrangements being as far as possible maintained;
- negotiate and conclude new Air Service Agreements providing routes for airlines incorporated and having their principal place of business in the Hong Kong Special Administrative Region and rights for overflights and technical stops; and
- negotiate and conclude provisional arrangements where no Air Service Agreement with a foreign state or other region is in force.

All scheduled air services to, from or through the Hong Kong Special Administrative Region which do not operate to, from or through the mainland of China shall be regulated by Air Service Agreements or provisional arrangements referred to in this paragraph.

The Central People's Government shall give the Hong Kong Special Administrative Region Government the authority to:

- negotiate and conclude with other authorities all arrangements concerning the implementation of the above Air Service Agreements and provisional arrangements;
- issue licences to airlines incorporated and having their principal place of business in the Hong Kong Special Administrative Region;
- designate such airlines under the above Air Service Agreements and provisional arrangements; and
- issue permits to foreign airlines for services other than those to, from or through the mainland of China.

X

The Hong Kong Special Administrative Region shall maintain the educational system previously practised in Hong Kong. The Hong Kong Special Administrative Region Government shall on its own decide policies in the fields of culture, education, science and technology, including policies regarding the educational system and its administration, the language of instruction, the allocation of funds, the examination system, the system of academic awards and the recognition of educational and technological qualifications. Institutions of all kinds, including those run by religious and community organisations, may retain their autonomy. They may continue to recruit staff and use teaching materials from outside the Hong Kong Special Administrative Region. Students shall enjoy freedom of choice of education and freedom to pursue their education outside the Hong Kong Special Administrative Region.

XI

Subject to the principle that foreign affairs are the responsibility of the Central People's Government, representatives of the Hong Kong Special Administrative Region Government may participate, as members of delegations of the Government of the People's Republic of China, in negotiations at the diplomatic level directly affecting the Hong Kong Special Administrative Region conducted by the Central People's Government. The Hong Kong Special Administrative Region may on its own, using the name "Hong Kong, China", maintain and develop relations and conclude and implement agreements with states, regions and relevant international organisations in the appropriate fields, including the economic, trade, financial and monetary, shipping, communications, touristic, cultural and sporting fields. Representatives of the Hong Kong Special Administrative Region Government may participate, as members of delegations of the Government of the People's Republic of China, in international organisations or conferences in appropriate fields limited to states and affecting the Hong Kong Special Administrative Region, or may attend in such other capacity as may be permitted by the Central People's Government and the organisation or conference concerned, and may express their views in the name of "Hong Kong, China". The Hong Kong Special Administrative Region may, using the name "Hong Kong, China", participate in international organisations and conferences not limited to states.

The application to the Hong Kong Special Administrative Region of international agreements to which the People's Republic of China is or becomes a party shall be decided by the Central People's Government, in accordance with the circumstances and needs of the Hong Kong Special Administrative Region, and after seeking the views of the Hong Kong Special Administrative Region Government. International agreements to which the

People's Republic of China is not a party but which are implemented in Hong Kong may remain implemented in the Hong Kong Special Administrative Region. The Central People's Government shall, as necessary, authorise or assist the Hong Kong Special Administrative Region Government to make appropriate arrangements for the application to the Hong Kong Special Administrative Region of other relevant international agreements. The Central People's Government shall take the necessary steps to ensure that the Hong Kong Special Administrative Region shall continue to retain its status in an appropriate capacity in those international organisations of which the People's Republic of China is a member and in which Hong Kong participates in one capacity or another. The Central People's Government shall, where necessary, facilitate the continued participation of the Hong Kong Special Administrative Region in an appropriate capacity in those international organisations in which Hong Kong is a participant in one capacity or another, but of which the People's Republic of China is not a member.

Foreign consular and other official or semi-official missions may be established in the Hong Kong Special Administrative Region with the approval of the Central People's Government. Consular and other official missions established in Hong Kong by states which have established formal diplomatic relations with the People's Republic of China may be maintained. According to the circumstances of each case, consular and other official missions of states having no formal diplomatic relations with the People's Republic of China may either be maintained or changed to semi-official missions. States not recognised by the People's Republic of China can only establish non-governmental institutions.

The United Kingdom may establish a Consulate-General in the Hong Kong Special Administrative Region.

XII

The maintenance of public order in the Hong Kong Special Administrative Region shall be the responsibility of the Hong Kong Special Administrative Region Government. Military forces sent by the Central People's Government to be stationed in the Hong Kong Special Administrative Region for the purpose of defence shall not interfere in the internal affairs of the Hong Kong Special Administrative Region. Expenditure for these military forces shall be borne by the Central People's Government.

XIII

The Hong Kong Special Administrative Region Government shall protect the rights and freedoms of inhabitants and other persons in the Hong Kong Special Administrative Region according to law. The Hong Kong Special Administrative Region Government shall maintain the rights and freedoms as provided for by the laws previously in force in Hong Kong, including freedom of the person, of speech, of the press, of assembly, of association, to form and join trade unions, of correspondence, of travel, of movement, of strike, of demonstration, of choice of occupation, of academic research, of belief, inviolability of the home, the freedom to marry and the right to raise a family freely.

Every person shall have the right to confidential legal advice, access to the courts, representation in the courts by lawyers of his choice, and to obtain judicial remedies. Every person shall have the right to challenge the actions of the executive in the courts.

Religious organisations and believers may maintain their relations with religious organisations and believers elsewhere, and schools, hospitals and welfare institutions run by religious organisations may be continued. The relationship between religious organisations in the Hong Kong Special Administrative Region and those in other parts of the People's Republic of China shall be based on the principles of non-subordination, non-interference and mutual respect.

The provisions of the International Covenant on Civil and Political Rights and the International Covenant on Economic, Social and Cultural Rights as applied to Hong Kong shall remain in force.

XIV

The following categories of persons shall have the right of abode in the Hong Kong Special Administrative Region, and, in accordance with the law of the Hong Kong Special Administrative Region, be qualified to obtain permanent identity cards issued by the Hong Kong Special Administrative Region Government, which state their right of abode:

- all Chinese nationals who were born or who have ordinarily resided in Hong Kong before or after the establishment of the Hong Kong Special Administrative Region for a continuous period of 7 years or more, and persons of Chinese nationality born outside Hong Kong of such Chinese nationals;
- all other persons who have ordinarily resided in Hong Kong before or after the establishment of the Hong Kong Special Administrative Region for a continuous period of 7 years or more and who have taken Hong Kong as their place of permanent residence before or after the establishment of the Hong Kong Special Administrative Region, and persons under 21 years of age who were born of such persons in Hong Kong before or after the establishment of the Hong Kong Special Administrative Region;
- any other persons who had the right of abode only in Hong Kong before the establishment of the Hong Kong Special Administrative Region.

The Central People's Government shall authorise the Hong Kong Special Administrative Region Government to issue, in accordance with the law, passports of the Hong Kong Special Administrative Region of the People's Republic of China to all Chinese nationals who hold permanent identity cards of the Hong Kong Special Administrative Region, and travel documents of the Hong Kong Special Administrative Region of the People's Republic of China to all other persons lawfully residing in the Hong Kong Special Administrative Region. The above passports and documents shall be valid for all states and regions and shall record the holder's right to return to the Hong Kong Special Administrative Region.

For the purpose of travelling to and from the Hong Kong Special Administrative Region, residents of the Hong Kong Special Administrative Region may use travel documents issued by the Hong Kong Special Administrative Region Government, or by other competent authorities of the People's Republic of China, or of other states. Holders of permanent identity cards of the Hong Kong Special Administrative Region may have this fact stated in their travel documents as evidence that the holders have the right of abode in the Hong Kong Special Administrative Region.

Entry into the Hong Kong Special Administrative Region of persons from other parts of China shall continue to be regulated in accordance with the present practice.

The Hong Kong Special Administrative Region Government may apply immigration controls on entry, stay in and departure from the Hong Kong Special Administrative Region by persons from foreign states and regions.

Unless restrained by law, holders of valid travel documents shall be free to leave the Hong Kong Special Administrative Region without special authorisation.

The Central People's Government shall assist or authorise the Hong Kong Special Administrative Region Government to conclude visa abolition agreements with states or regions.

ANNEX II

SINO-BRITISH JOINT LIAISON GROUP

1. In furtherance of their common aim and in order to ensure a smooth transfer of government in 1997, the Government of the United Kingdom and the Government of the People's Republic of China have agreed to continue their discussions in a friendly spirit and to develop the cooperative relationship which already exists between the two Governments over Hong Kong with a view to the effective implementation of the Joint Declaration.

2. In order to meet the requirements for liaison, consultation and the exchange of information, the two Governments have agreed to set up a Joint Liaison Group.

3. The functions of the Joint Liaison Group shall be:

(*a*) to conduct consultations on the implementation of the Joint Declaration;
(*b*) to discuss matters relating to the smooth transfer of government in 1997;
(*c*) to exchange information and conduct consultations on such subjects as may be agreed by the two sides.

Matters on which there is disagreement in the Joint Liaison Group shall be referred to the two Governments for solution through consultations.

4. Matters for consideration during the first half of the period between the establishment of the Joint Liaison Group and 1 July 1997 shall include:

(*a*) action to be taken by the two Governments to enable the Hong Kong Special Administrative Region to maintain its economic relations as a separate customs territory, and in particular to ensure the maintenance of Hong Kong's participation in the General Agreement on Tariffs and Trade, the Multifibre Arrangement and other international arrangements; and
(*b*) action to be taken by the two Governments to ensure the continued application of international rights and obligations affecting Hong Kong.

5. The two Governments have agreed that in the second half of the period between the establishment of the Joint Liaison Group and 1 July 1997 there will be need for closer cooperation, which will therefore be intensified during that period. Matters for consideration during this second period shall include:

(*a*) procedures to be adopted for the smooth transition in 1997;
(*b*) action to assist the Hong Kong Special Administrative Region to maintain and develop economic and cultural relations and conclude agreements on these matters with states, regions and relevant international organisations.

6. The Joint Liaison Group shall be an organ for liaison and not an organ of power. It shall play no part in the administration of Hong Kong or the Hong Kong Special Administrative Region. Nor shall it have any supervisory role over that administration. The members and supporting staff of the Joint Liaison Group shall only conduct activities within the scope of the functions of the Joint Liaison Group.

7. Each side shall designate a senior representative, who shall be of Ambassadorial rank, and four other members of the group. Each side may send up to 20 supporting staff.

8. The Joint Liaison Group shall be established on the entry into force of the Joint Declaration. From 1 July 1988 the Joint Liaison Group shall have its principal base in Hong Kong. The Joint Liaison Group shall continue its work until 1 January 2000.

9. The Joint Liaison Group shall meet in Beijing, London and Hong Kong. It shall meet at least once in each of the three locations in each year. The venue for each meeting shall be agreed between the two sides.

10. Members of the Joint Liaison Group shall enjoy diplomatic privileges and immunities as appropriate when in the three locations. Proceedings of the Joint Liaison Group shall remain confidential unless otherwise agreed between the two sides.

11. The Joint Liaison Group may by agreement between the two sides decide to set up specialist sub-groups to deal with particular subjects requiring expert assistance.

12. Meetings of the Joint Liaison Group and sub-groups may be attended by experts other than the members of the Joint Liaison Group. Each side shall determine the composition of its delegation to particular meetings of the Joint Liaison Group or sub-group in accordance with the subjects to be discussed and the venue chosen.

13. The working procedures of the Joint Liaison Group shall be discussed and decided upon by the two sides within the guidelines laid down in this Annex.

ANNEX III

LAND LEASES

The Government of the United Kingdom and the Government of the People's Republic of China have agreed that, with effect from the entry into force of the Joint Declaration, land leases in Hong Kong and other related matters shall be dealt with in accordance with the following provisions:

1. All leases of land granted or decided upon before the entry into force of the Joint Declaration and those granted thereafter in accordance with paragraph 2 or 3 of this Annex, and which extend beyond 30 June 1997, and all rights in relation to such leases shall continue to be recognised and protected under the law of the Hong Kong Special Administrative Region.

2. All leases of land granted by the British Hong Kong Government not containing a right of renewal that expire before 30 June 1997, except short term tenancies and leases for special purposes, may be extended if the lessee so wishes for a period expiring not later than 30 June 2047 without payment of an additional premium. An annual rent shall be charged from the date of extension equivalent to 3 per cent of the rateable value of the property at that date, adjusted in step with any changes in the rateable value thereafter. In the case of old schedule lots, village lots, small houses and similar rural holdings, where the property was on 30 June 1984 held by, or, in the case of small houses granted after that date, the property is granted to, a person descended through the male line from a person who was in 1898 a resident of an established village in Hong Kong, the rent shall remain unchanged so long as the property is held by that person or by one of his lawful successors in the male line. Where leases of land not having a right of renewal expire after 30 June 1997, they shall be dealt with in accordance with the relevant land laws and policies of the Hong Kong Special Administrative Region.

3. From the entry into force of the Joint Declaration until 30 June 1997, new leases of land may be granted by the British Hong Kong Government for terms expiring not later than 30 June 2047. Such leases shall be granted at a premium and nominal rental until 30 June 1997, after which date they shall not require payment of an additional premium but an annual rent equivalent to 3 per cent of the rateable value of the property at that date, adjusted in step with changes in the rateable value thereafter, shall be charged.

4. The total amount of new land to be granted under paragraph 3 of this Annex shall be limited to 50 hectares a year (excluding land to be granted to the Hong Kong Housing Authority for public rental housing) from the entry into force of the Joint Declaration until 30 June 1997.

5. Modifications of the conditions specified in leases granted by the British Hong Kong Government may continue to be granted before 1 July 1997 at a premium equivalent to the difference between the value of the land under the previous conditions and its value under the modified conditions.

6. From the entry into force of the Joint Declaration until 30 June 1997, premium income obtained by the British Hong Kong Government from land transactions shall, after deduction of the average cost of land production, be shared equally between the British Hong Kong Government and the future Hong Kong Special Administrative Region Government. All the income obtained by the British Hong Kong Government, including the amount of the above mentioned deduction, shall be put into the Capital Works Reserve Fund for the financing of land development and public works in Hong Kong. The Hong Kong Special Administrative Region Government's share of the premium income shall be deposited in banks incorporated in Hong Kong and shall not be drawn on except for the financing of land development and public works in Hong Kong in accordance with the provisions of paragraph 7(*d*) of this Annex.

7. A Land Commission shall be established in Hong Kong immediately upon the entry into force of the Joint Declaration. The Land Commission shall be composed of an equal number of officials designated respectively by the Government of the United Kingdom and the Government of the People's Republic of China together with necessary supporting staff. The officials of the two sides shall be responsible to their respective governments. The Land Commission shall be dissolved on 30 June 1997.

The terms of reference of the Land Commission shall be:

(*a*) to conduct consultations on the implementation of this Annex;

(*b*) to monitor observance of the limit specified in paragraph 4 of this Annex, the amount of land granted to the Hong Kong Housing Authority for public rental housing, and the division and use of premium income referred to in paragraph 6 of this Annex;

(*c*) to consider and decide on proposals from the British Hong Kong Government for increasing the limit referred to in paragraph 4 of this Annex;

(*d*) to examine proposals for drawing on the Hong Kong Special Administrative Region Government's share of premium income referred to in paragraph 6 of this Annex and to make recommendations to the Chinese side for decision.

Matters on which there is disagreement in the Land Commission shall be referred to the Government of the United Kingdom and the Government of the People's Republic of China for decision.

8. Specific details regarding the establishment of the Land Commission shall be finalised separately by the two sides through consultations.

EXCHANGE OF MEMORANDA

(A) UNITED KINGDOM MEMORANDUM

MEMORANDUM

In connection with the Joint Declaration of the Government of the United Kingdom of Great Britain and Northern Ireland and the Government of the People's Republic of China on the question of Hong Kong to be signed this day, the Government of the United Kingdom declares that, subject to the completion of the necessary amendments to the relevant United Kingdom legislation:

(*a*) All persons who on 30 June 1997 are, by virtue of a connection with Hong Kong, British Dependent Territories citizens (BDTCs) under the law in force in the United Kingdom will cease to be BDTCs with effect from 1 July 1997, but will be eligible to retain an appropriate status which, without conferring the right of abode in the United Kingdom, will entitle them to continue to use passports issued by the Government of the United Kingdom. This status will be acquired by such persons only if they hold or are included in such a British passport issued before 1 July 1997, except that eligible persons born on or after 1 January 1997 but before 1 July 1997 may obtain or be included in such a passport up to 31 December 1997.

(*b*) No person will acquire BDTC status on or after 1 July 1997 by virtue of a connection with Hong Kong. No person born on or after 1 July 1997 will acquire the status referred to as being appropriate in sub-paragraph (*a*).

(*c*) United Kingdom consular officials in the Hong Kong Special Administrative Region and elsewhere may renew and replace passports of persons mentioned in sub-paragraph (*a*) and may also issue them to persons, born before 1 July 1997 of such persons, who had previously been included in the passport of their parent.

(*d*) Those who have obtained or been included in passports issued by the Government of the United Kingdom under sub-paragraphs (*a*) and (*c*) will be entitled to receive, upon request, British consular services and protection when in third countries.

Beijing, 19 December 1984.

(Stamp of the British Embassy)

(B) CHINESE MEMORANDUM

Translation

MEMORANDUM

The Government of the People's Republic of China has received the memorandum from the Government of the United Kingdom of Great Britain and Northern Ireland dated 19 December 1984.

Under the Nationality Law of the People's Republic of China, all Hong Kong Chinese compatriots, whether they are holders of the "British Dependent Territories citizens' Passport" or not, are Chinese nationals.

Taking account of the historical background of Hong Kong and its realities, the competent authorities of the Government of the People's Republic of China will, with effect from 1 July 1997, permit Chinese nationals in Hong Kong who were previously called "British Dependent Territories citizens" to use travel documents issued by the Government of the United Kingdom for the purpose of travelling to other states and regions.

The above Chinese nationals will not be entitled to British consular protection in the Hong Kong Special Administrative Region and other parts of the People's Republic of China on account of their holding the above-mentioned British travel documents.

Beijing, 19 December 1984.

(Stamp of the Ministry of Foreign Affairs of the Central People's Government)

B

Background to the Negotiations Preceding the Sino-British Joint Declaration

History

During the nineteenth century Britain concluded three treaties with the then Chinese Government relating to Hong Kong: the Treaty of Nanking, signed in 1842 and ratified in 1843 under which Hong Kong Island was ceded in perpetuity; the Convention of Peking in 1860 under which the southern part of the Kowloon peninsula and Stonecutters Island were ceded in perpetuity; the Convention of 1898 under which the New Territories (comprising 92 per cent of the total land area of the territory) were leased to Britain for 99 years from 1 July 1898. It was the fact that the New Territories are subject to a lease with a fixed expiry date which lay behind the decision by the British Government to seek to enter negotiations with the Government of the People's Republic of China (referred to hereafter as "the Chinese Government") on Hong Kong's future.

The Chinese Government has consistently taken the view that the whole of Hong Kong is Chinese territory. Its position for many years was that the question of Hong Kong came into the category of unequal treaties left over from history; that it should be settled peacefully through negotiations when conditions were ripe; and that pending a settlement the status quo should be maintained. The Chinese Government made its view of Hong Kong's status clear in a letter to the Chairman of the United Nations Special Committee

Source: Bill Knight, ed., *Hong Kong: 1985*, Hong Kong: Goverment Publications Center, n.d., pp. 16–41.

on the Situation with regard to the Implementation of the Declaration on the Granting of Independence to Colonial Countries and Peoples in March 1972. This maintained that the settlement of the question of Hong Kong was a matter of China's sovereign right and that consequently Hong Kong should not be included in the list of colonial territories covered by the Declaration on the Granting of Independence to Colonial Countries and Peoples.

The Background to the Negotiations

In the late 1970's, as the period before the termination of the New Territories lease continued to shorten, concern about the future of Hong Kong began to be expressed both in the territory itself and among foreign investors. In particular there was increasing realisation of the problem posed by individual land leases granted in the New Territories, all of which are set to expire three days before the expiry of the New Territories lease in 1997. It was clear that the steadily shortening span of these leases and the inability of the Hong Kong Government to grant new ones extending beyond 1997 would be likely to deter investment and damage confidence.

The British Government had by this time, following a detailed examination of the problem conducted in consultation with the then Governor, concluded that confidence would begin to erode quickly in the early to mid-1980's if nothing was done to alleviate the uncertainty caused by the 1997 deadline. Accordingly, when the Governor of Hong Kong visited Peking in March 1979 at the invitation of the Chinese Minister of Foreign Trade, an attempt was made, on the initiative of the British Government, to solve the specific question of land leases expiring in 1997. These discussions did not result in measures to solve the problem.

In the course of the next two years there was increasing awareness of the need to remove the uncertainty which the 1997 deadline generated. The importance of the issue was publicly stressed by the senior Unofficial Member of the Executive Council in May 1982. In January 1982 Sir (then Mr) Humphrey Atkins, Lord Privy Seal, visited Peking and was given significant indications of Chinese policy towards Hong Kong by Chinese leaders, which confirmed the view of the British Government that negotiations should be opened with the Chinese Government.

The Prime Minister's Visit to China

Against this background the British Government decided that the Prime Minister's visit to China in September 1982 would provide an opportunity to open discussions with the Chinese Government on the future of Hong Kong. It was evident that the Chinese Government had reached the same conclusion, and substantive discussions took place during the visit. Following a meeting between the Prime Minister and Chairman Deng Xiaoping on 24 September 1982 the following joint statement was issued:

> "Today the leaders of both countries held far-reaching talks in a friendly atmosphere on the future of Hong Kong. Both leaders made clear their respective positions on this subject.
>
> They agreed to enter talks through diplomatic channels following the visit with the common aim of maintaining the stability and prosperity of Hong Kong."

The Course of the Negotiations

The Prime Minister's visit was followed by the first phase of negotiations conducted by the British Ambassador in Peking and the Chinese Foreign Ministry. These consisted of exchanges between the two sides on the basis on which the negotiations would be conducted, and on the agenda. On 1 July 1983 it was announced that the second phase of the talks would begin in Peking on 12 July. The pattern of negotiation in the second phase, which was continued until the end of the negotiations, was for formal rounds of talks to be held between delegations led by the British Ambassador in Peking and a Vice or Assistant Minister of the Chinese Foreign Ministry, supplemented as necessary by informal contacts between the two delegations. The Governor of Hong Kong took part in every round of formal talks as a member of the British delegation.

In the course of the negotiations the British Government explained in detail the systems which prevail in Hong Kong and the importance for these systems of the British administrative role and link. Following extensive discussion, however, it became clear that the continuation of British administration after 1997 would not be acceptable to China in any form. After full consultation with the Governor and the Executive Council of Hong Kong, the British Government therefore proposed that the two sides discuss on a conditional basis what effective measures other than continued British administration might be devised to maintain the stability and prosperity of Hong Kong and explore further the Chinese ideas about the future which had at that stage been explained to them, in order to see whether on this basis arrangements which would ensure lasting stability and prosperity for Hong Kong could be constructed. The Chinese Government was told that, if this process was successful, the British Government would consider recommending to Parliament a bilateral agreement enshrining the arrangements. The British Government also undertook in this event to assist in the implementation of such arrangements. Following this, the British Government sought to explore with the Chinese Government the implications of the Chinese Government's concept of Hong Kong as a Special Administrative Region of the People's Republic of China. In response, the Chinese side further elaborated its policies and ideas.

In April 1984 the two sides completed initial discussion of these matters. There were a number of outstanding unresolved points, but it was by then clear that an acceptable basis for an agreement might be possible. At the invitation of the Chinese Government the Secretary of State for Foreign and Commonwealth Affairs visited Peking from 15 to 18 April. During his meetings with Chinese leaders the two sides reviewed the course of the talks on the future of Hong Kong, and further progress was made. In Hong Kong on 20 April Sir Geoffrey Howe made a statement on the approach of the British Government to the negotiations. He said that it would not be realistic to think of an agreement that provided for continued British administration in Hong Kong after 1997: for that reason the British Government had been examining with the Chinese Government how it might be possible to arrive at arrangements that would secure for Hong Kong, after 1997, a high degree of autonomy under Chinese sovereignty, and that would preserve the way of life in Hong Kong, together with the essentials of the present systems. He made it clear that the British Government were working for a framework of arrangements that would provide for the maintenance of Hong Kong's flourishing and dynamic society, and an agreement in which such arrrangements would be formally set out.

After Sir Geoffrey Howe's visit in April 1984 negotiations continued. A working group was established on 21 June 1984 to meet full-time in Peking and consider documents tabled by both sides. From 27 to 31 July 1984 the Secretary of State for Foreign and Commonwealth Affairs again visited Peking. The visit was devoted almost entirely to the future of Hong Kong. Sir Geoffrey Howe announced in Hong Kong on 1 August that very substantial progress had been made towards agreement on the form and content of documents which would set out arrangements for Hong Kong's future with clarity and precision, in legally binding form.

Sir Geoffrey also announced on the same occasion that the two sides had agreed to establish a Sino-British Joint Liaison Group which would come into being when the agreement came into force and continue until the year 2000. It would meet in Peking, London and Hong Kong. It was agreed that the Group would not be an organ of power. Its functions would be: liaison, consultation on the implementation of the agreement, and exchange of information. It was agreed that it would play no part in the administration of Hong Kong. The British Government would continue to be responsible for the administration of Hong Kong up to 30 June 1997.

Following Sir Geoffrey Howe's visit the negotiations continued on the remaining unresolved issues and three further rounds of plenary talks took place. A further ad hoc working group was established in Peking on 24 August. By 18 September negotiators on both sides had approved the English and Chinese texts of the documents that make up the agreement and the associated Exchange of Memoranda. These were submitted to British Ministers and Chinese leaders for final approval. The texts were initialled by the two delegation leaders on 26 September and later that day were published simultaneously in Hong Kong, London and Peking.

Consultation with the People of Hong Kong: (I) In the course of the negotiations

From the beginning of the negotiations the British Government were conscious that the negotiations concerned the interests and future of the five and a half million people of Hong Kong. It was the consistent position of the British Government that any agreement with the Chinese Government on the future of the territory had to be acceptable to the people of Hong Kong as well as to the British Parliament and the Chinese Government.

The negotiations were conducted on a basis of confidentiality. This was crucial to their success, but the maintenance of confidentiality also caused much concern and anxiety among the people of Hong Kong who were understandably anxious to know what was being negotiated for their future. All members of the Executive Council, as the Governor's closest advisers, were kept fully informed on the negotiations and consulted on a continuing basis throughout the period. The Unofficial Members of the Executive and Legislative Councils (UMELCO) provided invaluable advice to the Governor and to Ministers on the course of the negotiations and on the attitude of the people of Hong Kong.

At a number of crucial points in the negotiations the Governor and Unofficial Members of the Executive Council visited London for consultations with the Prime Minister and other Ministers. British Ministers also paid a series of visits to Hong Kong, to consult the Governor, the Executive Council and the Unofficial Members of the Executive and Legislative Councils and to keep in touch with opinion in the territory. The Secretary of State for Foreign and Commonwealth Affairs was able to describe the approach of the British Government to the negotiations in his statement in Hong Kong on 20 April 1984, and to fill in more details of what might eventually be included in an agreement in a further statement in the territory on 1 August 1984. In the course of the negotiations, and in particular following the statement of 20 April, numerous individuals and groups in Hong Kong made specific proposals on what should be included in an eventual agreement. The Legislative Council of Hong Kong debated aspects of the future of the territory on a number of occasions. The British Government paid close attention to these expressions of opinion which the Hong Kong Government relayed to Ministers, and to views about the future expressed through a variety of channels – by and through UMELCO, through the press, through individual communications addressed to the British Government or the Hong Kong Government. In this way the British Government sought to take into account the views of the people of Hong Kong to the maximum extent possible during the negotiations.

In the same way the maintenance of confidentiality made the task of consulting Parliament on the negotiations more difficult. Despite this there were debates on Hong Kong in October and November 1983 and in May 1984, and part of the Foreign Affairs Debate in March 1984 was also devoted to Hong Kong. Members of Parliament kept in close touch with the people of Hong Kong, both through visits to the territory and through meetings with Hong Kong delegations visiting the United Kingdom.

Consultation with the People of Hong Kong: (II) After publication of the draft agreement

With the publication of the text of the draft agreement, many of the difficulties attendant on the process of consultation were removed. The British Government consistently recognised that an agreement on the future of Hong Kong must be acceptable to the people of Hong Kong as well as to Parliament. Accordingly, the people of Hong Kong were invited to comment on the overall acceptability of the draft agreement before it was submitted for approval by Parliament.

This process started on 26 September with the publication of a White Paper by the British Government and the Hong Kong Government. The paper explained the background to the preceding two years of negotiations and their course, included the text of the draft agreement and the associated memoranda on the status of persons after 30 June 1997 who at present are British Dependent Territories citizens, and related issues. It set these documents in the context of the negotiations.

The White Paper set out the British Government's view that the draft agreement was a good one, which they strongly commended to the people of Hong Kong. It went on to say that the British Government were confident that the agreement provided the necessary assurances about Hong Kong's future to allow the territory to continue to flourish, and to maintain its unique role in the world as a major trading and financial centre.

In presenting the White Paper at a special meeting of the Legislative Council held on the evening of 26 September 1984, the Governor, Sir Edward Youde, said that the draft agreement took account of Hong Kong's needs and the realities of history. It foresaw that change must come but that, in providing for change it provided also for the preservation of the essential elements in Hong Kong's society. In as far as was possible for governments to provide for the future, the agreement removed the uncertainty which had existed because of the 1997 deadline. It constituted a blueprint for a new stage in Hong Kong's development. As such, he commended the agreement to the Legislative Council and to the people of Hong Kong. He concluded by saying he had no doubt that the people of Hong Kong could make the agreement work and could build for themselves a successful future. Speaking a few hours later in New York, Sir Geoffrey Howe said that the Prime Minister and he had no doubt that the agreement was a good one which could be confidently commended to Hong Kong people and Parliament.

Shortly before the White Paper was published an Assessment Office was set up under the authority of the Governor, staffed by civil servants under a Commissioner, but separate from the ordinary machinery of the Hong Kong Government. The task of the Office was to provide the British Government with an analysis and assessment of opinion in Hong Kong on the draft agreement. The Office came into full operation on 26 September.

Two independent Monitors, Sir Patrick Nairne and Mr Justice Simon Li Fook-sean, were appointed by the Secretary of State for Foreign and Commonwealth Affairs. The Monitors were required to observe all aspects of the work of the Assessment Office and to submit an independent report to the Secretary of State whether they were satisfied that the Office had properly, accurately and impartially discharged its duties and faithfully followed the procedures set out in its terms of reference.

The period allowed for views to be expressed for the purposes of the Assessment Office extended for just over seven weeks and ended on 15 November. During this period all the major representative bodies in Hong Kong placed on record their view that the draft agreement was acceptable. These included the Executive Council, the Legislative Council, the Urban Council, all 18 district boards and the Heung Yee Kuk. Additionally, the Assessment Office took account of the views expressed in the media, by 430 representative organisations and groups and 1 815 individuals who made written submissions to the Office and 23 opinion polls which came to the Office's attention.

On 23 November the Commissioner of the Assessment Office submitted his report to the Governor. This was published in London and Hong Kong on 29 November. (An extract is annexed to this chapter at pages 31 to 38) This concluded that, although anxieties had been expressed by many who had submitted their views to the Assessment Office, most of the people of Hong Kong found the draft agreement acceptable. This conclusion was unreservedly endorsed by the report of the independent Monitors.

The last major expression of Hong Kong opinion came with the publication of a statement by the Unofficial Members of the Hong Kong Executive and Legislative Councils on 29 November. (It is annexed to this chapter at pages 39 to 41) This statement noted that the draft agreement was acceptable as a whole to the majority of the community. It also referred to concerns and points of detail which had been raised.

The final stage in the test of acceptability of the draft agreement came in early December when both Houses of Parliament debated the motion "that this House, having considered the views of the people of Hong Kong as set out in the reports laid before it, approves Her Majesty's Government's intention to sign the agreement on the future of Hong Kong negotiated with the Chinese Government". This motion was moved in the House of Commons on 5 December by the Secretary of State for Foreign and Commonwealth Affairs, Sir Geoffrey Howe, and in the House of Lords by the Minister of State, Baroness Young, on 10 December. On both occasions the motion was approved without a division. Both debates were attended by a delegation of Unofficial Members of the Executive and Legislative Councils and the Governor, Sir Edward Youde, was present for the debate in the House of Commons.

Signature of the Agreement

The British Government's requirement that any agreement on the future of Hong Kong must be acceptable to the people of Hong Kong as well as to Parliament had thus been met and the way was clear for the draft agreement to be signed. On 18 December the Prime Minister, Mrs Margaret Thatcher, accompanied by the Secretary of State, Sir Geoffrey Howe, arrived in Peking to sign the Agreement. The signature ceremony took place in the Great Hall of the People on 19 December in the presence of the Governor, Sir Edward Youde, and a representative group of observers from Hong Kong including the Senior Unofficial Member of the Executive Council, Sir S. Y. Chung, the Senior Unofficial Member of the Legislative Council, Sir (then Mr) Roger Lobo, other Members of the Executive and Legislative Councils and other prominent Hong Kong people drawn from a wide cross section of the Hong Kong community. Mrs Thatcher signed on behalf of the British Government and the Chinese Prime Minister, Mr Zhao Ziyang, signed on behalf of the Government of the People's Republic of China. President Li Xiannian and the Chairman of the Central Advisory Commission of the Communist Party, Mr Deng Xiaoping, were present at the ceremony.

On 20 December Mrs Thatcher and Sir Geoffrey Howe travelled to Hong Kong. Sir Geoffrey had discussions with the Executive Council and in the evening Mrs Thatcher addressed a joint session of the Executive and Legislative Councils. Her address concluded with these words:

> "The Agreement on its own cannot ensure a successful future for Hong Kong. So much lies, as it always has done, in your hands. You, the Hong Kong people, have earned the respect of the entire world for the astonishing success story which you have written. You have contributed resilience, imagination and sheer hard work. Above all you have shown the courage to adapt to changing circumstances. We have over 12 years to prepare together for the changes which lie ahead: I believe you will rise to that challenge and that the spirit, the enterprise and the prosperity of Hong Kong will flourish and endure".

ANNEX A

EXPLANATORY NOTE ON THE ANNEXES TO THE JOINT DECLARATION

Introduction

1. The following notes are intended to explain the material in the Annexes to the Joint Declaration and in the associated Exchange of Memoranda. They do not seek to be a comprehensive guide and do not include every point in the texts. They are designed to explain in simple terms, and to illustrate where appropriate, how the Annexes provide for the continuation of the essentials of Hong Kong's systems. Hong Kong is a highly developed industrial, commercial and financial centre and as such is a complex place.

Annex I: Elaboration by the Government of the People's Republic of China of its Basic Policies regarding Hong Kong

Section I: Constitutional Arrangements and Government Structure

2. When the People's Republic of China resumes the exercise of sovereignty over Hong Kong on 1 July 1997, Hong Kong will become a Special Administrative Region (SAR) of the People's Republic of China with a high degree of autonomy. A Basic Law to be enacted by the National People's Congress of the People's Republic of China will become the constitutional instrument for the Hong Kong SAR. The Letters Patent and the Royal Instructions, which have hitherto performed this function, will be revoked. As paragraph 3(12) of the Joint Declaration makes clear, the basic policies of the People's Republic of China as set out in the Joint Declaration and elaborated in this Annex will all be stipulated in the Basic Law.

3. This section of the Annex makes clear the important point that the Basic Law will stipulate that the socialist system and socialist policies practised in the rest of the People's

Republic of China will not be extended to the Hong Kong SAR and that Hong Kong's capitalist system and life-style will remain unchanged for 50 years after the establishment of the SAR.

4. The Annex also states that, except in relation to foreign and defence affairs, which are now the overall responsibility of the British Government, and will with effect from 1 July 1997 become the overall responsibility of the Central People's Government of the People's Republic of China, the Hong Kong SAR will enjoy a high degree of autonomy, including executive, legislative and independent judicial power. The SAR will also have authority to conduct its own external affairs in appropriate areas (including those relating to economic, trade, financial and monetary, shipping, communications, touristic, cultural and sporting matters) as amplified in section XI of this Annex, which deals with external relations. The SAR will enjoy a significant degree of autonomy in the maintenance and development of its air transport system as set out in section IX of this Annex, which deals with civil aviation.

5. The section of the Annex which deals with constitutional arrangements and government structure provides that the Hong Kong SAR will be under the direct authority of the Central People's Government. The SAR will therefore not be under the authority of any provincial Government.

6. This section of the Annex lays down the main elements of the structure of government in the Hong Kong SAR. It also states that the Government and legislature of the SAR will be composed of local inhabitants. The chief executive will be selected by election or through consultations held locally and be appointed by the Central People's Government. Officials of the rank equivalent to Secretaries will be nominated by the chief executive and appointed by the Central People's Government. The legislature will be elected.

7. Furthermore the Annex indicates that the executive authorities will be required to act in accordance with the law and will be accountable to the legislature; that both Chinese and English languages may be used in government and in the courts; and that, apart from the national flag and national emblem of the People's Republic of China, the SAR may use a regional flag and emblem of its own.

Section II: The Laws

8. This section of the Annex, which describes how the Hong Kong SAR will have its own system of laws, provides continuity of Hong Kong law beyond 1997. The law of the SAR will include the common law and laws passed by the legislature of the SAR. It will remain, as now, capable of adapting to changing conditions and will be free to take account of developments in the common law elsewhere. That this is so is reinforced by specific provisions in section III of this Annex providing that the courts of the SAR will be able to refer to precedents in other common law jurisdictions, that judges of the SAR may be recruited from other common law jurisdictions and that the SAR's court of final appeal may invite judges from other common law jurisdictions to sit on it.

9. Hong Kong laws and those enacted after 1 July 1997 by the legislature of the Hong Kong SAR will be valid unless they contravene the Basic Law. The policies stated in the Joint Declaration and in this Annex will be stipulated in the Basic Law.

10. Laws enacted in the Hong Kong SAR will, as now, have to be passed by the legislature, or under its authority in the form of delegated legislation. Such laws may amend the laws of

Hong Kong carried over in 1997 so long as the provisions of the Basic Law are not transgressed. After enactment, laws will have to be reported to the Standing Committee of the National People's Congress of the People's Republic of China for the record.

Section III: The Judicial System

11. The courts of Hong Kong consist of the Supreme Court, the District Courts, the Magistrates' Courts, and various statutory tribunals. The courts are at the heart of Hong Kong's legal system, which plays an important role in maintaining the stability and prosperity of Hong Kong. The Annex contains the very important provision for continuity of the judicial system.

12. The Annex indicates that the main change in the judicial system which will take place is the abolition of the system of appeal to the Privy Council and the substitution of arrangements for the final adjudication of disputes by a court of the Hong Kong SAR.

13. The independent exercise of judicial power and the obligation of the courts to decide cases in accordance with the law are both provided for in this section of the Annex. It also provides that the appointment of judges in the Hong Kong SAR will be subject to the recommendation of an independent commission similar to the existing Judicial Service Commission. The independence of the judiciary is protected by the provisions that judges of the SAR may only be removed from office on the grounds of inability or misbehaviour, and then only on the recommendation of a tribunal of judges of the SAR.

14. The Annex provides that the essentials of the system of appointment and removal of judges will remain unchanged, but the appointment and removal of judges of the highest rank will require the endorsement of the legislature of the Hong Kong SAR and have to be reported for the record to the Standing Committee of the National People's Congress.

15. At present the decision whether or not to prosecute in any particular case is the responsibility of the Attorney General. That responsibility is exercised independently free from government interference. The Annex provides that the responsibility will continue to be exercised in the SAR in the same independent way.

16. The Annex provides that local lawyers and also lawyers from outside Hong Kong, who contribute greatly both to the strength of the present legal system and to the success of Hong Kong as a commercial and financial centre, will continue to be able to practise law in Hong Kong. Provision is also made to enable arrangements to be continued whereby, for example, judgments obtained in Hong Kong may be enforced in foreign states, and evidence may be obtained overseas for use in proceedings in Hong Kong.

Section IV: The Public Service

17. This section of the Annex provides for the continuation in Hong Kong of an impartial, stable and effective public service. This is an essential factor in ensuring Hong Kong's future stability and prosperity.

18. Under the provisions of this section of the Annex serving officers will be able to continue in employment with the Hong Kong SAR Government on terms and conditions, including pay and pensions, no less favourable than before 1 July 1997. Special commissions dealing with pay and conditions of service will be retained. In addition, appointments and promotions will be made on the recommendations of a public service commission and on the basis of qualifications, experience and ability.

19. The Annex states that the Hong Kong SAR may employ foreign nationals in a number of capacities, namely as public officers (except at the highest levels), as advisers and in professional and technical posts.

20. It is explicitly provided that all pensions and other benefits due to those officers leaving the public service before or after 1 July 1997 or to their dependants will be paid by the Hong Kong SAR Government.

Section V: The Financial System

21. This section of the Annex provides for continuity in that the Government of the Hong Kong SAR will determine its own fiscal policy and manage and dispose of its financial resources, in accordance with Hong Kong's own needs. There will be no requirement to remit revenue to the Central People's Government. The Annex also makes clear that the predominant authority of the legislature in financial matters, and the system for independent and impartial audit of public accounts, will continue unchanged.

Section VI: The Economic System and External Economic Relations

22. The Annex deals together with these two subjects, which are both important for Hong Kong's export-oriented economy. Hong Kong's prosperity is heavily dependent on securing continued access to its principal export markets in the developed world. This section of the Annex provides reassurance both to the community at large in Hong Kong and to its trading partners that the basis for Hong Kong's flourishing free market economy will continue. It also ensures that Hong Kong's distinct position within the international trading community, on the basis of which Hong Kong enjoys its present rights of access, will continue.

23. The Annex provides for:

(*a*) Hong Kong's right to continue to determine its economic policies, including trade policy, in accordance with its own needs;

(*b*) the continuation of the free enterprise system, the free trade policies and the free port, which are the essentials of Hong Kong's consistent and successful economic policies;

(*c*) the continuation of individual rights and freedoms in economic matters, notably the freedoms of choice of occupation, of travel and of movement of capital, and the rights of individuals and companies to own and dispose of property.

All these essential requirements are met in this section of the Annex, read in conjunction with the appropriate paragraphs of section XIII, which deals with rights and freedoms. The right of the future Hong Kong SAR to decide its own economic policies is an essential part of the "one country, two systems" concept.

24. Hong Kong's participation in the General Agreement on Tariffs and Trade (GATT), through which it enjoys most favoured nation treatment in its major markets, has been an important element in its success as an exporter. Even in textiles and clothing, where the free trade principles of the GATT have been modified by the Multi-Fibre Arrangement (MFA) which is a negotiated derogation from the normal GATT rules, Hong Kong is able to develop its trade within the MFA and the bilateral agreements negotiated under its provisions. What is even more important, Hong Kong plays an active role in the GATT and the MFA. The continuation of Hong Kong's participation in the GATT and the MFA (if the latter is extended beyond 1986, in which year it expires) is, therefore, of prime importance: and that too is provided in this section of the Annex.

Section VII: The Monetary System

25. A freely convertible currency and the right to manage the Exchange Fund, which provides the backing for the note issue and is used to regulate the exchange value of the currency, are the essential elements of Hong Kong's monetary system. This section of the Annex clearly stipulates that these essential elements shall be maintained.

26. This section of the Annex also provides for the continuation of the arrangements by which currency is issued locally by designated banks under statutory authority.

27. The changes to the designs of bank notes and coins provided for in this section are a logical consequence of the fact that Hong Kong will become a Special Administrative Region of the People's Republic of China on 1 July 1997.

Section VIII: Shipping

28. A major factor in Hong Kong's trading success is its well-developed deep water port and the capacity to handle cargoes by up to date methods. Hong Kong's position as a major shipping centre will be preserved by this section of the Annex, which provides that systems of shipping management and shipping regulation will continue. Private shipping businesses and shipping-related businesses, including container terminals, may continue to operate freely.

29. The Annex states that the Hong Kong SAR will have its own shipping register and will issue certificates in the name of "Hong Kong, China".

30. The Annex also provides that merchant shipping will have free access to the ports of Hong Kong under the laws of the SAR.

Section IX: Civil Aviation

31. This section of the Annex makes clear that Hong Kong will continue as a major centre of regional and international air services, and that airlines and civil aviation related businesses will be able to continue operating.

32. Under the provisions of the Annex the Central People's Government of the People's Republic of China will negotiate agreements concerning air services from and to other points in China through the Hong Kong SAR. However there is also a provision that in dealing with such arrangements the Central People's Government will consult the SAR Government, take its interests into account and include its representatives in delegations to air service consultations with foreign governments. By virtue of section XI of the Annex, which deals with external relations, such representatives may also be included in delegations to appropriate international organisations. The Central People's Government will also consult the Hong Kong SAR Government about arrangements for air services between the SAR and other parts of China.

33. It is clearly provided that all scheduled air services touching the Hong Kong SAR which do not touch the mainland of China will be regulated by separate arrangements concluded by the SAR Government. For this purpose the SAR Government will be given specific authorisations from the Central People's Government to negotiate with foreign states and regions its own bilateral arrangements regulating air services. These will as far as possible maintain the rights previously enjoyed by Hong Kong. The SAR Government will also act under a general authority from the Central People's Government in negotiating all matters concerning the implementation of such bilateral arrangements and will issue its own operating permits for air services provided under these arrangements. The Annex also states that the SAR will have the authority to license local airlines, to keep its own aircraft register, to conduct the technical supervision of civil aviation and to manage airports in the SAR. In addition the general provisions in section II of the Annex, which deals with the laws of the SAR, provide for continuity of previously existing civil aviation laws beyond 1997.

34. Hong Kong's civil aviation industry will thus be able to continue to make an important contribution to the effective functioning of Hong Kong's economy in terms of servicing the needs of both business and tourism.

Section X: Culture and Education

35. This section of the Annex makes clear that Hong Kong's own system of education will be continued and that it will operate separately and differently from that in other parts of China. Although most of the funds for education in Hong Kong are provided by the Government, many educational institutes were founded and are run by community and religious organisations. Explicit provision is made for this system to be maintained.

36. This section also provides for continuity in the application of present educational standards, in the use of teaching materials from overseas and in the freedom to pursue education outside Hong Kong. It therefore provides a sound basis for Hong Kong to continue to develop an educational system which will ensure that the population will have the skills and expertise required to enable Hong Kong to maintain and improve its position in the fiercely competitive economic and trading environment within which Hong Kong operates.

37. Hong Kong has come to enjoy a varied cultural and intellectual life. This and other sections of the Annex provide for the present unique mix of cultural and intellectual influences to continue. Provision is made in section XI of the Annex, which deals with external relations, for Hong Kong to continue to participate in international sporting events.

Section XI: External Relations

38. This section of the Annex provides that, subject to the principle that foreign affairs are the responsibility of the Central People's Government, the Hong Kong SAR will manage on its own certain aspects of its external relations, in particular those in the economic field. This is particularly important, since Hong Kong's access to its principal overseas markets in the industrialised world, which is crucial to Hong Kong's industry, depends upon recognition of the separate nature of these interests.

39. In keeping with the general provisions for Hong Kong to be a Special Administrative Region under Chinese sovereignty, overall responsibility for foreign affairs will lie with the Central People's Government, just as overall responsibility for these matters at present lies with the British Government. At the same time the Hong Kong SAR will be able, under the provisions of this section of the Annex, to look after its own particular interests in certain areas by virtue of the power to be given to it to conclude agreements in appropriate fields and to be represented in the delegation of the People's Republic of China at negotiations of direct concern to Hong Kong.

40. The detailed method by which the provisions of the second paragraph of this section of the Annex, which deals with the application to the Hong Kong SAR of international agreements, will be implemented will have to be worked out during the transitional period and will be one of the matters to be considered by the Joint Liaison Group. There is a very large number of international agreements which apply to Hong Kong and whose continued application following the establishment of the Hong Kong SAR will need to be secured. This will require consultation with third countries.

41. The Annex provides for continuity of representation by all foreign states and organisations currently represented in Hong Kong, subject to the approval of the Central People's Government. Changes to the status of such missions may be required in order to take account of the existence or otherwise of formal relations between the People's Republic of China and a particular state. The United Kingdom will be represented in Hong Kong by a Consul-General after 1 July 1997.

Section XII: Defence, Security and Public Order

42. With the establishment of the Hong Kong SAR, the British garrison will be withdrawn and the Central People's Government of the People's Republic of China will be responsible for the SAR's defence. This section of the Annex makes clear that the maintenance of public order in the SAR will be the SAR Government's responsibility. It is also stated that military forces sent by the Central People's Government to be stationed in the SAR for the purpose of defence will not interfere in its internal affairs, and that expenditure for these military forces will be borne by the Central People's Government.

Section XIII: Rights and Freedoms

43. This section of the Annex explains that basic rights and freedoms will be protected in the Hong Kong SAR. It covers this important subject without an extended description of the rights and freedoms concerned by providing:

(*a*) that the rights and freedoms previously enjoyed under the laws of Hong Kong will be maintained by the SAR Government; and

(*b*) that the provisions of the International Covenants on Civil and Political Rights and on Economic, Social and Cultural Rights, as they apply to Hong Kong, will continue to apply to the Hong Kong SAR.

44. It is thus made clear that persons in the Hong Kong SAR will enjoy the same protection of the law against infringements of their basic rights as they did before the establishment of the SAR.

45. While not restricting the range of rights and freedoms the text mentions specifically some of the more important rights and freedoms presently enjoyed under the law.

46. The Covenants are too lengthy to reproduce here but they are public documents[1]. They apply to Hong Kong, with certain reservations, and, in accordance with this section of the Annex, will continue to do so after 30 June 1997. The Covenants were drafted by the United Nations Human Rights Commission and adopted by the United Nations General Assembly, and entered into force in 1976. They state a general consensus of nations on basic rights and identify in detail specific human rights and freedoms: including the right to work, to an adequate standard of living, to life and liberty, and freedom of expression, conscience, religion and association.

47. The reservations entered by the United Kingdom in respect of the application of the Covenants to Hong Kong, which are also public, took account of the realities of the social

Command 6702 Treaty Series No. 6 (1977)

and economic conditions in Hong Kong: for example, in relation to Hong Kong the United Kingdom made reservations relating to immigration and to the deportation of aliens.

Section XIV: Right of Abode, Travel Documents and Immigration

48. This section concerns the right of abode in the Hong Kong SAR, the travel documents to be used by residents of the SAR, and immigration matters. It provides for a high degree of continuity in these areas consistent with the change in Hong Kong's status on 1 July 1997.

49. The first paragraph defines the categories of people who will have the right of abode (including the right to enter, re-enter, live and work) in the Hong Kong SAR. These include:

(*a*) Chinese nationals who were born in Hong Kong or have lived there continuously for at least 7 years;

(*b*) Chinese nationals born outside Hong Kong to Chinese nationals who have the right of abode in Hong Kong;

(*c*) all non-Chinese nationals who have lived in Hong Kong continuously for at least 7 years and who have taken it as their place of permanent residence; and

(*d*) any others who had the right of abode only in Hong Kong before 1 July 1997.

Non-Chinese nationals born in Hong Kong to parents who have the right of abode there also have the right of abode but will retain it after the age of 21 only if they have met the requirements of seven years' residence and of taking Hong Kong as their place of permanent residence. The SAR Government will issue permanent identity cards to all those with the right of abode in the SAR. These cards will state the holder's right of abode.

50. This section of the Annex states that Chinese nationals who have the right of abode in the Hong Kong SAR will be eligible for passports issued by the SAR Government. Other persons who have the right of abode, or are otherwise lawfully resident, in the SAR will be eligible for other travel documents issued by the SAR Government. Both these categories of persons may also use travel documents issued by the competent authorities of the People's Republic of China or by other governments to travel to and from the SAR: these include passports issued by the United Kingdom (see paragraphs 63 to 64 below).

51. The Annex makes clear that the right to leave the Hong Kong SAR for any purpose, e.g. business, study or emigration, will be maintained subject to the normal exceptions under the law. To facilitate entry by SAR residents into third countries, all travel documents issued to them will either include a reference to their right to return to the SAR or refer to the fact that they hold a permanent identity card as evidence of their right of abode in the SAR. The SAR Government will be assisted or authorised by the Central People's Government to conclude agreements with states or regions which provide for the mutual abolition of visa requirements.

Annex II: Terms of Reference of the Sino-British Joint Liaison Group

52. As the Secretary of State for Foreign and Commonwealth Affairs emphasised in his press conference in Hong Kong on 1 August 1984, it is fully agreed between the British Government and the Chinese Government that the British Government will remain responsible for the administration of Hong Kong until 30 June 1997. Nonetheless there will, of course, be a number of areas relating to the implementation of the Joint Declaration where further consultation between the two Governments will be required after the Joint Declaration has entered into force. One obvious example in the future is the arrangements for Hong Kong's continued participation in international agreements and organisations. Such consultation will be facilitated by the Sino-British Joint Liaison Group, whose role and functions are clearly defined in Annex II.

Annex III: Land Leases
53. This Annex takes account of the important part which land plays in the development and economy of Hong Kong.

54. It considers existing leases under two main categories: those which continue beyond 30 June 1997 and those which expire before that date. In the case of the first category (mainly 75 year leases renewable for 75 years, and 999 year leases) the rights in the leases are recognised by the Annex and will be recognised and protected under the law of the SAR after 1997. These rights include the right of renewal in the case of renewable leases, as well as rights granted by the leaseholder to other persons, e.g. sub-leases, mortgages and rights of way.

55. Leases which expire before 30 June 1997 (mainly New Territories leases and 75 year non-renewable leases in the urban area) may be extended without premium until 2047. A rent of 3 per cent of current rateable value will be charged from the date of extension, except in the case of village land held by indigenous villagers who will continue to pay a nominal rent.

56. New leases running until 2047 may be issued by the Hong Kong Government in the period up to 30 June 1997. These will continue to be issued under the existing system of land disposal (i.e. by public auction, tender or private treaty grant). A premium will be payable and a nominal rent will be charged up to 30 June 1997. After that date, no additional premium will be payable but the rent will increase to 3 per cent of current rateable value.

57. The concept of charging a rent on the basis of rateable values follows that used since 1973 to fix rents on the renewal of leases. It has, however, been agreed that the rent will be based on current rateable values (i.e. a rent which will change as rateable values change) rather than based, as at present, on a fixed reference point (i.e. a rent which is based on the rateable value at the date of renewal and which remains unchanged for the whole term of the lease).

58. The amount of new land which may be granted by the Hong Kong Government will be limited to 50 hectares a year. The limit does not include land granted to the Housing Authority for the construction of public rental housing.

59. Modifications of lease conditions will continue to be dealt with by the Hong Kong Government in accordance with existing practice.

60. In recognition of the fact that leases which extend beyond June 1997 derive part of their value from the post-June 1997 portion of their term, the Annex provides for net premium income to be shared between the Hong Kong Government and the future SAR Government.

61. A Land Commission, consisting of an equal number of officials appointed by the British Government and the Chinese Government, will be set up. This Commission will monitor the implementation of the provisions in this Annex and will consider proposals for increasing the limit on the amount of new land which may be granted and for drawing on the SAR Government's share of premium income. It will not, however, consider individual land cases, nor will it be involved in deciding who should be issued with new leases. The Commission will be dissolved on 30 June 1997.

Associated Exchange of Memoranda

62. The status after 30 June 1997 of persons who are now British Dependent Territories citizens, and related issues, are covered in two Memoranda which were formally exchanged between the British and Chinese Governments on the same day as the signature of the Joint Declaration. These Memoranda set out the respective positions of the two Governments.

63. Since Hong Kong will no longer be a British dependent territory after 30 June 1997, it will not be appropriate for those who are British Dependent Territories citizens by virtue of a connection with Hong Kong to be described as such after that date. The United Kingdom Government will seek Parliamentary approval for legislation which will give such British Dependent Territories citizens the right to a new status, with an appropriate title. This status will not give them the right of abode in the United Kingdom, which they do not possess at present, but it will carry benefits similar to those enjoyed by British Dependent Territories citizens at present, including the entitlement to use British passports and to receive British consular services and protection in third countries. The status will not, however, be transmissible by descent. The United Kingdom Government has pledged to do all they can to secure for holders of these British passports the same access to other countries as that enjoyed at present by holders of British Dependent Territories citizen passports.

64. This new status will be acquired by former Hong Kong British Dependent Territories citizens only if they obtain a British passport before 1 July 1997. The only exceptions to this are:

(*a*) persons included in the passport of a parent before 1 July 1997 will be able to acquire this new status and will be able to obtain a British passport of their own after that date;

(*b*) persons who were born between 1 January and 30 June 1997 will be able to acquire this new status if they obtain a British passport, or are included in the passport of a parent, on or before 31 December 1997. Those who are included in the passport of a parent will be able to obtain a British passport of their own after that date.

65. The Chinese Memorandum states the Chinese Government's position that Hong Kong Chinese are Chinese nationals. It indicates, however, that those Chinese nationals who hold British travel documents may continue to use them after 1 July 1997. Such persons will not, of course, be entitled to consular protection by the United Kingdom Government in the Hong Kong SAR or in other parts of China.

ANNEX B

Extract from "Report of the Assessment Office on arrangements for testing the acceptability of the draft agreement on the future of the territory"

CHAPTER 3 OVERALL ASSESSMENT OF THE EXTENT OF ACCEPTABILITY

Part I: The Extent of Acceptability

3.1 Under the most important of its terms of reference, the Assessment Office is required to make an overall assessment of the extent of acceptability by the people of Hong Kong of the

draft agreement. After the most careful analysis and consideration of all the information received, the Office has concluded that most of the people of Hong Kong find the draft agreement acceptable.

3.2 All but a few have acknowledged the inevitability of the reversion of sovereignty over Hong Kong to China in 1997. The proposition that an agreement between Britain and China on the future of Hong Kong is preferable to there being no agreement, is generally understood and accepted. Furthermore, although anxieties and reservations have been expressed by many who have submitted their views, the detailed provisions of the draft agreement have been welcomed, whilst the assurances that they will be implemented have been noted.

3.3 The overall assessment and the views on which it is based are analysed in the following paragraphs.

Views Expressed in the Media

3.4 The extent and significance of media coverage monitored by the Office is described in paragraphs 2.10 and 2.11. Its depth and range have been remarkable. The overall picture from the media is one of general acceptance of the draft agreement. A small number of newspapers and magazines is known consistently to take a pro-Beijing or pro-Taiwan stand but the majority of the daily newspapers and magazines read by the bulk of the Hong Kong people have no discernible political leanings. These publications and the coverage given by radio and television have consistently taken the view that the draft agreement is acceptable in general terms. This view is illustrated by the following quotations:—

> "It has produced a document that, if nothing else, will be read by future generations as a landmark of good sense, human reasonableness, delicate compromise and high idealism. And if it succeeds, as we earnestly hope it will, not just Hongkong, but the world will be a better place."
>
> —South China Morning Post 27.9.84

> "The content of the draft agreement is better than expected."
>
> —(Translation)
> Oriental Daily 27.9.84

> "Meets the wishes of Hong Kong people."
>
> —(Translation)
> Ming Pao 27.9.84

> "The documents provide the most solid possible foundation on which the community of Hongkong and those who trade with and invest in Hongkong can go on building prosperity."
>
> —Derek Davies
> Far Eastern Economic Review 4.10.84

> "From recent observations, a vast majority of Hong Kong people find the draft agreement satisfactory."
>
> —(Translation)
> Joseph Cheng
> Wide Angle 16.10.84

Views Expressed by Representative Bodies

(A) *Executive Council*

3.5 At a press conference on 28 September 1984, members of the Executive Council promulgated their stand. Sir S. Y. Chung made an open statement describing to the general public why the members of the Executive Council endorsed the draft agreement and commended it to the people of Hong Kong.

(B) *Legislative Council*

3.6 The Legislative Council held two special meetings on 15 and 16 October 1984 respectively to debate the acceptability of the draft agreement. The Honourable R. H. Lobo moved a motion which reads as follows:—

> "That this Council endorses the draft agreement on the future of Hong Kong between the Governments of the United Kingdom of Great Britain and Northern Ireland and the People's Republic of China and commends it to the people of Hong Kong".

All but two members supported the motion.

(C) *Urban Council*

3.7 On 9 October 1984, the Urban Council at its meeting resolved:—

> "That this Council welcomes the draft agreement between the Government of the United Kingdom of Great Britain and Northern Ireland and the Government of the People's Republic of China on the future of Hong Kong."

Twenty-two members spoke in support of the motion; one abstained.

(D) *Heung Yee Kuk*

3.8 The New Territories Heung Yee Kuk at a special meeting on 16 October 1984 passed the following resolution:—

> "The New Territories Heung Yee Kuk appeals to the New Territories residents to support the draft agreement between the Government of the United Kingdom of Great Britain and Northern Ireland and the Government of the People's Republic of China on the future of Hong Kong."
>
> —(Translation)

(E) *District Boards*

3.9 All the 18 District Boards discussed and endorsed the draft agreement on the following dates:—

District Boards	*Date of Meeting*
Central and Western	4 October 1984
Eastern	18 October 1984
Islands	5 October 1984
Kowloon City	25 October 1984
Kwun Tong	29 October 1984
Mong Kok	8 November 1984
North	8 October 1984
Sai Kung	8 October 1984
Sha Tin	4 October 1984
Sham Shui Po	19 October 1984
Southern	19 October 1984

District Boards	*Date of Meeting*
Tai Po	4 October 1984
Tsuen Wan	9 October 1984
Tuen Mun	12 October 1984
Wan Chai	17 October 1984
Wong Tai Sin	22 October 1984
Yau Ma Tei	26 October 1984
Yuen Long	5 October 1984

3.10 Thus all the principal representative bodies have unequivocally placed on record their view that the draft agreement is acceptable(6).

Views Expressed by Organisations and Groups

3.11 The views expressed directly to the Office by the wide range of organisations described in paragraph 2.18 indicate that out of a total of 430 organisations, an overwhelming majority of 334 have placed on record the fact that in the view of the members they represent the draft agreement is acceptable. 33 organisations have declared that their members reject it. The remainder gave no clear indication of their position. From the response it is clear that the most influential organisations from the professional and business sectors, the religious community, the student population and the civil service, and amongst pressure groups and trade unions have come out generally in support of the draft agreement.

3.12 Some organisations have declared their unwillingness or inability to send their views directly to the Assessment Office, either because they disagreed with the concept of the Assessment Office, or they were unable to arrive at a consensus view. Amongst these were the Bar Association, the Law Society and the Hong Kong Observers. The Office has, nevertheless, taken their views as reported in the media into account(7).

3.13 . . . the Office received a number of informal collections of views from groups of people sharing a common background but not forming an organisation in the sense of being able to express a representative corporate view. There were 249 of these group submissions coming mainly from groups of civil servants, groups of students, people attending welfare agencies, staff of commercial firms, and various other groups. Altogether some 6 000 people expressed their views in this way and generally indicated clear support for the draft agreement. Of those who did not find the draft agreement acceptable, five groups of some 300 people in all used stencilled forms in identical terms expressing their rejection of the draft agreement, mainly on the grounds of total distrust of the communist regime in China.

Views Expressed by Individuals

3.14 This was the most difficult category to deal with in the context of assessing overall acceptability because of shades of opinions expressed and the tone of the language used;

---

(6) Copies of the views expressed and resolutions passed are available for public reference in the United Kingdom and Hong Kong.

(7) (*a*) *The Bar Association* was reported to have been unable to pass a resolution recommending ratification of the draft agreement.

(*b*) *The Law Society* declared that it would not give its views on the draft agreement to the Office as it did not feel a collective view would be appropriate.

(*c*) *The Hong Kong Observers* (a pressure group) whilst accepting the draft agreement, said the Office was "a farce".

in many cases, the writers simply asked questions, made suggestions, expressed concern or made comments on specific aspects. These concerns and comments have all been taken into account . . . But on the question of overall acceptability, just over 1 000 individuals have indicated a clear stand. Of these, 677 indicated positive acceptance of the draft agreement and 364 rejected it. The range of individual views is described in Part II of this chapter.

Opinion Surveys

3.15 The findings of various independent opinion surveys . . . indicated general acceptance of the draft agreement. Although the surveys were of varying reliability and validity, the consistency of the findings on the general question of overall acceptability is worthy of note.

3.16 The findings of some of the surveys may be of significance:—

(*a*) *Survey by the Survey Research Hong Kong Ltd. (SRH)*[8]*:* This survey which was carried out by a professional market research company, was based on a random sample of 6 124 respondents aged 18 or over throughout Hong Kong and door-to-door interviews were conducted. The published report of this major survey was not available to the Office at the time of writing this Report, nevertheless, the Office has studied the tabulations of survey data which were received on 15 November 1984. In answer to one of the main questions in the survey (after reading visual aids briefly describing various sections in the draft agreement): "Taking the agreement as a whole now, do you believe the terms of this agreement are a good thing for the people of Hong Kong or a bad thing for them?", 10% said "very good", 71% "quite good", 14% "good in some way not so good in others", 1% "not particularly good nor at all good" and 4% "don't know"

(*b*) *Survey by the Hong Kong Association for Continuing Education*[9]*:* 8 000 questionnaires were distributed, and 5 068 were completed and returned, 96% of which were by respondents aged 15–45. Of the respondents, 14% accepted the draft agreement unconditionally; 39% accepted it with some reservations and 44% accepted for want of a better alternative.

(*c*) *Survey by the New Hong Kong Researchers Ltd.*[10]*:* This was a street poll in which 4 616 respondents aged 20 or over were interviewed at various vantage points on Hong Kong Island and in Kowloon. 27% of the respondents did not understand the draft agreement, but 92% of those who did understand accepted it.

(*d*) *Survey by Radio Television Hong Kong:* This was a telephone survey seeking the views of elected District Board members on the draft agreement. 116 out of a total of 132 elected District Board members responded. 97% of them found the draft agreement acceptable.

---

(8) Survey Research Hong Kong Ltd. (SRH) is one of the largest market research companies in Hong Kong.

(9) Hong Kong Association for Continuing Education is a group interested in educational issues with about 200 individual members and about 30 organisation members.

(10) New Hong Kong Researchers Ltd. is a newly formed organisation with about 200 members, some being professionals, industrialists and businessmen.

(*e*) *Surveys involving young people:* Six surveys, covering a total of 4 200 respondents aged below 25, were conducted by student unions and organisations. All the topics in the draft agreement were found acceptable and the majority of respondents had confidence in Hong Kong's future but expressed a wish for direct elections and participation in drafting the Basic Law.

3.17 Notwithstanding the extent of the response in support of acceptance, it is necessary to pose the question of whether there is a "silent majority" whose views have not been heard. The Office is convinced by the evidence available that the views of the so-called "silent majority" have been reflected in the response received, and that those who have suggested this is not so are unaware of the range and depth of the response from the media, from organisations and groups and from individuals and also clearly in the independent opinion surveys described above.

3.18 The readings obtained by the Office from the views expressed in each of the main categories are consistent one with another. The overall picture which emerges can reasonably be said to be one which gives a true indication of Hong Kong opinion and supports the statement made in paragraph 3.1 above. The range of views is described in Part II of this chapter.

Part II: The Range of Views

3.19 In the following paragraphs the range of views on overall acceptability are summarised. Whilst acknowledging the overwhelming extent of overall acceptance, the Office, in examining the views expressed, has not underrated the degree to which those who have accepted the draft agreement have placed on record their concerns.

3.20 The favourable response to the draft agreement ranged from outright praise; to qualified acceptance; to acknowledgement that, in the light of the alternatives, it is the best that can be hoped for. Adverse reaction ranged from condemnation of certain parts of the draft agreement to total rejection.

3.21 The draft agreement was seen to provide a way by which sovereignty could be restored to China peacefully whilst, at the same time, it removed the uncertainties about the future, provided a sound basis for continued prosperity and stability and would preserve for fifty years the familiar life style. The concepts of "one country, two systems" and "the Hong Kong Special Administrative Region with a high degree of autonomy" were praised as imaginative and farsighted. People holding these views were optimistic that the draft agreement would work and that the two sides would honour their commitment to Hong Kong.

> "The agreement is a clear document and a good one in the light of present day politics. I salute and thank all who worked so hard for the millions living here."
>
> —An individual

> "The solution of the Hong Kong issue under the innovative guidance of the 'one country, two systems' concept will be conducive to maintaining the stability and prosperity of Hong Kong. Moreover, the success of this 'one country, two systems' arrangement may embody a more far-reaching international significance."
>
> —(Translation)
> Hong Kong Federation of Education Workers

"The White Paper also lays a solid foundation for the smooth resumption of sovereignty over Hong Kong by the People's Republic of China on 1 July 1997."

—Hong Kong Social Workers Association

3.22 Those whose acceptance was a qualified one expressed reservations about China's ability to implement the provisions of the draft agreement. The point was made that it was difficult to accept the assurances regarding implementation so far ahead, although they were prepared to give China the benefit of the doubt. They were concerned lest any reduction in Hong Kong's prosperity and thus its value to China after 1997 would remove the incentives for China to comply with the undertakings in the draft agreement. They were worried about the possibility of undue interference by China and stressed the importance of incorporating the basic principles of the draft agreement in the Basic Law with clarity and in detail. They insisted on the importance of participation by Hong Kong people in the drafting of the Basic Law and in the work of the Joint Liaison Group and the Land Commission. Notwithstanding these reservations, most took a pragmatic view towards the future and the common feeling was that it was up to the Hong Kong people to make it work.

"It is difficult to foresee the future. The draft agreement is a postdated cheque. The result can only be known when it is proved."

—An individual

"The worry about Hong Kong being governed by people from Beijing or from the left-wing cannot be removed simply by the initialling of the draft agreement."

—(Translation)
Lung Ying
Cheng Ming Magazine
October 1984

"China must give the Hong Kong people a role in the drafting of the Basic Law for the SAR . . . The Basic Law is as important a blueprint for Hongkong's future as is the Joint Declaration. What the Joint Declaration did not deal with in detail should be included in the Basic Law."

—HK Observers
South China Morning Post
29.10.84

"This is a historical moment for Hong Kong and we need to re-examine our roles and obligations. The Joint Declaration has only provided a basis; the future developments of Hong Kong depend on her people's continuous efforts and further commitments to be made on the existing foundation."

—(Translation)
University of Hong Kong Students' Union

3.23 In a number of cases, people expressed sadness at the severance of the link with Britain and the socio-economic system it has provided; disappointment at Britain's inability to maintain the *status quo*; resentment at the lack of involvement in the talks and frustration at the fact that the draft agreement could not be altered.

"I belong to the middle income group who do not have the means to emigrate to other countries and because I was born and educated in Hong Kong I would wish to stay in Hong Kong. For the purpose of your statistics you can classify me as one of those who would accept the draft agreement but I hope you will also take into account that I only accept it with much reluctance and with many reservations about the feasibility of its implementation. My heart is not truly at ease and I have no full confidence in our future. The whole thing has not been a very fair play to us because we have not had any say and there is no other alternative other than not to have an agreement at all."

—An individual

3.24 Although a few of the small number of organisations which have rejected the draft agreement have done so because of their inability to accept its specific provisions, most have scarcely touched upon those provisions, but rather have challenged the validity of the draft agreement and the right of Britain and China to determine the future of Hong Kong in this way. They have argued either for the *status quo*, or for Hong Kong to have the right of self-determination, or that any negotiations should have been with Taiwan and not with Beijing. They have stated that the PRC cannot be trusted to keep any promises made; the example of Tibet was quoted. The five groups of people who used stencilled proformas to communicate their views to the Office generally took the same line.

"They should render early support for the Hong Kong people to determine their own destiny by way of a referendum so as to avert the fate of future persecution by the communists."

—(Translation)
Cotton Bleaching & Dyeing Free Workers Union

"If Britain wants to abrogate or amend the treaties, she should approach the Republic of China as it is the legal party to these treaties."

—(Translation)
The Sun Yat Sen Memorial Association of Hong Kong Ltd

3.25 The minority of individuals who rejected the draft agreement did so because of a complete inability to trust in its implementation because of the basic incompatibility of the two systems, or because of China's past history of political upheavals, or because of past personal experience. In some cases, there was so strong a dislike of one or more of the specific aspects of the draft agreement that acceptability as a whole became impossible. The strongest feelings expressed came from those who considered themselves adversely affected by the provisions on nationality.

"The British Government ought to have compassion on those people who fled the cruelties of communist China to Hong Kong so as to assist in resettling them elsewhere."

—An individual

"Britain cannot simply rescind a historic and moral responsibility of looking after her subjects. These people are legally British and cannot be made stateless."

—An individual

Conclusion

3.26 The range of views expressed and summarised above reflects the uniqueness and complexity of the position in which the people of Hong Kong find themselves. The calmness with which the draft agreement was received and the reasoned response to it underlines its overall acceptability. There is a general feeling of relief and a wish to build Hong Kong's future on the foundation provided by the draft agreement.

ANNEX C

Statement issued by the Unofficial Members of the Hong Kong Executive and Legislative Councils on 29 November 1984

THE FUTURE OF HONG KONG

Introduction

Unofficial Members of the Executive Council and the Legislative Council* (UMELCO) have always been aware of the concern of the people of Hong Kong about their future, and on the arrival of the Governor in May 1982, the Senior Member stressed publicly the importance and urgency to the people of Hong Kong of the satisfactory resolution of this issue.

Since the Sino-British talks on the future of Hong Kong began in late 1982, UMELCO have received many representations about Hong Kong's future up to and beyond 1997.

Before the debates took place in the two Houses of British Parliament in May this year, UMELCO sent a delegation to London and issued a statement to reflect the anxieties and wishes of the people of Hong Kong: there they listed, *inter alia*, the four most important criteria by which the acceptability of the Sino-British Agreement to the people of Hong Kong would be judged.

Briefly, these are, *first*, that the Agreement must contain full details of the proposed administrative, legal, social and economic systems applicable in Hong Kong after 1997; *second*, that it must state that the provisions of the Basic Law will incorporate the relevant provisions of the Agreement; *third*, that it must provide adequate and workable assurances that the terms of the Agreement will be honoured; and *fourthly*, that the rights of Hong Kong British Nationals must be safeguarded.

Following its publication. UMELCO received a large number of representations from a wide cross-section of the community expressing their support. The South China Morning Post commissioned an independent research firm to conduct a survey, which showed that 82% of the community approved fully or in part of the statement. In addition, about 70% of the elected and appointed Unofficial Members of the 18 District Boards gave their support.

Three Unofficial Members went to Beijing in June this year and reflected to the Chinese leaders, including Chairman Deng, the anxieties and wishes of the people of Hong Kong. They also made three major proposals to the Chinese leaders, proposals which they considered would help to enhance the confidence of the people of Hong Kong about their future.

---

* The Governor consults the Executive Council in the execution of the powers and authorities granted to him by Letters Patent, and acts on its advice. At present, it consists of 4 Ex-officio Members, 2 Official Members and 10 Unofficial Members, appointed by the Governor.

The Legislative Council consists of 3 Ex-officio Members, 13 Official Members and 30 Unofficial Members. It enacts legislation and controls public expenditure.

The Unofficial Members are appointed from a wide spectrum of the community. Through their membership of over 300 boards and committees, including District Boards, the Urban Council and the Heung Yee Kuk, dealing with public affairs, with educational and legal matters, and with all facets of Hong Kong's economic and social life, Unofficial Members are in touch with all sectors of the community.

Apart from their duties in the two Councils, they monitor the effectiveness of the public administration, and consider complaints by members of the public against Government, for handling which they have far wider powers than is possessed by any Ombudsman.

These three major proposals were *first*, that the Sino-British Agreement must be detailed and binding and the Basic Law must be based on the Agreement; *second*, that the people of Hong Kong should participate in the drafting of the Basic Law and those sections relating to Hong Kong's internal affairs should be drafted in the territory, and not amended except at the initiation of Hong Kong; and *third*, that a committee of Chinese people of international standing should be appointed by China to monitor and advise on the drafting, implementation and subsequent amendments to the Basic Law.

Their trip to Beijing also received overwhelming support from the public. A second poll taken by the same independent research firm showed that eight out of ten agreed with the UMELCO visit to Beijing; 74% supported the *first*, 78% the *second*, and 61% the *third* major proposal.

Acceptability of Joint Declaration

Since its publication on 26 September 1984, all the Unofficial Members, with the exception of two Members in the Legislative Council, have endorsed and commended the Draft Agreement to the people of Hong Kong. The Draft Agreement or Joint Declaration, in their view, does meet substantially the four basic criteria contained in the UMELCO statement made in London in May. Furthermore, there are in the Joint Declaration many positive features which are to be welcomed and it contains much more detail than many people originally expected. It is a mutually binding agreement, freely negotiated and entered into between two sovereign states.

All the 18 District Boards, as well as the Urban Council and the Heung Yee Kuk, have found the draft Joint Declaration generally acceptable. Unofficial Members, in conjunction with some newspapers, commissioned an independent research firm to conduct a territory-wide survey covering 6 000 randomly selected adults above the age of 18. The results of this professional survey indicated that the majority of the people of Hong Kong found the Draft Agreement generally acceptable and that 90% of the respondents preferred the Agreement to no Agreement at all.

Whilst the Draft Agreement is acceptable as a whole to the majority of the community, some concern and points of detail have been raised. In particular, there is anxiety about interference from the Chinese Government; worry about conscription in the Hong Kong Special Administrative Region; uncertainty about the acceptability to third countries of the new form of British passport; doubt about the preservation of existing human rights and personal freedoms; fear about the stationing of PLA troops in Hong Kong; resentment about the termination of transmissibility of British nationality for Hong Kong BDTCs in 1997; reservations about possible incompatibility between the constitution of the People's Republic of China and the future Basic Law of Hong Kong; and concern about the faithful implementation of the Agreement and the policies of future Chinese leaders.

There are also very strong requests that the people of Hong Kong should not only be consulted on, but should actively participate in, the drafting of the Basic Law and that Hong Kong people should also sit on the Sino-British Joint Liaison Group.

The ultimate success of the Joint Declaration depends on people's confidence that it will be implemented faithfully and that matters of concern and questions of detail which have been raised are satisfactorily resolved and clarified by the two signatory Governments. Therefore, in accepting the Agreement, we urge both the British and Chinese Governments to take steps to reassure the people of Hong Kong in these respects.

Move to Representative Government

Given that Hong Kong will be a Special Administrative Region within China after 1997, with an elected legislature enjoying a high degree of autonomy, it is essential that a government structure consisting largely of local people is in place and in proper working order well before 1997. It is therefore necessary to move to a more representative form of government, transferring the powers of the present colonial government to the elected representatives of the people of Hong Kong.

In this respect, UMELCO welcome and support the basic proposals and the progressive approach outlined in both the Green and White Papers on the Further Development of Representative Government in Hong Kong. However, Unofficial Members echo the caution expressed in many quarters against any rapid or radical changes which may put at risk Hong Kong's *raison d'etre*, that is, stability and prosperity.

Hong Kong is not an independent state and can never be. Despite the promise of a high degree of autonomy, its subsidiary relationship with the Chinese Central Government must be understood and accepted. Parliamentary government as practised in the West, featuring adversarial politics, is not necessarily suited to Hong Kong, recognising Hong Kong's unique status and the political constraints placed upon it by this status. Hong Kong must, therefore, devise its own unique style of representative government, building on the proven elements which have been responsible for Hong Kong's success.

The Next Twelve Years

Most people in Hong Kong believe that only if stability and prosperity are maintained in the period prior to 1997 can there be any hope that stability and prosperity will be continued for fifty years after 1997. It is therefore generally felt that the next twelve years will be critical and crucial to Hong Kong's continual success beyond 1997. It is essential, therefore, that all concerned, Britain, China and the people of Hong Kong, play their part in furthering Hong Kong's stability and prosperity in the next 12 years.

The main task for Her Majesty's Government in the next twelve years is to ensure a smooth transition, so that 1997 does not represent an abrupt break with the past, but the continuation of a gradual process of evolution. To allay fears of Britain losing interest in Hong Kong, it is important that HMG continue to govern Hong Kong effectively. It must demonstrate its continual determination, resolve and commitment to Hong Kong's stability and prosperity.

The Chinese Government must demonstrate its willingness to listen to the views and wishes of the people of Hong Kong. In particular, given the great significance attached by the people of Hong Kong to the Basic Law, it is hoped that, as was suggested by the Unofficial Members to the Chinese leaders in Beijing in June this year, the people of Hong Kong should be consulted on, and participate in, the drafting of the Basic Law.

As for the people of Hong Kong, they understand that the aim of the draft agreement is the maintenance of Hong Kong's stability and prosperity, and that stability and prosperity are the product of, among other qualities, their energy, talent, industry and confidence. The Agreement provides a sound basis on which to continue to apply these attributes. The people of Hong Kong are ready and willing to take on the challenge of the new circumstances they face. Given understanding and sensitivity by the two signatory Governments and their firm commitment to implementing the Joint Declaration in both letter and spirit, the people of Hong Kong will succeed in maintaining Hong Kong's stability and prosperity, and in making the draft agreement work.

C

U. S. Secretary of State Shultz's Statement on Sino-British Joint Declaration

SECRETARY'S STATEMENT, SEPTEMBER 26, 1984

The U.S. Government welcomes the successful conclusion of 2 years of negotiations between the United Kingdom and the People's Republic of China over the future of Hong Kong.

The United States has a strong interest in the continued stability and prosperity of Hong Kong and believes the agreement will provide a solid foundation for Hong Kong's enduring future progress.

In this regard, we have noted statements by both sides indicating that Hong Kong's way of life will be guaranteed for 50 years from 1997 and that systems existing in Hong Kong will continue in the special administrative region.

We expect the American business communities, both in the United States and Hong Kong, will see in this agreement good reason for sustained confidence in the future of Hong Kong as an attractive and thriving commercial center.

The United States will provide any assistance it can, in close cooperation with the United Kingdom and the People's Republic of China, to maintain Hong Kong's appropriate participation in international bodies.

Source: Read to news correspondents, on behalf of Secretary Schultz, by acting Department spokesman Alan Romberg. *Department of State Bulletin*, Vol. 84, no. 2092 (Nov. 1984), p. 56.

D

The Further Development of Representative Government in Hong Kong

INTRODUCTION

The Green Paper

1. On July 18, 1984, the government published a Green Paper entitled *The Further Development of Representative Government in Hong Kong* and invited public comment on the proposals put forward in it.

2. The aims of the proposals were:

(*a*) to develop progressively a system of government the authority for which is firmly rooted in Hong Kong, which is able to represent authoritatively the views of the people of Hong Kong, and which is more directly accountable to the people of Hong Kong;

(*b*) to build this system on our existing institutions, which have served Hong Kong well, and, as far as possible, to preserve their best features, including the maintenance of the well established practice of government by consensus; and

(*c*) to allow for further development if that should be the wish of the community.

Public Response to the Green Paper

3. The government received and recorded comments from a wide range of sources during the two-month period allowed for public consultation on the Green Paper proposals. In addition to over 360 written submissions to the Government Secretariat from various organisations, groups and individuals, extensive consultation was carried on through the district offices. Many meetings and public discussions were attended by government officers, several surveys of public opinion were carried out and an assessment was made of views expressed extensively in the media. Comments were received from many members of district boards, area committees and mutual aid committees. Urban Councillors expressed their views in an open debate on September 4 and 6, 1984, which was followed up by a resolution from the Standing Committee of the Whole Council on September 27, 1984, and unofficial members of the Legislative Council commented on the proposals during the debate in the Legislative Council on August 2, 1984.

4. Public reaction was generally in favour of the aims of the Green Paper and the gradual and progressive nature of the proposals made in it. The need to ensure that the prosperity and stability of Hong Kong are not put at risk by introducing too many

Source: Bill Knight, ed., *Hong Kong: 1985*, Hong Kong: Government Publications Center, n.d., pp. 42–51; *White Paper*, November 21, 1984.

constitutional changes too rapidly was widely recognised. Many people supported the proposals as being a realistic and practical framework for the development of representative government at the central level during the next few years.

The White Paper

5. The purpose of this White Paper is to set out, in the light of public reaction, the government's intentions for 1985 with regard to the next stage of development of representative government in Hong Kong at the central level. The proposals in the Green Paper covered the period up to 1991. The revised plans for 1985 described in this White Paper include several of the original proposals concerning the composition of the Legislative Council in 1988.

6. In preparing the White Paper the government has recognised the need to keep in mind the provisions of the Draft Agreement on the Future of Hong Kong, and the plans have been framed accordingly.

THE LEGISLATIVE COUNCIL

The Electoral College

7. It was proposed in the Green Paper that:

(*a*) the electoral college should be composed of all the elected and, to start with, all the appointed members of the Urban Council, the new Regional Council and the district boards;

(*b*) it should be able to elect anyone who is a registered elector on the general electoral roll and who has been ordinarily resident in Hong Kong for a minimum of 10 years, not necessarily from among its own members; and

(*c*) that these arrangements should be introduced progressively, with six unofficial members being elected in 1985 and 12 in 1988.

8. There has been much comment on these proposals. One suggestion was for a single list of candidates. Another was for arrangements to be made which would ensure a reasonably balanced geographical distribution of members elected by the college. This might be achieved by dividing the members of the college into groups of districts, each of which would elect one member, with the Urban Council and Regional Council forming separate constituencies to elect one member each.

9. The government agrees that there should be a reasonably balanced geographical distribution. In consequence, in 1985. the district board members of the electoral college will be grouped into 10 geographical constituencies each based on one, two or three districts and representing roughly 500 000 people each; and members of the Urban Council and Regional Council will form two special constituencies. Thus the electoral college will return 12 unofficial members to the Legislative Council in the 1985 elections instead of the six members originally proposed in the Green Paper.

10. For the electoral college elections a list of all members of the Urban and Regional Councils and of the district boards will be published as the electoral college roll. The qualifications to be a candidate for election to the Legislative Council by the electoral college will be the same as those in the Electòral Provisions Ordinance for election to the Urban Council and the district boards. namely; a candidate must be a registered voter on the general electoral roll with a minimum of 10 years residence in Hong Kong.

11. Further details of these proposals are given at Appendix A.

Appointed Unofficial Members

19. It was proposed in the Green Paper that the number of appointed unofficial members should be reduced progressively to 23 in 1985 and 16 in 1988. Public comment on this proposal varied widely from support for the retention of appointed unofficial members indefinitely to suggestions that they should be removed from the council completely as soon as possible.

20. If an element of continuity is to be maintained in the Legislative Council it would be unwise to reduce appreciably or too hastily the number of appointed members at this stage, for their experience in the workings of the council should not be lost. The introduction of 24 elected members into a council of the present size would require a significant reduction in the number of appointed unofficial members. It has therefore been decided to increase the overall size of the council to 56 and to reduce the number of appointed unofficial members to 22 in 1985. The increase in the overall size of the council is supported by the public view that the council should be larger in order to meet the wide and diverse needs of present-day Hong Kong.

Official Members

21. It was proposed in the Green Paper that the three *ex-officio* members of the Legislative Council, the Chief Secretary, the Financial Secretary and the Attorney General, should remain on the council, but that the overall number of official members should be reduced progressively to 13 in 1985 and 10 in 1988.

22. The general view was in favour of this proposal. It is now intended that the reduction to 10 will take place in 1985 in line with the increase in the number of elected members. This will still allow for a reasonable number of officials to remain in the Legislative Council at this stage to assist in the conduct of the business of the council.

The Composition of the Legislative Council

23. The composition of the Legislative Council in 1985 and 1988 proposed in the Green Paper was as follows:

	1985	*1988*
(*a*) Elected by electoral college	6	12
(*b*) Elected by functional constituencies	6	12
(*c*) Appointed by the Governor	23	16
(*d*) Official members	13	10
Total	48	50

24. As a result of the changes which have been made to the original proposals, the composition of the council in 1985 will now be as set out below. The additional seats required to cater for the increase in elected membership have been partially offset by a small reduction in seats for appointed and official members.

	1985
(*a*) Elected by electoral college	12
(*b*) Elected by functional constituencies	12
(*c*) Appointed by the Governor	22
(*d*) Official members	10
Total	56

Direct Elections

25. The relative merits of direct and indirect elections attracted considerable public interest and comment. However, there was little evidence of support in public comment on the Green Paper for any move towards direct elections in 1985. With few exceptions the bulk of public response from all sources suggested a cautious approach with a gradual start by introducing a very small number of directly elected members in 1988 and building up to a significant number of directly elected members by 1997. Proposals that the Legislative Council's unofficial members should all be returned by direct elections were in the minority. There was considerable general public concern that too rapid progress towards direct elections could place the future stability and prosperity of Hong Kong in jeopardy. In summary, there was strong public support for the idea of direct elections but little support for such elections in the immediate future.

The Review

26. It was proposed in the Green Paper that a review should take place in 1989, after the second elections to the Legislative Council had been held in 1988, with a view to deciding, in particular, the future position of appointed unofficial members and other possible mixes of members elected by the electoral college and the functional constituencies. It was further stated that other types of electoral arrangements including the possibility of direct elections, might be considered in the review.

27. There was strong public support for the idea that there should be a review and that it should occur before 1989. It was argued that this should take place before the 1988 elections and the second phase of development. This would give an opportunity for further consultation about future development including such questions as the introduction of direct elections.

28. Since some of the Green Paper proposals concerning the composition of the Legislative Council have been brought forward from 1988 to 1985, it has been argued that the review should be held after 1988 in order to allow time for the new arrangements to settle down. On the other hand, there was strong public feeling that the timing of the review should be brought forward. There will also be a need to consider matters such as direct elections and other issues raised in the Green Paper and subsequently in public debate. After careful consideration the government has decided to bring forward the review to 1987.

THE EXECUTIVE COUNCIL

29. It was proposed in the Green Paper that the majority of appointed unofficial members of the Executive Council should be replaced progressively by members elected by the unofficial members of the Legislative Council, but the number of *ex-officio* members should remain at four.

30. There was much less comment on the Executive Council proposals than on those about the Legislative Council. An alternative proposal was made that any future Chief Executive should be free to choose his own Executive Council.

31. It is not proposed to make any changes affecting the Executive Council in 1985. The issue will remain open for further public discussion and consideration.

A Ministerial System

32. In response to the Green Paper a substantial number of suggestions were made that unofficial members of the Executive Council should be given more power and authority to control and supervise the policies and the operations of the government through some form of ministerial system in future.

33. This issue, like that concerning the position of the Governor, raises important constitutional questions. It is not a matter that need be decided in the immediate future nor is it the only way of proceeding. The whole subject will be addressed further at a later stage.

THE GOVERNOR

34. Only one proposal was made in the Green Paper with regard to the position of the Governor, namely, that in due course he should be replaced as President of the Legislative Council by a presiding officer elected by the unofficial members of the Legislative Council from among their own number.

35. Although the proposal to replace the Governor as President of the Legislative Council by an elected presiding officer was, on the whole, reasonably well received, it seems clear that the general view is in favour of making no significant changes in the position of the Governor during the next few years. Public opinion seems to favour caution as far as the immediate future is concerned.

36. It is therefore proposed to reconsider the Governor's position as President of the Legislative Council in the review in 1987.

37. As regards the position of the Governor in general, the Green Paper stated that the Governor will continue to be appointed formally by the Queen until 1997 and there was strong public support for this. Since the Green Paper was published the Draft Agreement on the Future of Hong Kong has been initialled in Peking. Any proposals for change in the position and role of the Governor will need to take into account the provisions of the Joint Declaration and these important issues will be considered at a later stage.

OTHER RELATED MATTERS

Civic Education

38. An opinion which has been expressed strongly by many organisations and individual members of the public is that arrangements should be made for the people of Hong Kong to be educated more effectively and comprehensively in political and constitutional matters so that they will be able to understand better all the implications and complexities of proposals for the development of the system of government in Hong Kong.

39. The Education Department has been promoting civic education in schools for many years through Social Studies and Economic and Public Affairs courses. It is the intention to develop these further in a new syllabus covering Government and Public Affairs. Civic education will be pursued both through the formal school curriculum and extra-curricular activities, such as current affairs clubs, debating societies and visits for senior students to district boards, the Urban Council, the UMELCO Office, government departments and the Legislative Council.

40. It is also important that adults should be given the opportunity to receive more civic education and encouragement will be given to other educational institutions and organisations to provide more courses in constitutional and public affairs for the general public.

Remuneration for Unofficial Members of the Legislative Council

41. Several suggestions were made that unofficial members of the Legislative Council should be provided with adequate remuneration so as to enable them to devote the proper amount of time and attention to their duties as councillors. This would also help to ensure that prospective candidates for the Legislative Council are not prevented from standing for election for financial reasons.

42. Although arrangements already exist for certain expenses to be reimbursed to unofficial members, it is now proposed that a standard rate of remuneration as well as payment of expenses should be provided. The level is now under consideration, with a view to introducing the scheme when the first elected unofficial members join the Legislative Council.

LEGISLATION

43. In order to implement the changes in the composition and method of selection of the Legislative and Executive Councils it will be necessary to make some amendments to the two main constitutional instruments, the Letters Patent and the Royal Instructions. The intention is to effect these in stages, as and when necessary.

44. It will also be necessary to enact legislation in Hong Kong to cover the holding of elections to the Legislative Council by the electoral college and the functional constituencies and who may vote in them. This legislation is now being drafted and will be published for debate in the Legislative Council early next year. As there is a degree of public familiarity with the legislation governing elections to the Urban Council and district boards, and in order to minimise possible confusion and misunderstanding, the electoral legislation will be framed on broadly similar lines.

45. In order to give sufficient time for preparation of this complex legislation and for all the necessary administrative arrangements for the holding of the elections to be made, it is now intended to hold the first electoral college and functional constituency elections to the Legislative Council in September 1985, instead of July as originally proposed in the Green Paper.

SUMMARY

46. A summary of the government's intentions and legislative proposals relating to the further development of representative government at the central level in Hong Kong is as follows:

Main Aims

(*a*) The main aims are to develop progressively a system of representative government at the central level which is more directly accountable to the people of Hong Kong and is firmly rooted in Hong Kong; to base this system on our existing institutions, as far as possible, and to preserve their best features; and to allow for further development later on. The objectives described in this White Paper are intended to cover only the next stage in the development of representative government in Hong Kong. Further developments will be considered later in the light of experience.

The Legislative Council

(*b*) In 1985, 24 Unofficial members of the Legislative Council will be elected:
 (i) by an electoral college composed of all members of the Urban Council, the new Regional Council, and the district boards, and
 (ii) by specific functional constituencies.

(*c*) The district board members of the electoral college will be grouped into 10 geographical constituencies. Members of the Urban Council and Regional Council will form two special constituencies. Thus 12 unofficial members will be elected to the Legislative Council from the electoral college in 1985.

(*d*) In 1985 there will be nine functional constituencies returning 12 members to the Legislative Council on the basis set out in paragraph 14.

(*e*) The number of appointed unofficial members of the council will be reduced to 22 in 1985.

(*f*) The number of official members of the council will be reduced to 10 in 1985.

(*g*) The composition of the Legislative Council in 1985 will be:
 (i) 12 unofficial members elected by the electoral college,
 (ii) 12 unofficial members elected by functional constituencies,
 (iii) 22 unofficial members appointed directly by the Governor,
 (iv) 10 official members (including the three *ex-officio* members), making a total of 56 members.

(*h*) A review to assess progress made in the development of representative government will be carried out in 1987. Further consideration will be given to direct elections in the context of the review.

The Executive Council

(*j*) No conclusions have been reached about the development of the Executive Council, nor about the introduction of a ministerial system and these matters will be considered further at a later stage.

The Governor

(*k*) The position of the Governor as President of the Legislative Council will be considered further in the review in 1987. The general position of the Governor will need to be addressed at a later stage.

Other Related Matters

(*l*) Development of Government and Public Affairs courses in schools will continue and encouragement will be given to other educational institutions and organisations to provide more courses in civic education for the general public.

(*m*) Unofficial members of the Legislative Council will receive suitable remuneration and expenses for their services.

Legislation

(*n*) The first elections will be postponed from July to September 1985 to allow for the enactment of the necessary legislation and for the necessary administrative arrangements to be made.

APPENDIX A

The Electoral College

The electoral college will comprise all members of the district boards, the Urban Council and the new Regional Council. The college will elect 12 unofficial members to the Legislative Council in September 1985.

2. In order to achieve a more balanced and adequate representation the district boards will be grouped into 10 geographical constituencies each representing approximately 500 000 people.

3. The remaining two seats will be provided by the two special constituencies formed respectively by members of the Urban Council and the Regional Council. The interests of the Heung Yee Kuk will be represented through the Regional Council.

4. Details of the 12 constituencies formed from the electoral college are in the table below.

	Constituency	*Population (000)*	*Grouping*	*Population (000)*
1.	East Island	696	Eastern District	481
			Wan Chai District	215
2.	West Island	507	Central and Western District	272
			Southern District	235
3.	Kwun Tong	663	Kwun Tong District	663
4.	Wong Tai Sin	452	Wong Tai Sin District	452
5.	Kowloon City	441	Kowloon City District	441
6.	Sham Shui Po	435	Sham Shui Po District	435
7.	South Kowloon	389	Mong Kok District	215
			Yau Ma Tei District	174
8.	East New Territories	524	North District	134
			Tai Po District	109
			Sha Tin District	281
9.	West New Territories	459	Yuen Long District	238
			Tuen Mun District	221
10.	South New Territories	726	Tsuen Wan District (Including Tsing Yi)	654
			Island District	37
			Sai Kung District	35
11.	Urban Council			
12.	Regional Council			

APPENDIX B

Functional Constituencies

Nine functional constituencies will return an overall total of 12 unofficial members to the Legislative Council in the elections planned for September 1985.

2. The commercial, industrial, and labour constituencies will each return two unofficial members to the Legislative Council. The remaining six constituencies will each return one unofficial member.

3. Details of the nine functional constituencies are in the table below.

	Constituency	Representative Organisations	No. of Seats	Total Seats
1.	Commercial	Hong Kong General Chamber of Commerce	1	
		Chinese General Chamber of Commerce	1	
				2
2.	Industrial	Federation of Hong Kong Industries	1	
		Chinese Manufacturers Association	1	
				2
3.	Financial	Hong Kong Association of Banks	1	
				1
4.	Labour	All Registered Employee Trade Unions	2	
				2
5.	Social Services	Hong Kong Council of Social Services	1	
				1
6.	Medical	Hong Kong Medical Association	1	
				1
7.	Education	Electoral rolls compiled from: statutory lists, as well as membership/staff lists of institutions and relevant professional bodies	1	
				1
8.	Legal		1	
				1
9.	Engineers and associated professions		1	
				1
		Total		12

E

Statement by the Hong Kong Government on the New Exchange-Rate System

IMPORTANT MESSAGE TO BANKS AND DEPOSIT-TAKING COMPANIES FOR THE ATTENTION OF CHIEF EXECUTIVES

Government Measures to Stabilise the Exchange Rate: Explanatory Note

1. The Financial Secretary has today announced two steps designed to stabilise the exchange rate of the Hong Kong dollar. One step is the removal of interest tax on Hong Kong dollar deposits with financial institutions; the other involves revised arrangements for the issue and redemption of banknotes. This message concerns the latter.

2. The central element in the new arrangements is that, following agreement between the Government and the two note-issuing banks, Certificates of Indebtedness, which are issued by the Hong Kong Government Exchange Fund to the note-issuing banks to be held as cover for their note issues, will henceforth be issued and redeemed only against payment in US dollars, at the fixed exchange of US $1 = HK $7.80. The forces of competition and arbitrage should then ensure, as they do at present, that approximately the same rate of exchange is available on transactions in all types of instrument. In other words, exchange rates quoted in the market for the US dollar will be close to the rate of $7.80 fixed for certificates of indebtedness.

3. To assist the smooth and equitable functioning of this arrangement, the note-issuing banks have agreed with the Government that they should provide notes to, and accept them from, other banks on the same basis as they themselves deal with the Exchange Fund—i.e., against payments in US dollars at the rate of US $1 = HK $7.80. The note-issuing banks will be notifying other banks individually of the consequent revisions to their procedures for providing notes and for taking them back.

4. It should be stressed that the market rate will hold close to the announced rate

Source: Monetary Affairs Branch, Hong Kong Government, October 15, 1983.

without any need for increased transactions in bank notes. The mere fact that deposits are convertible (at maturity, where relevant) into notes and that HK$ notes are ultimately convertible (via certificates of indebtedness) into foreign currency will, assisted by the forces of competition and arbitrage, ensure convertibility between HK$ deposits and foreign currency deposits at a rate determined principally by the fixed rate for certificates of indebtedness, without any intermediate transactions in notes having to take place.

5. Neither DTC's nor any other bank customers should expect there to be any change in the manner in which they draw notes from, or deposit notes with, banks. The new arrangements do not affect bank customers directly. Customers will merely find that the quoted exchange rate is close to $7.80, whether for exchanging notes or for other foreign exchange transactions. As a result of the Government fixing the rate for certificates of indebtedness, the exchange rate available to bank customers will also remain stable.

6. As regards broader implications, essentially the new scheme transfers the impact of any adjustment to balance of payments pressures away from the exchange rate and onto the banking system, and more specifically onto the liquid reserve base of the banks and onto the level of interest rates paid and charged on HK$ deposits and loans. Thus, for example, a capital inflow may lead to increases in liquidity and lower interest rates, while a capital outflow may give rise to a squeeze on liquidity and higher HK$ interest rates, instead of leading, as at present, to depreciation of the currency. In the event of an outflow the impact might be more severe on some banks than on others, and the consequences for other sectors, such as DTCs [Deposit-Taking Companies] and corporate or individual borrowers, might be painful. The Government will be monitoring the situation carefully, particularly in its initial stages. The Commissioner of Banking and of Deposit-Taking Companies will keep a close watch on the effects of the scheme on individual banks and DTCs; the Government would be prepared to consider action to mitigate any difficulties that might arise in particular cases.

F

Structure of Hong Kong Basic Law

PREAMBLE

1. Hong Kong's *territory* [new text, hereinafter abbreviated as n.t.] and historical background, the signing of the Sino-British Joint Declaration [n.t.] and the resolution of the Hong Kong question.

2. The setting up of the Hong Kong Special Administrative Region (HKSAR) under the guiding principle of "one country, two systems."

3. Drawing up the Basic Law for the HKSAR under Article 31 of the Constitution to safeguard state sovereignty and the prosperity and stability of Hong Kong.

CHAPTER 1

General Principles

1. The HKSAR is an inseparable part of the People's Republic of China. *Authorized by the National People's Congress* [originally, "under the leadership of the Central People's Government"], the HKSAR shall enjoy a high degree of autonomy.

Source: Adopted at the Second Session of the Basic Law Drafting Committee (BLDC) on April 22, 1985, held in Beijing.

Note: Substantial changes were made on the structure initially submitted by the BLDC Secretariat for discussion. The initial draft was revised three times during the five-day session before it was finally and unanimously adopted. Views not included in the final version will be written into a memorandum for consideration by the five subgroups.

In this unofficial translation of the draft structure, changes made on the first and second revised drafts are in italics.

2. The government and legislature shall be composed of local inhabitants.

3. Socialist system and policies [n.t.] shall not be practiced in the HKSAR. Hong Kong's capitalist system and lifestyle shall remain unchanged for 50 years.

4. The ownership of private property shall be protected. The ownership of enterprises and the legal right of inheritance [n.t.] shall be protected.

5. The right of ownership, management and disposal of land.

6. *The right of ownership, management and disposal of natural resources* [n.t.].

7. The laws previously in force [originally "legal system"] shall remain basically unchanged.

8. Languages and scripts.

CHAPTER 2

Relationship between the Central Government and the SAR

1. The HKSAR shall be under the direct authority of the Central People's Convention.

2. Foreign Affairs shall be managed by the Central Government (HKSAR shall dispose of those external affairs as specified in Chapter 7 and other related clauses).

3. The Central Government is responsible for affairs concerning defence and garrison [deletion of "relationship between defence and security"].

4. The HKSAR shall be vested with administrative power (The *executive power* of HKSAR in matters of personnel, security [n.t.], government finance, taxation, finance, currency, *postal service* [n.t.], industry and commerce, trade, tariffs, education, science, culture, *immigration*, [n.t.] and other fields).

5. The HKSAR shall be vested with legislative power [rewritten].

6. The HKSAR shall be vested with independent judicial power, including that of final adjudication [rewritten].

7. *Other powers authorized by the National People's Congress and the State Council* [n.t.].

8. *HKSAR representatives and their participation in the administration of national affairs* [rewritten].

9. *The relationship between all the departments of the Central government as well as provincial, autonomous region and municipal governments and the HKSAR (but there shall not be interference in the internal affairs of the HKSAR).*

CHAPTER 3

The Fundamental Rights and Duties of Hong Kong Inhabitants

1. The definition of Hong Kong inhabitants.

2. Right to vote and stand for election.

3. Freedom of speech, of the press, of assembly, of association, of forming and joining trade unions, of strike and of demonstration.

4. Freedom of the person.

5. Inviolability of the home and freedom of correspondence.

6. Freedom of movement and exit and entry *across the national boundary* [n.t.].

7. Freedom of religion and belief.

8. Freedom of choice of occupation and of academic research.

9. The right to have secret legal advice, to take legal proceedings, to choose lawyers as proxy at court and to have judicial compensation. The inhabitants are entitled to appeal to court against conducts of administrative departments [n.t.].

10. The right to benefit from social welfare in accordance with law [n.t.]. Welfare benefits of retired or resigned public servants shall be protected.

11. The right to marry and the right to raise a family.

12. The provisions of the International Covenant on Civil and Political Rights and the International Covenant on Economic, Social and Cultural Rights as applied to Hong Kong shall remain in force [n.t.].

13. *Other rights and freedoms as provided by the Common Law* [n.t.].

14. The legal rights of other persons living in Hong Kong shall be protected [n.t.].

15. *The legal rights of the original inhabitants in the New Territories shall be protected* [n.t.].

16. *It is the duty of the Hong Kong inhabitants to abide by the Basic Law and other laws of the SAR* [rewritten].

CHAPTER 4

HKSAR Political Structure

1. The chief executive
   i. His selection, appointment and dismissal [n.t.].
   ii. His term of office.
   iii. His powers and duties.
2. The executive authorities
   i. The formation of the executive organization, and the selection [n.t.], appointment and dismissal of the members.
   ii. The term of office of chief officials [n.t.].
   iii. Powers and duties.
   [Deletion of "Departments under the organization" and "Public servants of the executive organization."
   iv. Relationship between the executive organization and legislature.
3. The Legislature
   i. Method of composition and formation.
   ii. Term of office of the members [n.t.].
   iii. Powers and duties.
   iv. Its convention and law-making procedures.
   v. Rights, powers and duties of members of the legislature.
4. The Judiciary
   i. Its organizational structure.
   ii. Rights and duties.
   iii. The appointment and dismissal of judges and other judicial officers.
   iv. Independent trial.
   v. The jury system.
   vi. Principles of defence.
   vii. Criminal prosecution.

viii. Judicial links [originally "relationship"] with other provinces, autonomous regions and municipalities.
ix. Mutual assistance of the judiciaries [deletion of "... between the SAR and overseas"].
[Deletion of "Supervisory authorities."]
5. District and regional administration.
Functions and organization of district and regional administration [rewritten].
6. *Public servants* [n.t.].

CHAPTER 5

HKSAR Economy

1. Financial management and taxation policy.

2. Financial system and policy (international [n.t.] financial centre; issuing and circulation of the Hong Kong currency; no exchange control. Market for foreign exchange, gold, securities and futures shall remain open).

3. Free trade policy (free port, the independent customs territory and the right as a separate unit [n.t.] to fill export quota and to negotiate tariff preferences and other related arrangements, and to issue certificates of origin).

4. *Industrial policies on manufacturing and other industries* [rewritten].

5. Policies on commerce, tourism and real estates [n.t.].

6. Shipping and civil aviation management.

CHAPTER 6

HKSAR Education, Science, *Technology*, Culture, *Sports and Religion* [n.t.]

1. Education policy and system.
2. Science and technology policy.
3. Cultural policy. *Sports promotion* [n.t.].
4. *Religion policy* [n.t.].
5. The accreditation of professional standards and qualifications.
6. *Other social affairs* [n.t.].

CHAPTER 7

HKSAR External Affairs

1. Participation in related diplomatic negotiations.

2. Participation in international organizations and conferences: conclusion and implementation of related international treaties [n.t.].

3. The application of international treaties in Hong Kong.

4. The issuing of passports and other travel documents.

5. Matters of visa abolition with states and regions.

6. The establishment of official or semi-official economic and trade missions in countries and regions [n.t.].

7. Conditions and procedures of setting up offices by countries and regions [n.t.]. in Hong Kong.

CHAPTER 8

HKSAR Flag and Emblem

1. Apart from displaying the National Flag and National Emblem, the HKSAR may use a Regional Flag and Emblem of its own.

2. The Flag of the HKSAR.

3. The Emblem of the HKSAR.

CHAPTER 9

The *Legal Status* [n.t.] of the HKSAR Basic Law and its Interpretation and Amendment

1. *The legal status of the Basic Law and its relationship with the Constitution* [n.t.].

2. Interpretation of the Basic Law.

3. Amendments to the Basic Law.

CHAPTER 10

Appendix

1. The formation of the first HKSAR government [originally "...executive authority and first legislature"].

2. The continued validity of original laws, documents and contracts.

3. The enactment of the Basic Law.

Selected Bibliography

Adley, Robert. *All Change Hong Kong*. Poole: Blandford Press, 1984.

Amnesty International. *China: Violations of Human Rights*. London: Amnesty International Publications, 1984.

Ashton, Basil, et al., "Famine in China, 1958–61." *Population and Development Review* 10, no. 4 (Dec. 1984): 613–46.

Baker, Hugh D. R. "Life in the Cities: The Emergence of Hong Kong Man." *China Quarterly*, no. 95 (Sept. 1983): 469–79.

Balfour, S. F. "Hong Kong before the British." *Journal of the Hong Kong Branch of the Royal Asiatic Society* 10 (1970): 134–79.

Beazer, William F. *The Commercial Future of Hong Kong*. New York: Praeger Publishers, 1978.

Beeching, Jack. *The Chinese Opium Wars*. London: Hutchinson & Co., 1975.

Benton, Gregor. *The Hong Kong Crisis*. London: Pluto Press, 1983.

Bernstein, Thomas P. "China in 1984: The Year of Hong Kong." *Asian Survey* 25, no. 1 (Jan. 1985): 33–50.

Birch, Alan, Y. C. Jao, and Elizabeth Sinn. *Research Materials for Hong Kong Studies*. Hong Kong: Centre of Asian Studies, University of Hong Kong, 1984.

Blaustein, Albert P. "Drafting a New Constitution for the Hong Kong Special Administrative Region." Paper presented at the conference "Hong Kong and 1997: Strategies for the Future," Dec. 6–8, 1984, at the Centre of Asian Studies, University of Hong Kong.

Bonavia, David. *Hong Kong and 1997: The Final Settlement*. 2d ed. Hong Kong: South China Morning Post, 1985.

Bond, Michael H. "Coping with the Threat of Westernization in Hong Kong." Paper presented at the symposium "Alternative Models of Development," May 2–

Note: Complied by George L. Hicks and edited by Hungdah Chiu. Articles or news items in *Asiaweek*; *Asian Wall Street Journal*; *Far Eastern Economic Review*; *Foreign Broadcast Information Service, China*; *Hong Kong Standard*; *Ming Pao Daily News*; and *South China Morning Post* are not included.

5, 1984. Third Asian regional meeting of the Association of Cross-Cultural Psychology, Kuala Lumpur.

———. "Inter-Group Relations in Hong Kong." Paper presented at the conference "Interethnic Conflict and Aggression," May 5–12, 1985, at the East-West Center, Honolulu.

Brim, John Anthony. *Local Systems and Modernizing Change in the New Territories of Hong Kong.* Ann Arbor: University Microfilms, 1971.

Bueno de Mesquita, Bruce, David Newman, and Alvin Rabushka. *Forecasting Political Events: The Future of Hong Kong.* New Haven: Yale University Press, 1985.

Burns, John P. "Immigration from China and the Future of Hong Kong." Paper presented for the "Spring 1985 Regional Seminar in Chinese Studies," April 12–13, 1985, at the University of California, Berkeley.

Burns, John P., and J. H. Bacon-Shone. "The Localization of the Hong Kong Civil Service." Paper presented at the conference "Hong Kong and 1997: Strategies for the Future," Dec. 6–8, 1984, at the Centre of Asian Studies, University of Hong Kong.

Butler, Stuart M. "How Guam Can Become America's Hong Kong," Heritage Foundation Asian Studies Center, *Backgrounder*, no. 1 (Apr. 19, 1983).

Catron, Gary. "Hong Kong and Chinese Foreign Policy, 1955–60." *China Quarterly*, no. 51 (July 1972): 405–24.

Cha, Louis. *On Hong Kong's Future: A Collection of Ming Pao's Editorials.* Hong Kong: Ming Pao Daily News, 1984.

Chau, L. C. "Industrial Growth and Employment in Hong Kong." *Philippine Economic Journal* 15, nos. 1/2 (1976): 82–138.

Chen, Albert. "Further Aspects of the Autonomy of Hong Kong under the PRC Constitution." *Hong Kong Law Journal* 14, part 3 (Sept. 1984): 341–47.

———. "Hong Kong's Legal System: Adaptation for 1997 and Beyond." Paper presented at the conference "Hong Kong and 1997: Strategies for the Future," Dec. 6–8, 1984, at the Centre of Asian Studies, University of Hong Kong.

Chen, Edward K. Y. "Hong Kong Case Study." *World Development* 12, nos. 5/6 (May/June 1984): 481–90.

———. "The Newly Industrializing Countries in Asia: Growth Experience and Prospects." Discussion paper no. 55 (April 1985), Department of Economics, University of Hong Kong.

Cheng, Chu-yuan. "Hong Kong's Prosperity: Foundation and Prospects." *Journal of Chinese Studies* 2, no. 1 (April 1985): 155–63.

Cheng, Joseph Y. S., "Goals of Government Expenditure in a Laissez-Faire Political Economy: Hong Kong in the 1970's." *Asian Survey* 19, no 7 (July 1979): 695–706.

———. "The Future of Hong Kong: A Study of the Hong Kong People's Attitudes." *Australian Journal of Chinese Affairs*, no. 12 (July 1984): 113–42.

———. ed. *Hong Kong: In Search of a Future.* Hong Kong: Oxford University Press, 1984.

Cheng, Tong-yung. *The Economy of Hong Kong.* 2d ed. Hong Kong: Far East Publications, 1982.

Cheong, W. E. *Mandarins and Merchants.* London: Curzon Press, 1979.

Ching, Frank. *Hong Kong and China: For Better or for Worse.* New York: China Council of the Asia Society and the Foreign Policy Association, 1985.

Chiu, Hungdah. "Prospects for the Unification of China: An Analysis of the Views of the Republic of China on Taiwan." *Asian Survey* 23, no. 10 (Oct. 1983): 1081–94.

———. "The 1982 Chinese Constitution and the Rule of Law." *Review of Socialist Law* 11, no. 2 (1985): 143–60.

———. "The Hong Kong Agreement and American Foreign Policy." *Issues & Studies* 22, no. 6 (June 1986): 76–91.

———. "The 1984 Sino-British Settlement on Hong Kong: Problems and Analysis." *Journal of Chinese Studies* 2, no. 1 (Apr. 1985): 95–112.

Chiu, T. N. *The Port of Hong Kong.* Hong Kong: Hong Kong University Press, 1973.

Chow, Steven C., and Gastav F. Papanek. "Laissez-Faire, Growth, and Equity—Hong Kong." *Economic Journal* 91, no. 362 (June 1981): 466–85.

Clarke, W. S. "Hong Kong under the Chinese Constitution." *Hong Kong Law Journal* 14, part 1 (Jan. 1984): 71–81.

———. "The Constitution of Hong Kong and 1997." Paper presented at the conference "Hong Kong and 1997: Strategies for the Future," Dec. 6–8, 1984, at the Centre of Asian Studies, University of Hong Kong.

Coates, Austin. *Prelude to Hong Kong.* London: Routlege & Kegan Paul, 1966.

Collins, Charles. *Public Administration in Hong Kong.* London: Royal Institute of International Affairs, 1952.

The Constitution of the People's Republic of China. Beijing: Foreign Languages Press, 1983.

Cooper, Eugene. *The Wood-Carvers of Hong Kong.* Cambridge: Cambridge University Press, 1980.

———. "Karl Marx's Other Island: The Evolution of Peripheral Capitalism in Hong Kong." *Bulletin of Concerned Asian Scholars* 14, no. 1 (Jan. 1982): 25–31.

Copper, John F. "The Lessons of Playing Tough with China." Heritage Foundation Asian Studies Center, *Backgrounder*, no. 4 (Aug. 23, 1983).

Covin, David Leroy. *Political Culture as an Analytical Instrument: An Examination of Refugees in Hong Kong.* Ann Arbor: University Microfilms, 1971.

Crisswell, Colin. *The Taipans: Hong Kong's Merchant Princes.* Hong Kong: Oxford University Press, 1981.

Davies, Derek. *Asia 1985 Yearbook.* Hong Kong: Far Eastern Economic Review, 1984.

Davies, S. N. G. "Review of *Society and Politics in Hong Kong* by Lau Siu-kai." *Hong Kong Law Journal* 13, part 2 (May 1983): 246–54.

Dicks, Anthony. "Treaty, Grant, Usage, or Sufferance? Some Legal Aspects of the Status of Hong Kong." *China Quarterly*, no. 95 (Sept. 1983): 427–55.

Dittmer, Lowell. "Ideology and Organization in Post-Mao China." *Asian Survey* 24, no. 3 (Mar. 1984): 349–66.

Dwyer, D. J., and Chuen-yun Lai. *The Small Industries in Hong Kong: Patterns and Policies.* Hull, Que.: University of Hull Publications, 1967.

———. eds. *Asian Urbanization.* Hong Kong: Hong Kong University Press, 1971.

Editorial. "The Legal System, the Constitution, and the Future of Hong Kong." *Hong Kong Law Journal* 14, part 2 (May 1984): 137–41.

Emmons, Charles F. "Public Opinion and Political Participation in Pre–1997 Hong Kong." Paper presented at the conference "Hong Kong and 1997: Strategies for the Future," Dec. 6–8, 1984, at the Centre of Asian Studies, University of Hong Kong.

Endacott, G. B. *Government and People in Hong Kong, 1841–1962.* Hong Kong: Hong Kong University Press, 1964.

———. *A History of Hong Kong.* 2d ed. Hong Kong: Oxford University Press, 1973.

England, Joe, and John Rear. *Chinese Labour under British Rule.* Hong Hong: Oxford University Press, 1975.

———. *Industrial Relations and Law in Hong Kong.* Hong Kong: Oxford University Press, 1981.

Epstein, Israel. *From Opium War to Liberation.* Hong Kong: Joint Publishing Co., 1980.

Evans, Dafydd M. E. "The Foundation of Hong Kong: A Chapter of Accidents." Paper presented at week-end symposium, Nov. 25–26, 1972, at the Royal Asiatic Society, Hong Kong Branch.

Fairbank, John K. *Trade and Diplomacy on the China Coast: The Opening of the Treaty Ports, 1842–1864.* Cambridge, Mass.: Harvard University Press: Stanford, Calif.: Stanford University Press, 1953.

———. *China's Response to the West.* Cambridge, Mass.: Harvard University Press, 1954.

———. "The Creation of the Treaty System." In *Cambridge History of China: Late Ch'ing, 1800–1911*, Vol. 10, Part 1, edited by John K. Fairbank. Cambridge: Cambridge University Press, 1978.

Faure, David, James Hayes, and Alan Birch. *From Village to City.* Hong Kong: Centre of Asian Studies, University of Hong Kong, 1984.

Fay, Peter Ward. *The Opium War, 1840–1842.* Chapel Hill: University of North Carolina Press, 1975.

Finer, Samuel. "Hong Kong 1997: When the Kissing Has to Stop." *Political Quarterly*, forthcoming.

Fransman, Martin. "Learning and the Capital Goods Sector under Free Trade: The Case of Hong Kong." *World Development* 10, no. 11 (Nov. 1982): 991–1014.

Fu, Jin. "China's Recovery of Xianggang [Hong Kong] Area Fully Accords with International Law." *Beijing Review*, 26, no. 39 (Sept. 26, 1983): 14–19, 25.

Geiger, Theodore, and Frances M. Geiger. *The Development Progress of Hong Kong and Singapore.* Washington, D.C.: National Planning Association: London: Macmillan, 1973.

Gillingham, Paul. *At the Peak: Hong Kong between the Wars.* Hong Kong: Macmillan, 1983.

Grantham, Alexander. *Via Ports*, Hong Kong: Hong Kong University Press, 1965.

Greenberg, Michael. *British Trade and the Opening of China, 1800–42.* Cambridge: Cambridge University Press, 1951.

Greenwood, John. "Stabilization of the Hong Kong Dollar." *Asian Monetary Monitor* 7, no. 6 (Nov. 1983): pp. 9–37.

———. "Operation of the New Exchange Rate." *Asian Monetary Monitor* 8, no. 1 (Jan. 1984): pp. 2–12.

———. "The Monetary Framework Underlying the Hong Kong Dollar Stabilization Scheme." *China Quarterly*, no. 99 (Sept. 1984): 631–36.

———. "Why the HK$/US$ Linked Rate System Should Not Be Changed." *Asian Monetary Monitor* 8, no. 6 (Nov. 1984): pp. 2–17.

———. "Experiments in Financial Liberalization and Innovation in Seven East Asian Economies." Paper presented at the "Second International Conference of the Institute for Monetary and Economic Studies," May 29–31, 1985, at the Bank of Japan, Tokyo.

Guldin, Gregory E. "Seven-Veiled Ethnicity: A Hong Kong Chinese Folk Model." *Journal of Chinese Studies* 1, no. 2 (June 1984): 139–56.

Harding, Harry. "Reform in China: A Mid-Course Assessment." *Journal of Northeast Asian Studies* 3, no. 2 (Summer 1984): 3–26.

———, ed. *China's Foreign Relations in the 1980's*. New Haven: Yale University Press, 1984.

Harrell, Stevan. "Why Do the Chinese Work So Hard?" *Modern China* 11, no. 2 (Apr. 1985): 203–26.

Harris, Peter. *Hong Kong: A Study in Bureaucratic Politics*. Hong Kong: Heinemann Educational Books, 1978.

Hayes, James. "Hong Kong: A Tale of Two Cities." Paper presented at week-end symposium, Nov. 25–26, 1972, at the Royal Asiatic Society, Hong Kong Branch.

———. *The Hong Kong Region, 1850–1911*. Hamden: Anchor Books, 1977.

———. *The Rural Communities of Hong Kong*. Hong Kong: Oxford University Press, 1983.

Her Majesty's Government. *A Draft Agreement between the Government of the United Kingdom of Great Britain and Northern Ireland and the Government of the People's Republic of China on the Future of Hong Kong*. London, 1984.

Hinton, Harold C. "For the U.S., Risks and Rewards as China Modernizes." Heritage Foundation Asian Studies Center, *Backgrounder*, no. 28 (May 17, 1985).

Ho, Alfred K. "Trade and Economic Development of the People's Republic of China." *Journal of Chinese Studies* 1, no. 2 (June 1984): 203–20.

Ho, H. C. Y. "Income Redistribution through the Government Budget in Hong Kong." *Southeast Asian Journal of Social Science* 4, no. 1 (1975): 99–112.

Ho, Suk-ching. "An Attitudinal Survey of Foreign Investors in Hong Kong." *Contemporary Southeast Asia* 7, no. 1 (June 1985): 48–57.

Ho, Y. K., and C. K. Law, eds. *The Hong Kong Financial Markets: Empirical Evidence*. Hong Kong: University Publisher and Printer, 1983.

Hong Kong—China Risk. Published fortnightly by Asiabanking since Jan. 1984.

Hong Kong Government. *Green Paper: The Further Development of Representative Government in Hong Kong*. Hong Kong: Hong Kong Government Printer, July 1984.

———. *White Paper: The Further Development of Representative Government in Hong Kong*. Hong Kong: Hong Kong Government Printer, November 1984.

———. *1984 Economic Background*. Hong Kong: Hong Kong Government Printer, 1985.

———. *1985 Economic Prospects*. Hong Kong: Hong Kong Government Printer, 1985.

———. *Powers and Privileges Bill: The Amended Text.* Hong Kong: Hong Kong Government Printer, 1985.

Hong Kong Observers. *The Hong Kong Observers Poll.* Hong Kong: Survey Research Hong Kong, 1982.

———. *Pressure Points.* Hong Kong: Summerson (HK) Educational Research Centre, 1983.

Hook, Brian. "The Government of Hong Kong: Change within Tradition." *China Quarterly*, no. 95 (Sept. 1983): 491–511.

Hopkins, Keith, ed. *Hong Kong: The Industrial Colony.* Hong Kong: Oxford University Press, 1971.

Howe, Christopher. "Growth, Public Policy and Hong Kong's Relationship with China." *China Quarterly*, no. 95 (Sept. 1983): 512–33.

Hsia, Ronald, Henry Ho, and Ewin Lim. *The Structure and Growth of the Hong Kong Economy.* Wiesbaden: Otto Harrassowitz, 1975.

Hsia, Ronald, Henry Ho, Ewin Lim, and Laurence Chau. *Industrialization, Employment and Income Distribution.* London: Croom Helm, 1978.

Hsing, Mo-huan. "A Critical Evaluation of the Existing NI/GDP Estimates in Hong Kong." *Developing Economies* 17, no. 1 (March 1979): 80–109.

Hsing, Mo-huan, and Yin-ping Ho. "The National Income and Social Accounts of Hong Kong, 1950–75." Hong Kong: Economic Research Centre, Chinese University of Hong Kong. Photocopy, 1982.

Hsu, Immanuel C. Y. "Late Ch'ing Foreign Relations, 1866–1905." In *Cambridge History of China: Late Ch'ing, 1800–1911*, Vol. 11, Part 2, edited by John K. Fairbank, and Kwang-ching Liu. Cambridge: Cambridge University Press, 1980.

———. *The Risk of Modern China*, 3d ed. New York and London: Oxford University Press, 1983.

Hughes, Richard. *Borrowed Time, Borrowed Place: Hong Kong.* 2d ed. London: Andre Deutsch, 1976.

Jao, Y. C. *Banking and Currency in Hong Kong.* London: Macmillan, 1974.

———. "The Rise of Hong Kong as a Financial Centre." *Asian Survey* 19, no. 7 (July 1979): 674–94.

———. "Hong Kong: Economic Prospects to 1987." *Economist Intelligence Unit.* Special Report, no. 156 (1983).

———. "Hong Kong's Role in Financing China's Modernization." In *China and Hong Kong: The Economic Nexus*, edited by A. J. Youngsen. Hong Kong: Oxford University Press, 1983.

———. "The Enigma of Hong Kong's Financial Transactions with China." *Asian Monetary Monitor* 8, no. 3 (May 1984): 26–31.

———. "Hong Kong Dollar Looking for Political Parity." *Asia Banking* (Sept. 1984): 47–55.

———. "The Monetary System of and the Future of Hong Kong." Paper presented at the conference "Hong Kong and 1997: Strategies for the Future," Dec. 6–8, 1984, at the Centre of Asian Studies, University of Hong Kong.

Jarvie, I. C. *Hong Kong: A Society in Transition.* London: Routledge & Kegan Paul, 1969.

Johnson, Chalmers. "The Mousetrapping of Hong Kong: A Game in Which Nobody Wins." *Asian Survey* 24, no. 9 (Sept. 1984): 887–909.

Johnson, Graham E. "The Production Responsibility System in Chinese Agriculture: Some Examples from Guangdon." *Pacific Affairs* 55, no. 3 (Fall 1982): 430–51.

Jones, Dorothy E., and Marc Frons. "Why Y. K. Pao Is so High on Hong Kong." *Business Week* (May 20, 1985), 53–54.

Jones, John F., ed. *The Common Welfare: Hong Kong's Social Services*. Hong Kong: Chinese University Press, 1981.

Jones, Susan Mann. "Misunderstanding the Chinese Economy." *Journal of Asian Studies* 40, no. 3 (May 1981): 539–58.

Kallgren, Joyce. "China in 1983: The Turmoil of Modernization." *Asian Survey* 24, no. 1 (Jan. 1984): 60–80

Karamanian, Susan L. "Legal Aspects of the Sino-British Draft Agreement on the Future of Hong Kong." *Texas International Law Journal* 20, no. 1 (Winter 1985): 167–88.

King, Ambrose Y. C. "Administrative Absorption of Politics in Hong Kong: Emphasis on the Grass Roots Level." *Asian Survey* 15, no. 5 (May 1975): 422–39.

King, Ambrose Y. C. and Rance P. L. Lee. *Social Life and Development in Hong Kong*. Hong Kong: Chinese University Press, 1981.

Knight, Bill, ed. *Hong Kong: 1985*. Hong Kong: Government Publications Center, n.d.

Lamb, H. K. *A Date with Fate: Hong Kong 1997*. Hong Kong: Lincoln Green Publishing, 1984.

Lardy, Nicholas R. "Consumption and Living Standards in China, 1978–83." *China Quarterly*, no. 100 (Dec. 1984): 849–65.

Lasater, Martin L. "Assessing the Taiwan Relations Act." Heritage Foundation Asian Studies Center, *Backgrounder*, no. 20 (Dec. 14, 1984).

———. "Hong Kong's Future—and Taiwan's." Heritage Foundation, *Executive Memorandum*, no. 65 (Oct. 3, 1985).

Lau, Chan Kit-ching. "The Hong Kong Question during the Pacific War (1941–45)." *Journal of Imperial and Commonwealth History* 2, no. 1 (Oct. 1973): 56–78.

Lau, Siu-kai. "Government Intermediate Organizations and Grass-Roots Politics in Hong Kong." *Asian Survey* 21, no. 8 (Aug. 1981): 865–84.

———. "Local Administrative Reform in Hong Kong: Promises and Limitations." *Asian Survey* 22, no. 9 (Sept. 1982): 858–73.

———. *Society and Politics in Hong Kong*. Hong Kong: Chinese University Press, 1982.

———. "Bureaucratic Rule and Emergent Political Issues in Hong Kong." *World Politics* 35 (July 1983): 544–62.

———. "Political Reform and Political Development in Hong Kong: Dilemmas and Choices." Paper presented at the conference "Hong Kong and 1997: Strategies for the Future," Dec. 6–8, 1984, at the Centre of Asian Studies, University of Hong Kong.

Lau, Siu-kai, and Hsin-chi Kuan. *The District Board Elections in Hong Kong*. Hong Kong: Chinese University of Hong Kong, 1983.

———. "The 1985 District Board Election in Hong Kong: The Limits of Political

Mobilization in a Dependent Polity." Department of Sociology, Chinese University of Hong Kong. Photocopy, 1985.

Lau, Siu-kai, Hsin-chi Kuan, and Kam-fai Ho. *Leaders, Officials and Citizens in Urban Service Delivery: Comparative Studies in Four Localities of Hong Kong*. Hong Kong: Chinese University, 1983.

Law, Cheung-Kwok. "A Test of the Efficient Market Hypothesis with Respect to the Recent Behavior of the Hong Kong Stock Market." *Developing Economies*, 20, no. 1 (Mar. 1982): 61–72.

Lee, Jane. "Pressure Groups and Political Participation in Hong Kong." Seminar paper, Research School of Pacific Studies, Australian National University, 1984.

Lee, Rance. "The Folklore of Corruption in Hong Kong." *Asian Survey* 21, no. 3 (Mar. 1981): 355–68.

———. ed. *Corruption and Its Control in Hong Kong*. Hong Kong: Chinese University Press, 1981.

Leng, Shao-chaun, and Hungdah Chiu. *Criminal Justice in Post-Mao China, Analysis and Documents*. Albany: State University of New York Press, 1984.

Lethbridge, H. J. "Caste, Clans and Race in Hong Kong before the Japanese Occupation." Paper presented at the week-end symposium, Nov. 25–26 , 1972 of the Royal Asiatic Society, Hong Kong Branch.

———. *Hong Kong: Stability and Choice*. Hong Kong: Oxford University Press, 1978.

———. *Hard Graft in Hong Kong*. Hong Kong: Oxford University Press, 1985.

———. ed. *The Business Environment of Hong Kong*. Hong Kong: Oxford University Press, 1984.

Leung, Chi-keung, J. W. Cushman, and Wang Gungwu, eds. *Hong Kong: Dilemmas of Growth*, Hong Kong: Centre of Asian Studies, University of Hong Kong, 1980.

Lewis, D. K., *The Prospects for Hong Kong*, London: Institute for the Study of Conflict, 1982.

Lewis, W. A. *The Evolution of the International Economic Order*, Princeton, N.J.: Princeton University Press, 1978.

Lin, Tzong-biau, Rance P. L. Lee, and Udo-Ernst Simonis, eds. *Hong Kong: Economic, Social and Political Studies in Development*. New York: M. E. Sharpe, 1979.

Lin, Tzong-biau, and Victor Mak. *Trade Barriers and the Promotion of Hong Kong Exports*. Hong Kong: Chinese University Press, 1980.

Lin, Tzong-biau, Victor Mak, and Yin-ping Ho. *Manufactured Exports and Employment in Hong Kong*. Hong Kong: Chinese University Press, 1980.

Lin, Tzong-biau, and Yin-ping Ho. "Export Instabilities and Employment Fluctuations in Hong Kong's Manufacturing Industries," *Developing Economies*, Vol. 17, no. 2 (June 1979), pp. 182–202.

Liu, Alan. "Problems in Communications in China's Modernization." *Asian Survey* 22, no. 5 (May 1982): 481–99.

Lo, Hsiang-lin. *Hong Kong and Western Cultures*. Honolulu: East-West Center Press, 1973.

Lockett, Martin, and Craig R. Littler. "Trends in Chinese Enterprise Management, 1978–1982." *World Development* 11, no. 8 (Aug. 1983): 683–704.

Luard, Evan. *Britain and China*. London: Chatto & Windus, 1962.
McGee, T. G. *Hawkers in Hong Kong*. Hong Kong: Centre of Asian Studies, University of Hong Kong, 1973.
Macpherson, I. F. C. *Report of the Assessment Office*. Hong Kong: Assessment Office, 1984.
———. *Report of the Assessment Office: Submissions made by Organizations to the Assessment Office*. 2 vols. Hong Kong: Assessment Office, 1984.
Mancall, Mark. *China at the Center: 300 Years of Foreign Policy*. New York: Free Press, 1984.
Menezes, Victor. "Hong Kong: Financial Centre for the Future." Paper presented at the conference "Hong Kong and 1997: Strategies for the Future," Dec. 6–8, 1984, at the Centre of Asian Studies, University of Hong Kong.
Miners, N. J. *The Government and Politics of Hong Kong*. 3d ed. Hong Kong: Oxford University Press, 1981.
———. "Alternative Governmental Structure for a Future Self-Governing Hong Kong." Paper presented at the conference "Hong Kong and 1997: Strategies for the Future," Dec. 6–8, 1984, at the Centre of Asian Studies, University of Hong Kong."
Moore, Robert Lloyd. *Modernization and Westernization in Hong Kong: Patterns of Culture Change in an Urban Setting*. Ann Arbor: University Microfilms, 1981.
Morgan, Maria Chan. "Controlling the Bureaucracy in Post-Mao China." *Asian Survey* 21, no. 12 (Dec. 1981): 1223–36.
Morkre, Morrie E. "Rent-Seeking and Hong Kong's Textile Quota System." *Developing Economies* 17, no. 1 (Mar. 1979): 110–18.
Mosher, Steven W. *Broken Earth: The Rural Chinese*. New York: Free Press, 1983.
———. *In Human Rights, China Remains in the Maoist Era*. Heritage Foundation Asian Studies Center, *Backgrounder*, no. 30 (June 19, 1985).
Mushkat, Miron. *The Making of the Hong Kong Administrative Class*. Hong Kong: Centre of Asian Studies, University of Hong Kong, 1982.
Mushkat, Roda. "The Transition from British to Chinese Rule in Hong Kong: A Discussion of Salient International Legal Issues." *Denver Journal of International Law and Policy* 14, nos. 2 and 3 (Winter/Spring 1986): 171–206.
Nairne, Patrick. *Reports on the Work of the Assessment Office*. Hong Kong: Assessment Office, 1984.
Nakajima, Mineo. *Hong Kong: A City State in Transition*. Tokyo: Current Events News Agency, 1985 (in Japanese).
Nyaw, Mee-kau, and Chan-leong Chan. "Structure and Development Strategies of the Manufacturing Industries in Singapore and Hong Kong." *Asian Survey* 22, no. 5 (Sept. 1982): 449–69.
Overholt, William H. "Hong Kong and the Crisis of Sovereignty." *Asian Survey* 24, no. 4 (Apr. 1984): 471–84.
———. "Hong Kong after the Chinese-British Agreement." *Current History* 84, no. 503 (Sept. 1985): 256–59, 274–75.
Pang, Eng Fong. "Distinctive Features of Two City-States' Development." Paper presented at the symposium "In Search of an East Asian Development Model," June 28–30, 1985, at the Council on Religion and International Affairs, New York.

Parsons, Melinda J., ed. *Hong Kong 1984*. Hong Kong: Hong Kong Government Printer, 1984.

Patel, D. K. "One Country, Two Systems: Prospects for Hong Kong's Economy under Chinese Sovereignty." Paper presented at the conference "Hong Kong and 1997: Strategies for the Future," Dec. 6–8, 1984, at the Centre of Asian Studies, University of Hong Kong.

Pye, Lucian W. *The Dynamics of Chinese Politics*. Cambridge: Oelgeschlager, Gunn & Hain, 1981.

———. *Chinese Commercial Negotiating Style*. Cambridge: Oelgeschlager, Gunn & Hain, 1982.

———. "The International Position of Hong Kong." *China Quarterly* no. 95 (Sept. 1983): 456–68.

Rabushka, Alvin. *Value for Money: The Hong Kong Budgetary Process*. Stanford, Calif.: Hoover Institution Press, 1976.

———. *Hong Kong: A Study in Economic Freedom*. Chicago: University of Chicago Press, 1979.

———. "China, Taiwan, and Hong Kong: Economic Development in Three Chinas," Stanford, Calif.: Hoover Institution, Stanford University. Mimeo, 1985.

———. "Hong Kong's Prospects for 1997." Stanford, Calif.: Hoover Institution on War, Revolution, and Peace, Stanford University. Photocopy, 1985.

Reynolds, Paul D. *China's International Banking and Financial System*. New York: Praeger Publishers, 1982.

Riedel, James. *The Industrialization of Hong Kong*. Tubingen: J. C. B. Mohr, 1974.

Salaff, Janet W. *Working Daughters of Hong Kong*. Cambridge: Cambridge University Press, 1981.

Saw, Swee-hock, and Wing-kin Chiu. "Population Growth and Redistribution in Hong Kong, 1844–1975." *Southeast Asian Journal of Social Science* 4, no. 1 (1975): 123–30.

Scott, Ian. "Administering the New Towns of Hong Kong." *Asian Survey* 22, no. 7 (July 1982): 659–75.

———. "The Sino-British Agreement and Political Power in Hong Kong." Paper presented at the workshop "The Future of Hong Kong." Apr. 19, 1985, at the University Joint Centre on Modern Eastern Asia, University of Toronto-York, Toronto.

Scott, Ian, and John P. Burns, eds. *The Hong Kong Civil Service: Personnel Policies and Practices*. Hong Kong: Oxford University Press, 1984.

Scott, Robert Haney. *Saving Hong Kong's Dollar*. Hong Kong: University Publishers & Printer, 1984.

Scurfield, R. G. "An Evaluation of Hong Kong Government's Policy of 'Positive Non-Intervention' in the Economic Sphere." *East Asia* 3 (1985): 136–52.

Shively, Aliza M., and Stan Shively. "Value Changes during a Period of Modernization: The Case of Hong Kong." Hong Kong: Social Research Centre, University of Hong Kong. Photocopy, 1972.

Sit, Victor F. S. "Dynamism in Small Industries: The Case of Hong Kong." *Asian Survey* 22, no. 4 (Apr. 1982): 399–409.

———. *Made in Hong Kong*. Hong Kong: Summerson Eastern Publishers, 1983.

———. ed. *Urban Hong Kong*. Hong Kong: Summerson Eastern Publishers, 1981.

Sit, Victor F. S., Sui-Lun Wong, and Tsin-sing Kiang. *Small Scale Industry in a*

Laissez-Faire Economy: A Hong Kong Case Study. Hong Kong: Hong Kong University Press, 1979.

Smith, Carl T. "English-Educated Chinese Elites in Nineteenth-Century Hong Kong." Paper presented at week-end symposium, Nov. 25–26, 1972 at the Royal Asiatic Society, Hong Kong Branch.

Stoltenberg, Clyde D. "China's Special Economic Zones: The Development and Prospects." *Asian Survey* 24, no. 6 (June 1984): 637–54.

Survey Research (HK). *Researching the 1997 Agreement*. 6 vols. Hong Kong: Survey Research (HK), 1984.

Szczepanik, E. *The Economic Growth of Hong Kong*. London: Royal Institute of International Affairs, 1958.

Tier, Mark. *How to Get a Second Passport*. Hong Kong: WMA Publishing Co., 1984.

Tomita, Teruhiko. "Japanese Management in Hong Kong." *Southeast Asian Studies* 22, no. 4 (1985): 61–75.

Turner, H. A. et al. *The Last Colony: But Whose?* Cambridge: Cambridge University Press, 1980.

United Kingdom. Parliamentary Debates (Commons) 1984. Vol. 19, no. 22: Vol. 60, no. 162: Vol. 65, no. 202: Vol. 69, nos. 22 and 23.

———. 1985. Vol. 70, no. 36: Vol. 71, no. 43: Vol. 72, nos. 55 and 56.

United Kingdom. Parliamentary Debates (Lords) 1984. Vol. 452, no. 127: Vol. 456, no. 177: Vol. 458, no. 17.

———. 1985. Vol. 459, no. 40: Vol. 460, no. 46.

Walden, John. *Excellency, Your Gap is Showing*. Hong Kong: Corporate Communications, 1983.

Waley, Arthur. *The Opium War through Chinese Eyes*. London: George Allen & Unwin, 1958.

Wang, Kwan-yin, ed. *Shenzhen Special Economic Zone*. Hong Kong: Hong Kong Geographical Association, 1982.

Ward, Barbara E. *Through Other Eyes: Essays in Understanding 'Conscious Models'—Mostly in Hong Kong*. Hong Kong: Chinese University Press, 1985.

Watson, James L. "Rural Society: Hong Kong's New Territories." *China Quarterly*, no. 95 (Sept. 1983): 480–90.

Wells, Lewis T., Jr. "Foreign Investment from the Third World: The Experience of Chinese Firms from Hong Kong." *Columbia Journal of World Business* 13, no. 1 (Spring 1978): 39–49.

Wesley-Smith, Peter. "Proposed Establishment of a 'China Office' in Hong Kong." *Journal of Oriental Studies* 19, no. 2 (1981): 175–84.

———. *Unequal Treaty 1898–1997: China, Great Britain, and Hong Kong's New Territories*. 2d ed. Hong Kong: Oxford University Press, 1983.

Wolosh, C. M., ed. *The Hong Kong Exporter and Far Eastern Importer*, Hong Kong: C. M. Wolosh, 1985.

Wong, Siu-lun. "*Industrial Entrepreneurship and Ethnicity: A Study of the Shanghainese Cotton Spinners in Hong Kong.*" Ph.D. diss., University of Oxford, 1979.

World Bank. *World Development Report*. New York: Oxford University Press, 1985.

Woronoff, Jon. *Hong Kong: Capitalist Paradise*. Hong Kong: Heinemann Educational Books, 1980.

Wu, C. *Societal Guidance and Development: A Case Study of Hong Kong*. Ann Arbor: University Microfilms, 1973.

Wu, Yuan-li. "The Future of Hong Kong before and after 1997." *American Asian Review* 11, no 4 (Winter 1984): 13–23.

Young, John D. "China's Role in Two Hong Kong Disturbances: A Scenario for the Future?" *Journal of Oriental Studies* 19, no. 2 (1981): 158–74.

Youngsen, A. J. *Hong Kong: Economic Growth and Policy*. Hong Kong: Oxford University Press, 1982.

———. ed. *China and Hong Kong: The Economic Nexus*. Hong Kong: Oxford University Press, 1983.

Index

About the Editors and Contributors

AN-CHIA WU is Research Fellow at the Institute of International Relations, National Chengchi University, Taipei, and Associate Editor of *Issues and Studies*. He is the author of *Historiographical Studies in Mainland China after 1976* and *Collection on Chinese Communist Historiography*.

GEORGE L. HICKS is an Australian economist and businessman working in Hong Kong. He is coauthor of *Trade and Growth in the Philippines*. Currently, he is collaborating with others on the book *The Chinese Family Business*.

HSIN-CHI KUAN is Senior Lecturer in Government and Public Administration, Head of the Department of Journalism and Communication, and Dean of Faculty of Social Sciences at the Chinese University of Hong Kong. He is the author of *The Non-Proliferation Treaty and the Federal Republic of Germany*. His articles have appeared in *Hong Kong Law Journal*, *The Journal of Commonwealth and Comparative Politics*, and *Studies in Comparative Communism*.

HUNGDAH CHIU is Professor of Law at the University of Maryland. He is the author of *The Capacity of International Organizations to Conclude Treaties*, *The People's Republic of China and the Law of Treaties*, and coauthor of *People's China and International Law: A Documentary Study*, and *Criminal Justice in Post-Mao China: Analysis and Documents*. He has edited *China and the Question of Taiwan* (Praeger, 1973), *China and the Taiwan Issue* (Praeger, 1979), and co-edited *Agreements of the People's Republic of China, 1949–1967: A Calendar*, *Law in Chinese Foreign Policy*, and *China: Seventy Years after the 1911 Hsin-hai Revolution*. He has also contributed many articles to various journals.

Y. C. JAO is Reader in Economics at the University of Hong Kong, where he also served as Dean of the Faculty of Social Sciences from 1978–1981. He is the author of *Banking and Currency in Hong Kong: A Study of Postwar Financial Development* and *Hong Kong: Economic Prospects to 1987*, coauthor of *Financial Structures and Monetary Policies in Southeast Asia*, co-editor of *Hong Kong and 1997: Strategies for the Future* and *China's Special Economic Zones: Policies, Problems, and Prospects*, and a contributor to *China and Hong Kong: the Economic Nexus*.

SIU-KAI LAU is Senior Lecturer in Sociology and Director of the Center for Hong Kong Studies at the Chinese University of Hong Kong. He is the author of *Society and Politics in Hong Kong* and a number of articles in *World Politics, Human Organization, Journal of Marriage and the Family, Asian Survey*, and *Journal of Commonwealth and Comparative Politics*.

TA-LING LEE is Professor of History at Southern Connecticut State University. He is the author of *Foundations of the Chinese Revolution, 1905–1912* and *Digest of Social Science Research on China*, and coauthor of *The Revenge of Heaven: Journal of a Young Chinese*.

YUAN-LI WU is Professor of Economics at the University of San Francisco and Consultant to the Hoover Institution, Stanford University. He is the author of many studies spanning several decades. Among his recent publications are *U.S. Policy and Strategic Interests in the Western Pacific, Planners and Entrepreneurs in the PRC: Sources of Systemic Instability and their Political Implications* and *Becoming an Industrialized Nation: ROC's Development on Taiwan* (Praeger, 1985), and coauthor of *Human Rights in Post-Mao China*.

www.ingramcontent.com/pod-product-compliance
Ingram Content Group UK Ltd.
Pitfield, Milton Keynes, MK11 3LW, UK
UKHW021543041026
15470UKWH00019B/866

9 780899 302416